EVANGELICALS &
TRUTH

A CREATIVE PROPOSAL FOR A POSTMODERN AGE

PETER HICKS

APOLLOS

APOLLOS (an imprint of Inter-Varsity Press)
38 De Montfort Street, Leicester LE1 7GP, England

First published 1998

British Library Cataloguing in Publication Data
A catalogue record for this book is available from the British Library.

ISBN 0-85111-457-1

Set in Bembo

Typeset in Great Britain by Parker Typesetting Service, Leicester
Printed in Great Britain by Creative Print and Design Group.

CONTENTS

PART 1

Introductory

Part 1 seeks to provide an introduction to the issue of truth and to evangelicals. Readers who already know enough about these two topics may well choose to skip these three chapters and go straight to Part 2. Others, for whom the history of philosophy is unknown territory, may also be tempted to skip chapters 2 and 3. That would probably not be wise, since those chapters contain important background material for the rest of the book. In them I have attempted to present the issues as clearly and simply as possible, and readers with no philosophical background should be able to grasp the general principles of the debate on truth without too much difficulty.

1. Truth and evangelicals

This is a book about evangelical Christianity and truth. It is not a book about what evangelicals believe to be true, but rather about the foundational concepts of truth on which evangelicals, consciously or otherwise, have based their beliefs. Rather than answering the question 'What is true for evangelicals?' it explores the issue 'What is truth for evangelicals?' in the sense of 'What do evangelicals mean, or what are they doing, when they say that this or that is true?'

Truth

There was a time when for most people the issue of the nature of truth was not a problem. Almost everyone agreed that there was such a thing as truth, and that it was more or less fixed, and in part (at least) knowable. It was something outside of us, and it existed independently of us. We could discover it, grasp it, accept it. But even if we failed to discover it, it would still be there; it did not depend on us for its existence or truthfulness. Further, it held within it a kind of authority. We did not control it; in many ways it controlled us. The correct attitude was to be open to it, and even to submit humbly to it.

Of course, not everyone agreed on which things were true. One might believe the Earth was flat, another that it was spherical. But, even so, those who disagreed in this way still agreed that behind their disagreement, and independent of it, there was the truth: the Earth was either flat or spherical (or neither); and if it was true that it was flat it was not true that it was spherical, and so on. Further, it was generally possible to think of some way of checking which of the two conflicting beliefs was true. For example, you could get in a ship and sail in a reasonably straight line and see if you fell off the edge or came back to where you started.

Because the truth was outside of us and discoverable and checkable, we could build a body of knowledge and understanding about the world. We could communicate and debate, and come to agreement over what is true. And once the truth had been settled, it would stay that way; truth was unchanging and eternal. As time went by we would amass more and more truth, a great body of knowledge, making us (in Bacon's phrase) 'lords and possessors of nature'.

This view of truth had four basic components. One was *objectivity*: truth is outside of us and independent of us. Another was *universality*: truth is the same the world over and for all people; cultural differences, for example, did not affect it. A third was *eternity*: truths last for ever; the truth that 'Socrates drank a cup of hemlock' remains a truth two thousand years and more after the event, and will remain a truth for ever. Indeed, the 'Socrates drank hemlock' truth can be said to have existed even before Socrates lifted the cup, although it may have had to be expressed as 'It is true that Socrates will drink hemlock'; so it is an eternal truth 'backwards' in time as well as 'forwards'. A fourth component was *intelligibility*: we as human beings are able to discover, comprehend and know the truth.

This is the concept of truth on which western culture and society have been built. Largely formulated by Plato, it dominated all subsequent thinking down to the twentieth century, and, in particular, provided the basis for the Enlightenment and the rise of modern science. Although, as we shall see, it is now officially discredited and rejected, its results are all around us and its present influence is still very wide indeed.

But although this concept of truth, which we shall call the traditional western concept, or simply the traditional concept, has been dominant for two millennia and more, it would be wrong to assume either that it has been monochrome or that it has been the only concept of truth available in the West. Within its basic parameters there has been much variety, as different thinkers stressed different aspects, or attempted different tasks, or set themselves to solve problems which arose out of the concept. Alternative approaches to truth were occasionally put forward, only to be overwhelmed by the dominant concept. Hebrew thinkers, for example, seem to have had an approach to truth which, while sharing Plato's conviction that truth was somehow rooted in the Divine Being, saw it as something much more alive and personal; and from ancient times there has been a succession of sceptical schools of thought, claiming that knowledge and truth in the accepted sense were unobtainable, and offering alternative approaches.

The twentieth century has seen the collapse of the traditional concept of truth. Over two thousand years of dominance have ended in the shattering of the structure into a tangled mass of problems and unresolved issues. A range of new concepts of truth and approaches to truth are being put forward, but it seems unlikely that in the foreseeable future any one of them will get anywhere near to taking the dominant position the traditional concept held for so long. The established structure has gone; uncertainty and relativism have taken its place.

The revolution that has occurred at this most basic level of human understanding and thought is parallel to, but deeper than, the paradigm shift from the Newtonian view of the universe to that which we hold today. When the Newtonian paradigm was rejected, a new paradigm was available to take its place; but in the area of truth the problem is compounded because the old view has been rejected and we do not know what will or can take its place.

Not that we did not have warning of the coming crisis. There have always been cracks in the traditional structure. They started appearing clearly in the seventeenth century. In the eighteenth century, philosophers were beginning to realize that repair might not be possible. In the nineteenth, there were those who were sure it was impossible. But though their arguments were strong, the message of those arguments was for the most part not heard. After all, the traditional concept was working magnificently. Basing all our thinking on it, we were making one discovery after another; knowledge was increasing; in every area of investigation we were making impressive progress; we were rapidly becoming lords and possessors of nature. It was easy to conclude that if modern culture and science presupposed the traditional concept of truth, and if modern culture and science were magnificent in their success and fruitfulness, then the traditional concept of truth must be true. So why listen to the scepticism of the philosophers?

Nietzsche, in 1882, was aware of this when he wrote his well-known 'madman' passage. After his graphic description of the world without the fixed points provided by the traditional concept of truth, the madman realizes that his audience cannot receive his message.

'I come too early,' he said then; 'my time has not yet come. This tremendous event is still on its way, still wandering – it has not yet reached the ears of man. Lightning and thunder require time, the light of the stars requires time, deeds require time even after they are done, before they can be seen and heard.'[1]

Throughout the twentieth century the effect of the collapse of the traditional concept has been increasingly felt. But even now most of us are cushioned from its full impact by the continued acceptance and use of the outworkings of the traditional view. We are much more aware of the problems than previous generations, but we still base much of our daily living and the structures of society on traditional concepts of what is true.

For some, the prospect before us is dark. Nietzsche wrote: 'Do we not feel the breath of empty space? Has it not become colder? Is not night and more night coming on all the while?'[2] His words were echoed by many in the twentieth century. But others are less gloomy. For them, it has to be possible to find a new theory to replace the old structures. Possible accounts of how truth functions are being worked out and offered as alternatives. More radically, new approaches to what truth is are being explored. Many are willing to incorporate elements of relativism and pragmatism into their approach. Others still seek to present concepts of truth that have at least some of the objectivity and universality that was at the heart of the old system. Just a few would feel that the collapse of the traditional structure is not final. For them a pattern that has worked so well for so long cannot be totally wrong and should not be allowed to be lost. Something can be salvaged from the wreckage, and a revised structure reinstated. To this possibility we shall return later in the book.

In chapters 2 and 3 we shall explore in more detail the story of the collapse of the traditional western concept of truth. In the rest of this chapter we turn to one specific section of western culture, evangelical Christianity, whose concept of truth and reaction to the collapse of the traditional concept will occupy us for much of the rest of the book.

Evangelicalism

It is generally accepted that evangelicalism as a modern movement started in the eighteenth century with the spiritual awakening that is usually associated with the Wesleys. The roots of the movement undoubtedly go back further. Some would claim that the Reformation itself was the beginning of evangelicalism; the term 'evangelical' is used by historians and in parts of continental Europe as a synonym for 'Protestant'. David Bebbington, in his *Evangelicals in Modern Britain*, cites Sir Thomas More as referring to the advocates of the Reformation as 'Evaungelicalles' in 1531.[3] Evangelical writers have generally claimed that the movement was based firmly upon the principles of the Reformation, remaining true to them when others have looked like losing sight of them. In this sense, evangelicals, they believe, are the true heirs of the Reformation. Whatever validity this claim may have, an awareness of evangelicalism's Reformation roots is essential to an understanding of its development, and in chapter 4 we shall be looking at the concept of truth held by the Reformers. Even so, our main interest will be the period from the eighteenth century to the twentieth.

The eighteenth-century spiritual awakening can be traced back to the 1730s with Howell Harris in Wales, Jonathan Edwards in Massachusetts, and George Whitefield in England. The Wesleys followed at the end of the decade, and soon the fires of spiritual renewal were spreading rapidly. Large numbers of new churches were started, and the growth in church membership well outstripped the population growth. In the early years it was the Dissenters who grew most rapidly; but by the beginning of the nineteenth century, evangelicalism was making major inroads into all Protestant denominations in Britain and America. By the middle of the century the Church of England had an evangelical archbishop (J. B. Sumner, 1848–62), and almost all Protestant denominations had a majority of evangelicals in their membership. According to the 1851 religious census, church attendance on a given Sunday was 35% of the population of England and Wales; half of these were evangelical Nonconformists. In Scotland, Presbyterianism was almost totally evangelical.[4] In America, the eighteenth-century Great Awakening, which started as an indigenous movement and spread extensively under the preaching of Wesley and Whitefield, resulted in evangelical ascendency not just in most of the denominations in the nineteenth century, but also in American culture, politics, science, and education. In 1850, for example, the vast majority of American colleges had evangelical clergymen as their presidents. William McLoughlin has claimed that the story of American evangelicalism in the nineteenth century is the story of America itself.[5]

The period of nineteenth-century evangelical ascendency in Britain and America peaked around the 1870s. After that, the movement's influence, though not necessarily its numbers, went into decline. But, meanwhile, evangelicals had been at the front of missionary vision and outreach, and by the end of the nineteenth century the movement had spread to most parts of the world. In Australia, for example, the Anglican clergyman who sailed with the first boatload of English convicts was an evangelical, as were almost all the early Anglican clergy there; when other denominations started sending ministers and evangelists, they too were generally evangelical. Evangelicals were at the front of nineteenth-century missionary advance into Africa and Asia. The Pentecostalism which spread rapidly in the twentieth century, especially in South America, is basically evangelical in its ethos, as is the charismatic movement which followed it. So too are several of the twentieth-century indigenous Christian movements that have produced very substantial growth, for example in China, South Korea, and some parts of Africa. Worldwide evangelicals now total well over 500 million, making up the bulk of Protestantism, almost one quarter of Christendom, and 8% of the total world population. Growth worldwide over the thirty years 1965–95 has averaged 4.5% annually, with the highest growth in the non-western world; some 70% of evangelicals now live outside the West.[6]

Evangelicalism, like most religious movements, has never been mono-chrome. From the start it has included Calvinists and Arminians, confession-alists and non-confessionalists, baptists and paedobaptists, and so on. It has always spanned the denominations, and it has always contained a variety of views on ecclesiology, liturgy, eschatology, and the like. Despite the attempts of some within its ranks, it has generally been committed to change and development; according to Bebbington, the changes through its nearly three centuries of history have been substantial. Even so, he singles out four emphases which he suggests can be regarded as the distinctive marks of evangelicalism: conversion, the centrality of the cross, activism, and the Bible.[7]

In the eighteenth and nineteenth centuries, evangelicalism put its main stress on a personal *conversion* experience and *the cross*. Typically, a survey of texts used by evangelical preachers on a Sunday in March 1896 found that the text most commonly used was Galatians 2:20: 'I am crucified with Christ: nevertheless I live; yet not I, but Christ liveth in me: and the life which I now live in the flesh I live by the faith of the Son of God, who loved me, and gave himself for me' (AV). In the nineteenth century the awareness grew that the personal experience of conversion must give rise to good works of evangelism and social concern, and the *activism* already present in Methodism became a dominant feature of the movement. Towards the end of the nineteenth century *the Bible* became a major focus of attention. Evangelicals saw themselves as defenders of the Bible and of the historic Christian doctrines against their attackers. This tended to direct their activity away from the social and cultural focus; but the stress on conversion and the cross has remained at the heart of evangelicalism even when 'the battle for the Bible' has been at its height. John Stott, perhaps the leading spokesman for evangelicals in the last quarter of the twentieth century, has characterized them as 'Bible people' and 'gospel people'.

The stress on *conversion*, for evangelicals, has its roots in the Reformation doctrine of justification by faith. Salvation, for them, is God's gift, and it is received by each individual through faith. Thus the experience of conversion, of turning to God in repentance and faith and receiving Christ and the fruit of his work, is of crucial importance. Before it the individual is cut off from God; after it a whole new relationship has begun, the person is 'born again'. Though evangelicals, and in particular Anglican evangelicals, have always allowed that the conversion experience can be a slow and gradual one, much evangelical preaching has been directed towards a dramatic moment of conversion, whether or not as the climax of a process. Charles Wesley, whose spiritual search was a lengthy one, had just such an experience:

Long my imprisoned spirit lay
Fast bound in sin and nature's night.
Thine eye diffused a quickening ray;
I woke, the dungeon flamed with light.
My chains fell off, my heart was free,
I rose, went forth, and followed thee.

The experience of conversion, particularly in the eighteenth and nine-teenth centuries, was often a deeply emotional one, involving conviction of sin and giving rise to joy, peace, and a new outlook on the whole of life.

In keeping with the western tradition of Christendom, evangelicals have made the doctrine of *the cross* the focal point of all their doctrine. It was Christ's atoning work on the cross that was the climax of the incarnation and all his work. As with Bunyan's Pilgrim, it is at the cross that we find salvation. John Wesley specifically stated that nothing in the Christian system is of greater importance than the doctrine of the atonement.[8] Paul's statement in Galatians 6:14, 'God forbid that I should glory, save in the cross of our Lord Jesus Christ' (AV) was a rallying-cry for evangelicals. For two centuries their understanding of atonement was almost exclusively in substitutionary terms; in the twentieth century, though substitutionary ideas remain central, there has been a developing willingness to accept that no one theory of the atonement can do it full justice.

Activism was a clear distinguishing mark of evangelicalism in the eighteenth and nineteenth centuries. John Wesley set the pace, with his 250,000 and more miles of travel, his 40,000 sermons, and his 400 publications. In contrast to the relaxed life of the non-evangelical clergy of the day, Methodist ministers and evangelists were committed to a whirlwind of activity, evangelistic, pastoral, and social, making up a working week of 90 to 100 hours. Bebbington cites the case of Thomas Chalmers:

In his early ministry he was not an evangelical. After the satisfactory discharge of his duties, Chalmers commented at the time, 'a minister may enjoy five days in the week of uninterrupted leisure'. After his conversion, by contrast, Chalmers was reputed to have visited 11,000 homes in his Glasgow parish during a single year.[9]

Activism was not limited to local evangelism and pastoral care. The evangelical vision was of a world won for Christ, and a Christian Britain or a Christian America. Tremendous energies, much money, and many lives were invested in overseas missionary activity; and many evangelicals, from William Booth to Lord Shaftesbury, worked tirelessly to transform society into something approaching the Christian ideal.

The fourth characteristic of evangelicals is their high view of *the Bible*. Though, again, the outworkings of this view have varied considerably, the conviction that the Bible is not only authoritative, but dependable, has remained central. As can be seen in these statements from Wesley and the Lausanne Covenant, evangelicals have taken the Bible as God's revelation and a key means through which we find not only truth about God, but God himself.

I want to know one thing, the way to heaven; how to land safe on that happy shore. God Himself hath condescended to teach the way; for this very end He came down from heaven. He hath written it down in a book! O give me that book. At any price, give me the Book of God! I have it; here is knowledge enough for me. Let me be *homo unius libri* [a man of one book]. Here then I am, far from the busy ways of men. I sit down alone: only God is here. In His presence I open, I read His book; for this end, to find the way to heaven.[10]

2. *The Authority and Power of the Bible*
We affirm the divine inspiration, truthfulness and authority of both Old and New Testament Scriptures in their entirety as the only written Word of God, without error in all that it affirms, and the only infallible rule of faith and practice. We also affirm the power of God's Word to accomplish his purpose of salvation. The message of the Bible is addressed to all mankind. For God's revelation in Christ and in Scripture is unchangeable. Through it the Holy Spirit still speaks today. He illumines the minds of God's people in every culture to perceive its truth freshly through their own eyes and thus discloses to the whole church ever more of the many-colored wisdom of God.[11]

At times this respect for the Bible has given rise to an unimaginative literalism; though this has not always been the case, and in the latter part of the twentieth century evangelicals have played a significant role in the development of biblical scholarship and hermeneutics. As we shall see later in the book, the evangelical approach to Scripture, though correctly described by terms like 'verbal inspiration', is one which has always found something richer than just propositional truth in the pages of the Bible.

The way to heaven is written by God in a book that is the Word of God, inspired, truthful, authoritative, and powerful. At the heart of that book is the message of the cross, an event in history through which the incarnate God took on himself the sins of the world. Through the cross is made possible a life-changing experience, an encounter in which what happened there becomes part of the believer, with radical implications not just for the individual but for society. These are core themes of evangelicalism, and to them we shall be returning as we explore the concept of truth which evangelicals have been using as they have preached and lived these beliefs. In common with most people, their concept of truth has almost always been presupposed rather than acknowledged; just as we generally use words to express our thoughts without stopping to reflect on etymology, so most of the time we use truth systems without stopping to analyse their epistemology. But inevitably presuppositions about the nature of truth underlie all statements that we claim to be true; evangelicalism's claim to have truth from God necessarily rests on such presuppositions.

Before we start investigating these, we shall turn back to the traditional western concept of truth, seeking to understand it more fully, and to trace the reasons for its collapse. We need to do this in order to be able to assess the extent of its influence on the development of evangelicalism.

2. Plato to postmodernism 1

Surveying over two thousand years of philosophy in a couple of chapters is a hard task, even if we limit ourselves to a single philosophical topic, that of truth. It can be done only at the risk of considerable oversimplification. Sadly, simplicity has never been a virtue philosophers have taken very seriously. To try to describe any given philosophical approach in a few simple sentences seems doomed to distort it.

Nevertheless, an overall pattern in the development of the concept of truth can be traced. Perhaps it can best be summarized by seeing how thinkers at different stages would have answered four questions.[1] I call them the *objectivity question*, the *relational question*, the *certainty question*, and the *ultimate justification question*.

The objectivity question asks, 'Is truth objective?' Is it something just in the mind, or is there something more to it, something independent of the mind? Would 'Water boils at 100°C at sea level' be true even if no-one believed it? The question of the objectivity of truth is closely related to the question 'Is reality objective?' Many of those who have denied the objectivity of truth have had to concede that since we cannot know objective truth about the world, we cannot know that there *is* an objective world.

The relational question asks, 'What is the relationship between human persons and the truth? What is it in us that enables us to relate to it, and how do we do it?'

The certainty question asks, 'Can we know truth for sure? Can we say, "This is a fact", "This proposition is true", "I know this"?'

The ultimate justification question asks, 'What is the ultimate justification for any given truth?' There may be immediate reasons why we hold a truth: we know water boils at 100°C because we were taught it at school. But we can always ask, 'Why do we believe what our physics teachers told us?' Then we can ask 'Why?' of that answer, and 'Why?' of the answer to that answer. To stop us going on for ever, we need an ultimate justification, a final authority, that we accept as sufficient in itself.

We shall divide the period into five sections, well aware that there was a great deal of development within those sections and that they generally overlapped. We start with the legacy of Plato; then we look briefly at the medieval period, the Renaissance, the period that is variously known as the Enlightenment or the Age of Reason or the modern period, and end up with postmodernism.

The legacy of Plato

There is a saying attributed to A. N. Whitehead, an influential modern British philosopher, that the history of western philosophy is no more than a series of footnotes to the philosophy of **Plato** (*c.* 428–*c.* 348 BC).[2] Certainly, Plato, and those after him who continued to develop Platonism in its various forms, have dominated western concepts of truth right down to the twentieth century. It would be wrong, however, to think that Plato personally established a set of doctrines about knowledge and truth which have stood virtually unchallenged ever since; in his writings he leaves many issues open, and at times even seems to contradict himself. What he did was set up a basic framework within which he and his followers explored the concepts of knowledge and truth. From this we can pick out four significant emphases, before we look briefly at Augustine, whose thinking was influenced by Neoplatonism.

1. *Truth is intimately linked with reality and goodness.* Reality, what is real, is what truly exists. We may mistakenly believe there is a cat on the mat, but we truly know that there is a cat on the mat only if there is a real cat on a real mat. Plato would never have accepted the twentieth-century division between the epistemological and the moral, between fact and value, truth and goodness. For him if we get something wrong, that is bad; if we get it right, and so have a true understanding of reality, that has got to be good. Underlying this, of course, was the conviction that reality in itself (as opposed to our mistaken views of reality) is necessarily good. Indeed, of the three, goodness is the key concept, which gives substance to reality and truth.[3]

2. *Truth is something outside of us.* We do not create or control it; rather, we look for it, find it, accept it; Plato used words like 'aim at it', 'pursue it', 'seek

it', 'discover it', 'grasp it', 'attain it'.[4] It would still exist and be the same even if no-one ever found it or believed it.

3. *Human beings have an ability to know truth.* This ability is not something we pick up as we go along; it is something innate. We have something in us, in our intellect or reason, which conforms to the reason or intellect which lies at the heart of the universe. But this ability is something much more than just reason. It is an ability which covers emotions and moral commitment and aesthetics – indeed, each part of the human person. A philosopher (humanity at its most ideal) was not, for Plato, just a thinking machine. He (they were all male in Plato's day) was a *lover* of wisdom;[5] and wisdom for Plato was not limited to 'scientific' facts; it was the 'vision of truth'; it was reality, and beauty and goodness. Plato was more at home speaking of knowledge as love of beauty or goodness, than as awareness of facts.[6]

4. *Underlying all reality and truth are 'forms' or 'ideas', the highest of which is the Form of the Good, the source of all truth and knowledge.* Much of our knowing is tainted with error, but the more we move from our immediate perceptions of things in the world to the forms which lie behind them, the more we grasp the truth. Just what the forms were, and how they might relate to any concept of God, was a matter of considerable debate for many centuries. Plato himself in some ways gave God-like status to the Form of the Good, and subsequent Platonism continued to develop the concept of one supreme and ultimate deity in place of the traditional Greek concept of many gods, a development which was understandably welcomed by Christians, who were eager to stress that God is the source of all reality. For them the world existed because he made it and held it in being. All truth must have its source in him; his knowledge must comprehend all that is knowable.[7]

Augustine (354–430), in his *Confessions*, recorded how (through reading the Platonists and especially the Neoplatonist Plotinus) he came to realize that truth is to be located in God.[8] Indeed, in his dialogue *De libero arbitrio*, working from Neoplatonist premises, he was able to claim that if we can establish that truth exists, then God must exist.[9]

Much (if not all) truth, for Augustine, came through 'illumination'. To know a thing truly requires something much stronger than the fallible acquaintance we have with objects about which we form mere beliefs. Certain knowledge and apprehension of truth require direct contact with the real thing, the perfect immutable truth that exists nowhere else than in the very mind of God. So, in the last analysis, true knowledge can be attained only as God reveals his divine ideas to us; we are able to see only when his light shines.[10]

In some passages Augustine seems to suggest that some ordinary truths can be known without specific divine illumination; these include the sort of statements whose truth seems obvious to all (such as '2 + 2 = 4', 'I exist' or 'To each should be given his own'),[11] and the truths that we accept on the testimony of others. But, even with these, the concept of the necessity of God as the source of truth is never far away; mathematical or moral truths are seen to be true because he decreed them and made our intellects in such a way that we could grasp them.

Our God-given intellects also have a role to play in the area of testimony, and specifically in the testimony to God's revelation in the Scriptures. Reason and philosophy may take us so far,[12] but revelation was essential to find the fullness of divine truth. But how do we know that the revelation is true? When we first believe it we do not; we have to start by taking it on trust – hence Augustine's well-known saying, 'Understanding is the reward of faith. Seek therefore not to understand in order that you may believe, but to believe in order that you may understand.'[13] This is not a call to blind fideism; Augustine was convinced that the act of faith would in time be rewarded by divine illumination. In any case, he argued that we should seek to justify what we at first accept by faith through the subsequent use of God-given reason.

In summary, then, the tradition of Plato and the Neoplatonists, culminating in Augustine's Christianized version, answered the *objective question* with a firm commitment to the objectivity of truth, which is to be linked with God. On the *relational question* they held that we all have an innate capacity to relate to the truth, not just intellectually, but emotionally and personally as well; and Augustine added that our relationship is dependent in many, if not all, cases on the truth itself reaching out to us, in the form of divine illumination. To the *certainty question* they replied that sure and certain knowledge was available, though they tended to suggest that only the philosopher or the believing Christian had full access to it. *Ultimate justification* rested, for them, in the divine origin of truth, expressed obliquely in Plato's conviction that ultimate reality is good and so divine, and more specifically in Augustine's identification of the truth with God.

The Middle Ages

Thinkers in the medieval period (which spans the 900 years or so up to the beginnings of the Renaissance) broadly accepted the approach to truth taken by the Platonists and Augustine, though there was much debate over details. The status of the forms, and so of truth itself, particularly in relation to God, was keenly debated. The debate came to be focused in the issue of the status of universals. Broadly speaking, the medieval period gave the same answers to our four questions as the earlier period. But two key figures at the end of the period, Anselm and Aquinas, while remaining generally within the tradition, each changed certain emphases and made distinctive contributions to the development of the debate.

Anselm (1033–1109) agreed with Augustine that truth is objective, that truth and reality (being) and goodness are inseparably related and that truth is ultimately to be identified with God. Despite a very high trust in the powers of reason,[14] Anselm was particularly concerned with practical issues; instead of limiting the concept of truth to the area of thought or intellectual knowledge, he was eager to extend it to the area of the will and of action; we must not just know the truth, we must choose and do it as well. This was an emphasis that was particularly to the fore in the Hebrew approach to truth,[15] though it was never absent from the Greek tradition; Plato, for instance, held it strongly. But in the development of Neoplatonism and the thinking of the Middle Ages, it had perhaps given way at least partly to the view of truth as something to be contemplated rather than lived, a view Anselm firmly rejected. In that God is truth, we as God's creatures attain to truth and rightness as we conform not just our thinking, but also our choosing and living, to his truth.[16]

Anselm's stress on truth as something we do rather than just believe or know did not attract many followers. This was partly because the centuries that came after him saw an increasing tendency to stress the role of reason over against that of will or action, culminating in the Enlightenment conviction that knowledge and truth were to be defined solely in rational terms. A further factor is that Anselm's philosophy was in due course overshadowed and ousted by the success of the philosophy of perhaps the greatest thinker of the late medieval period, Thomas Aquinas.

Aquinas (1225–74) claimed to be a true successor of Augustine; but he was suspicious of the way Platonism was being applied by some of the thinkers of his day. The works of Aristotle (384–322 BC), Plato's disciple who had challenged and developed much of Plato's philosophy, had long been neglected in favour of those of Plato himself as mediated by the Neoplatonists and Augustine. But they had recently been rediscovered, and Aquinas saw in them a much more satisfactory way of marrying the essential Platonic philosophy with Christian theology.

Once again, Aquinas accepted that both reality and truth are objective, and that both depend upon God for their existence; were it not for God, truth would not exist and we would not be able to know it.[17] But in practice, for Aquinas, any role that God plays in our knowledge of truth turns out to be very small. Like Anselm, Aquinas put a high value on the role of human reason. For him it was able to give us truth over a very wide range of topics without any specific divine intervention or activity. Aquinas, following Aristotle, was especially interested in exploring what the human mind could discover about the world around us through careful observation and reasoning. In the event, there seems no limit to what it can discover. Even in the area of theology, reason is, according to Aquinas, able to establish foundational truths about God, quite apart from the Christian revelation.[18] Given this, the long debates since the time of Augustine on how we can know the divine forms or how divine truth illuminates human minds seem to be a waste of time. The fact is, for Aquinas, that we have natural powers which enable us to achieve reliable knowledge and truth. Why then waste time seeking to know the forms when we have direct and dependable knowledge of ordinary individual things? Truth comes from our experience of things around us in the world, not from some distant world of forms; truth, primarily, is something in the human mind or intellect.[19]

The Renaissance

Though the work of Aquinas was very influential, it was by no means universally accepted, and debates about the relationship of God's truth to what we know as truth continued through the next two centuries, often involving the most complex and obscure arguments. But the spirit of the age was changing. Europe was being awakened in a new movement we know as the Renaissance; old traditions were being questioned; a new confidence in human powers was arising, and especially in the powers of human reason. We have already seen this in Anselm and Aquinas, with their stress on the increasingly autonomous role of reason. It was expressed, too, in the academic complexities of the debates of the rationalistic scholastics who followed Aquinas. It was seen in the early stirrings of the mindset that was to give rise to the beginnings of modern science: a willingness to challenge long-held explanations (especially those given by the theologians) with theories based on direct observation of the world around us. It is seen also in the stirrings of dissent that heralded the Reformation, the questioning of centuries of authoritative church tradition and teaching. The Reformation both expressed it and further unleashed it, stressing, as it did, the right of even ploughboys to seek and find truth and reality for themselves. The way was being prepared for the Age of Reason, when all else was to be subjected to the human intellect, when reason was to become the sole arbiter of all truth. Granted, at first, reason was acknowledged as God-given and God-inspired. But increasingly it became an autonomous reason; a reason which questioned and challenged and rejected, not just the authority of the church and centuries of accepted tradition, but the very role of God in matters of reality and truth.

The Renaissance, then, was a period of transition. But its answers to our four questions have a familiar ring. Truth remained *objective*, and something that we can know for *certain*. God continued to have an essential role in the *ultimate justification* of knowledge and truth. But it was becoming a much less active role; the Renaissance confidence in human powers, and in particular our reason, saw us as able to discover the truth unaided. In answer to the *relational question*, the key was steadily becoming our reason: something that God has given us, but which we are free to use without any reference to its source.

By the end of the Renaissance period the stage has been set for the modern experiment in which reason was given total and final authority in every area, an experiment which our current postmodern age tells us has ended in disastrous failure.

3. Plato to postmodernism 2

The modern period

The start of the modern period is hard to fix definitively, since, as we have seen, its roots go through the Renaissance and right back into the Middle Ages. But it seems reasonable to follow the tradition of placing it at the dawn of the Age of Reason or Enlightenment as expressed in the philosophies of Bacon and Descartes.

Francis Bacon (1561–1626) saw himself as rejecting all the philosophies that had gone before him, and replacing them with a new approach to knowledge and truth. He was conscious of living at the dawn of a great new era of discovery whose heralds were Marco Polo, Galileo, William Caxton, and the like. A new world was opening up; a new age was dawning; and the fusty metaphysics and irrelevant arguments of the late medieval philosophers – not to mention their Platonist forebears – were worse than useless. Traditions, erroneous philosophies, even established beliefs, all 'idols of the mind', are to be challenged; we have lost our mastery over the world, and we must regain it by a 'Great Instauration' or restoration, until we become again 'lords and possessors of nature'.[1]

The key to Bacon's new philosophy was reason. Faith and revelation have their place in religion (Bacon, like Descartes, was a Christian believer); but in the natural order reason, particularly exercised through inductive logic which observes and classifies and draws conclusions from careful observation of the world around us, was the only tool we need to establish the truth.

It is always easier to ask questions than to provide answers, to doubt than to prove a case. Even in Descartes's day the new tool of unfettered reason was being used more to further the arguments of the sceptics than to build constructive philosophies.[2] **René Descartes** (1596–1650) set himself to face the doubts put forward by the sceptics, and, through the use of reason, not just to answer them, but to build a whole system of knowledge and truth. But where Bacon's system, though wholly based on reason, had incorporated empirical observation, Descartes claimed to have established his total system of knowledge using reason alone as his tool. Using mathematical, and so deductive, logic as his model, he established by rational argument first his own existence, since, even if he is doubting, he still must exist; then the existence of God, by a form of the ontological argument; and then, since God must be perfect and a perfect God would not deceive us, the truth of 'whatever we conceive very clearly and very distinctly'.[3]

So God remains in Descartes's philosophy as the ultimate guarantor of it all. The *Fourth Meditation* concludes with the words:

> Every clear and distinct perception is something; so it cannot come from nothingness, but must have God for its author; God, I say, the supremely Perfect, who it is absurd should be deceitful; therefore it is indubitably true.

But in a sense even Descartes's God had become subject to reason. He was a God established by reason, and he was subject to reason in the sense that the criterion for his nature and activity was that they should be rational. Descartes, for all his talk of God, was firmly committed to the basic agenda of the modern period: that human reason should be the only authority.

How then would Bacon and Descartes have answered our four questions? For them truth was still *objective*, and they were still confident that *certainty* was attainable: despite the sceptics, they were full of optimism at the discoveries and developments of their age that were unlocking the secrets of nature, and conquering the world around them. The answer to the question of *ultimate justification*, however, was changing. Though still theoretically it was a God who would not let us be deceived, in practice God was gradually being dethroned and being made subject to reason. On the *relational question* the stress on the role of reason in establishing truth had meant that knowing truth was now becoming increasingly a matter of just the intellect.

In the two centuries following Bacon and Descartes, philosophers continued to work out the implications of the Enlightenment's confidence in reason. The initial benefits, of course, were enormous and very impressive.

The inductive method in particular led to one discovery after another; modern science brought tremendous benefits to the human race. Reason certainly appeared to be justified by her works. But the philosophical problems raised were serious and refused to go away. Basically, they arose from the question of *ultimate justification*. As God's role as the ultimate guarantor of reality and truth became more and more nominal, reason was increasingly looked on as its own ultimate justification. Superficially this seemed an easy and obvious assumption to make; but in the event it raised profound difficulties. Quite apart from appearing to be a case of pulling yourself up by your own bootlaces, reason in the event seemed to be far better at destroying its own authority than at justifying it; the rational arguments of the sceptics were more powerful and effective than those of the philosophers who tried to find a lasting justification for our confidence in reason. The philosophy of the rest of the modern period is the story of a developing realization that if we are to answer the *ultimate justification* question by making reason our ultimate authority, then our answer to the *objective* question has to change; truth ceases to be objective. That in turn changes our answer to the *certainty* question; if truth is no longer objective, we can no longer be sure of it; it ceases to be fixed and factual. Though the modern period continued to act as though it was built on the foundation of firm, factual, objective truth (and as a result made tremendous developments in knowledge and understanding), philosophers were increasingly aware that the foundation in fact did not exist.

A significant step in this process was made in the philosophy of **John Locke** (1632–1704). Like Bacon, Locke was a firm empiricist, believing that the basic data of all knowledge come to us through our five senses. But he was fully committed to the Enlightenment's total confidence in reason: 'Reason must be our last judge and guide in everything.'[4] A committed Christian, he nevertheless subjected everything, including his faith, to the test of reason,[5] and was strongly opposed to 'enthusiasm' (a form of Christianity that claimed that God communicates directly to the individual) on the grounds that it failed to subject revelation to reason. John Wesley was still a baby in the year that Locke died, but it was his form of religion, and the evangelical revival which followed it, that was most frequently attacked for 'enthusiasm' in the eighteenth century.

A key concept in Locke's philosophy was his theory of ideas. It was this theory that took the first clear steps in the abolition of objective truth. Locke was aware of this, and sought to resist the implications of his theory, even to the extent at times of being inconsistent with it. This theory stated that the objects of our knowledge are not things in the world around us, but ideas in our minds.

It is evident the mind knows not things immediately, but only by the intervention of the ideas it has of them. Our knowledge therefore is real only so far as there is a conformity between our ideas and the reality of things. But what shall be here the criterion? How shall the mind, when it perceives nothing but its own ideas, know that they agree with things themselves?[6]

How indeed? Locke tried to answer this question with a number of suggestions, including the intervention of God. But many thinkers were not convinced by his answers, and his philosophy, which was extremely influential, is generally seen as taking a crucial step away from the traditional view of truth as objective.

The next significant name in the development of British philosophy was **George Berkeley** (1685–1753). He was not as worried as Locke was over the realization that we cannot observe objects in the world around us, but instead only be aware of our ideas or impressions of them. But, rather than agree with Locke that the external material world is the reality and our ideas about it are derivative and so somehow insubstantial and unreliable, he took the radical step of asserting that it is the world that is derivative, and our ideas or minds the reality. The objects in the world do not shape our thinking; our thinking gives existence to the objects.[7] This approach provided Berkeley with a dramatic opportunity to reverse the trend towards the ousting of God as the answer to the *ultimate justification* question. If everything depends on mind, and our human minds are very limited in what they can perceive and think, the mind of God must necessarily play the key role in maintaining a coherent universe.

Berkeley, then, accepted that we can know only our own ideas, not objects in the world around us; but he avoided the sceptical implications of this by retaining God as the *ultimate justification*. But the tide was running too strongly in the other direction. In **David Hume** (1711–76), the next great British philosopher, we find an almost complete rejection of the role of God and an almost complete scepticism as a result. We can never, Hume said, get behind our impressions and ideas; we can only ever be aware of or know our thought or experience, never the object that lies behind it. Further, in a devastating critique of causation, which, philosophically speaking, took away the basis of the whole modern scientific enterprise, he destroyed the argument that our impressions or ideas are somehow caused by the objects in the world, so providing us with at least some link between them. Causation, claimed Hume, cannot be defended rationally; it is only a psychological convenience.[8] Hume was very willing to admit that we have to live as though the principle of causation works, and assume that our ideas are accurate representations of real things in a real world, at least for most of the time. He did not live as a sceptic; indeed, he could not. But what he was claiming was that there is no way of defending belief in an external world or objective knowledge on rational grounds, that is, by using reason as our *ultimate justification*. The central tenet of the modern period, the primacy of reason, was shown to be inadequate. Bertrand Russell comments:

> Hume's philosophy, whether true or false, represents the bankruptcy of eighteenth-century reasonableness. He starts out, like Locke, with the intention of being sensible and empirical, taking nothing on trust, but seeking whatever instruction is to be obtained from experience and observation. But having a better intellect than Locke's, a greater acuteness in analysis, and a smaller capacity for accepting comfortable inconsistencies, he arrives at the disastrous conclusion that from experience and observation nothing is to be learnt. There is no such thing as a rational belief: 'If we believe that fire warms, or water refreshes, 'tis only because it costs us too much pains to think otherwise.' We cannot help believing, but no belief can be grounded in reason . . . The growth of unreason throughout the nineteenth century and what has passed of the twentieth is a natural sequel to Hume's destruction of empiricism.[9]

Hume's findings alarmed **Immanuel Kant** (1724–1804) and caused him to work on a masterly critique of reason, and especially of its limits. He claimed to have answered Hume's scepticism, but in fact his victory was a very limited one, since he conceded Hume's basic point that on the basis of reason (as normally understood) we can never have knowledge of things in the world around us, things as they are in themselves.

> To avoid all misapprehension, it is necessary to explain, as clearly as possible, what our view is regarding the fundamental constitution of sensible knowledge in general.
> What we have meant to say is that all our intuition is nothing but the representation of appearance: that the things which we intuit are not in themselves what we intuit them as being, nor their relations so constituted in themselves as they appear to us, and that if the subject, or even only the subjective constitution of the senses in general, be removed, the whole constitution and all the relations of objects in space and time, nay space and time themselves, would vanish. As appearances, they cannot exist in themselves, but only in us. What objects may be in themselves, and apart from all this receptivity of our sensibility, remains completely unknown to us.[10]

So we have lost things as they are in themselves; we have lost the external objective world and objective truth about it. But, says Kant, rather than lamenting their loss or trying to reverse it, we should accept it and adapt our concept of knowledge and truth accordingly. This he sought to do, making a change so radical that he claimed it was the philosophical equivalent of what Copernicus did for the understanding of astronomy.

> Hitherto it has been assumed that all our knowledge must conform to objects. But all attempts to extend our knowledge of objects by establishing something in regard to them *a priori*, by means of concepts, have, on this assumption, ended in failure. We must therefore make trial whether we may not have more success in the tasks of metaphysics, if we suppose that objects must conform to our knowledge. This would agree better with what is desired, namely, that it should be possible to have knowledge of objects *a priori*, determining something in regard to them prior to their being given. We should then be proceeding precisely on the lines of Copernicus' primary hypothesis. Failing of discovering satisfactory progress in explaining the movement of the heavenly bodies on the supposition that they all revolved round the spectator, he tried whether he might not have better success if he made the spectator to revolve and the stars to remain at rest.[11]

This 'Copernican revolution' was radical, and it set the trend not just for continental philosophy, which, following Kant, tended to move into strongly subjective concepts of truth, but, less directly, for all western thinking in the last two hundred years. No longer is truth outside of us, something we discover and receive and submit to; it is something inside us, private, subjective. No longer does it shape us; we shape it. For all Kant's claim to a Copernican revolution, he has in fact done the reverse of what Copernicus did; Copernicus moved us from being the centre of the universe around which everything else revolved, and gave us a somewhat humbler position; Kant made the individual thinking subject the centre of the universe, the key to everything else.

Though Kant denied that normal human reason can give us knowledge of objective truth, he did go on to suggest that we can have some sort of knowledge of things in the real world, things in themselves, and even of God. This was not through ordinary reason or the intellect but through a faculty which, confusingly, he also called reason,[12] but which was in fact much more akin to feeling or faith or intuition (in the usual sense of the word). He made it clear that this second sort of reason was utterly different from the first; they functioned on different planes, and the different planes never intersect.

Kant's contribution to our understanding of truth was both a continuation of the process of the application of the Enlightenment's concept of reason, and a watershed that set the trend for all that followed him. Perhaps the most significant thing about it is that he took what until then had been a major article of scepticism – that if we follow reason as our authority or *ultimate justification*, we have to surrender objective truth – and made it a central tenet of respected philosophical thought. Western philosophy, in its bid to enthrone reason, has accepted that it has lost *objective truth*, and so it can no longer have *certainty*.

After Kant a few philosophers sought to resist his conclusions, and find ways of retaining objective truth. The majority, however, were willing to follow his lead. One stream broadly accepted his approach, but turned their attention particularly to his concept of a higher reason, and, in so doing, tended to move away from the Enlightenment's central stress on ordinary (scientific) reason. These were the philosophers who stressed will or feeling as central, including the Romantics and the Transcendentalists. They in effect raised again the *relational* question. Rejecting the established agenda of the Age of Reason to make the rational intellect the sole means by which we apprehend truth, they harked back to the earlier traditions and claimed that, while the intellect may be the proper tool for exploring the natural or phenomenal world around us, other aspects of the human person could discover 'real' or 'higher truth', a different sort of truth. Alongside or above our reason, they claimed, we have faculties or abilities like intuition, the soul, the will, feeling, and so on. The problem here, however, was that just as Kant's two types of reason never intersected, no way was found of integrating the higher sort of truth with ordinary 'scientific' truth; a great gulf was fixed between value and fact, between soul and body, between morals and science, between things in themselves and our personal experience. In course of time this sort of approach tended to lose favour, largely because of the increasing tendency to reject any concept of the soul or the inner person with its so-called ability to discover truth.

The division between ordinary 'truth' and 'higher truth' was welcomed by many philosophical theologians as a way out of the many problems that the Age of Reason had posed for those who had accepted the traditional truths of Christianity. Throughout its history Christianity had integrated the historical with the supernatural, facts with values, theology with science. In an Age of Reason, believers were only too willing to allow all Christianity's claims to be subjected to the scrutiny of reason; indeed, much energy was spent by Christian believers from Locke onwards seeking to demonstrate the reason-ableness of Christianity, showing not just that all its beliefs and tenets were rational, but even that most, if not all, the truths of religion could be discovered with the power of reason unaided by supernatural revelation.

Reason was not, however, used just to defend Christianity. In their conviction that reason's authority was ultimate, believers, every bit as much as sceptics, used it to critique the biblical accounts, both those that contained elements of the supernatural and those that claimed to give historical or scientific truth. The result was a growing uneasiness with the supernatural elements of Christianity (which fitted badly into an age that sought to reduce everything to a level that could be explained by natural reason) and a growing acceptance that there were areas of apparent conflict between the findings of reason and the claims of revelation.

Faced with this, the suggestion that there could be more than one type of truth offered a way of keeping absolute confidence in reason but at the same time retaining at least some elements of Christianity. Religion could be moved to the plane of 'higher reason'. There is such a thing as theological truth, but it is completely different from ordinary truth. Religious claims do not belong to the world of facts and of science, but to that of values and morals and theology. If we say 'Jesus rose from the dead', we are not making a statement about a physical event in the ordinary world at a specific point in history; we are stating a higher truth, something theologically true that has no relationship to history, fact, or physics. This, of course, entailed a radical reinterpretation of the Bible, and a rejection of huge parts of its teaching. It also meant that the role of God was greatly changed; no longer could he be a God who acts in history, who intervenes supernaturally in incarnation, salvation, answers to prayer, and so on. As a result, for some he became much less immanent or relevant, a deistic rather than a theistic being. Others moved in the direction of pantheism; if God ceases to be supernatural, then the only God we can have has to be a form of divinized nature. It was against these two elements of the rejection of the Bible and the removal of a supernatural God that evangelicals particularly reacted.

The loss of the traditional God of Christianity and its implications were graphically described by the atheist **Friedrich Nietzsche** (1844–1900) in the passage referred to in chapter 1. Though published in 1882, it marks the dividing line between the Enlightenment or modern period and what is called the postmodern period, the period in which the Enlightenment's vision of reason as the *ultimate justification* of knowledge and truth has been recognized as a failure and has been abandoned. Conscious postmodernism did not, of course, start in 1882; Nietzsche recognized that philosophical developments take time to permeate into ordinary life, and there are still large parts of our thinking it has not yet reached. But Nietzsche is right: once God has been removed as the *ultimate justification* of knowledge and truth, no horizons remain; reason cannot provide an alternative; all that is left is the irrationality of madness.

Have you not heard of that madman who lit a lantern in the bright morning hours, ran to the market place, and cried incessantly, 'I seek God! I seek God!' As many of those who do not believe in God were standing around just then, he provoked much laughter. Why, did he get lost? said one. Or is he hiding? Is he afraid of us? Has he gone on a voyage? or emigrated? Thus they yelled and laughed. The madman jumped into their midst and pierced them with his glances.

'Whither is God?' he cried. 'I shall tell you. *We have killed him* – you and I. All of us are his murderers. But how have we done this? How were we able to drink up the sea? Who gave us the sponge to wipe away the entire horizon? What did we do when we unchained this earth from its sun? Whither is it moving now? Whither are we moving now? Away from all suns? Are we not plunging continually? Backward, sideward, forward, in all directions? Is there any up or down left? Are we not straying as through an infinite nothing? Do we not feel the breath of empty space? Has it not become colder? Is not night and more night coming on all the while? Must not lanterns be lit in the morning? Do we not hear anything yet of the noise of the grave-diggers who are burying God? Do we not smell anything yet of God's decomposition? Gods too decompose. God is dead. God remains dead. And we have killed him. How shall we, the murderers of all murderers, comfort ourselves? What was holiest and most powerful of all that the world has yet owned has bled to death under our knives. Who will wipe this blood off us? What water is there for us to cleanse ourselves? What festivals of atonement, what sacred games shall we have to invent? Is not the greatness of this deed too great for us? Must not we ourselves become gods simply to seem worthy of it? There never has been a greater deed; and whoever will be born after us – for the sake of this deed he will be part of a higher history than all history hitherto.'

Here the madman fell silent and looked again at his listeners; and they too were silent and stared at him in astonishment. At last he threw his lantern on the ground, and it broke and went out. 'I come too early,' he said then; 'my time has not yet come. This tremendous event is still on its way, still wandering – it has not yet reached the ears of man. Lightning and thunder require time, the light of the stars requires time, deeds require time even after they are done, before they can be seen and heard. This deed is still more distant from them than the most distant stars – *and yet they have done it themselves.*'[13]

Postmodernism

Postmodernism is best seen as a reaction against modernism rather than as a positive movement in itself; indeed, for many postmoderns, the very concept of a 'positive movement' is to be rejected along with all the other failed gods of the Enlightenment or modern period. So it is characterized chiefly by negatives, by the rejection of reason, opposition to the dominance of the scientific worldview, the removal of boundaries and the demolition of structures, and, in particular, the denial of absolutes, whether moral or political or cultural or epistemological

The chief source of postmodernism is the collapse of modernism; we have traced this as far as Nietzsche, and now need to look briefly at two twentieth-century philosophies which have paved the way for postmodernism: existentialism and the philosophy of Wittgenstein and his followers.

Existentialism can trace its roots back to **Søren Kierkegaard** (1813–55) and Nietzsche in the nineteenth century, but it is mainly a twentieth-century phenomenon characterized by a rejection of objectivity and the 'scientific' approach which makes us into rational machines, and a stress on human persons as existing, sharing in Being, free, and making creative authenticating choices. Rather than develop well-argued systems of philosophy, many existentialists communicated their ideas, or perhaps rather their feelings, by story or literary device, emphasizing that existentialism is a way of life rather than a set of dogmas. Though there are exceptions, the picture painted by the existentialists is a gloomy one; though we have the power to authenticate ourselves by creative choice, the human condition for the most part is full of absurdity, dread and despair.

The topic of truth is not very prominent in existentialist literature. Being and existence and being human are far more important than knowledge; but for the most part they follow Kierkegaard's urgent call to subjective rather than objective truth:

> 'Truth is subjectivity' . . . When subjectivity is the truth, the conceptual determination of the truth must include an expression for the antithesis to objectivity, a memento of the fork in the road where the way springs off; this expression will at the same time serve as an indication of the tension of the subjective inwardness. Here is such a definition of truth: *An objective uncertainty held fast in an appropriation-process of the most passionate inwardness is the truth*, the highest truth attainable for an *existing* individual.[14]

Kierkegaard retained a role for God in his thinking, though he fully accepted Kant's dichotomy and placed him far beyond the reach of ordinary reason; but mainstream existentialism has allowed no role for God. This fact, and the minimizing of reason, are at the heart of both existentialism's hopelessness and its challenge: to be truly human in a universe where God is dead and reason offers only absurdity, we are called upon to create meaning and authenticity for ourselves.

In the early years of the twentieth century, Enlightenment rationalism made one last brief appearance on the philosophical stage, in the form of *logical positivism*. This focused on meaning or meaningfulness rather than truth, and offered as a criterion of a proposition's meaningfulness that it should be open to 'scientific' verification, or verification by the five empirical senses. If such verification was not possible, as, for instance in the realms of ethics or aesthetics or theology, then those propositions were to be dismissed as meaningless.

One of logical positivism's early supporters was **Ludwig Wittgenstein** (1889–1951). He was also one of the earliest philosophers to realize its inadequacy, and to abandon it – with the result that he passed through a period of almost existentialist despair, and for a time gave up philosophy altogether. But later in life he developed a new philosophy, which recognized that so far from there being just one meaningful way of looking at things (the scientific), there were many. Using the concept of 'language-games', he pointed out that we use language in a wide variety of ways, each way authentic and meaningful in its particular context. But just as we do not play chess according to the rules of rugby, so we do not impose the rules of, say, scientific discourse when telling a joke, or reading poetry, or telling a story. Each context has its own rules; each has its own way of determining meaning and truth.

Here is a development of the post-Kantian dichotomy; instead of ordinary truth and 'higher' truth, we have all sorts of truth: poetic truth, storybook truth, scientific truth, moral truth, and, of course, theological truth. There is no right or wrong way of using language; there is no limit to the games we can play with it. This was a liberating concept, particularly for many theologians, who were happy to be able to claim theological truth for their beliefs, even though they may be historically or scientifically false or meaningless. Others were less happy, discerning that Wittgenstein was in fact opening up the concept of meaning and truth far too widely. Any claim, provided it can be given a context in which it functions, is to be accepted as true in its own way. The logical development of Wittgenstein is relativism and pluralism, and the loss of any claim to objective truth.

The abandonment of objective truth and the acceptance of relativism are basic to postmodernism.[15] As a movement, it is wide-ranging, covering culture and architecture and sociological issues. But its attitude to truth and knowledge is crucial. In reply to our four questions, postmodernism decisively rejects any concept of *objective truth*, and so of *certainty*. On the *ultimate justification* question the postmodernist replies that no justification is necessary; the rejection of all overarching explanatory systems, or metanarratives, is one of the central features of postmodernism; we can never get beyond our subjective way of seeing things; there is no ultimate explanation. Jean-François Lyotard writes, 'Simplifying to the extreme, I define *postmodern* as incredulity toward metanarratives.'[16] This rejection of explanation is a direct result of the failure of Enlightenment reason to provide justification; if reason has failed (and the very concept of justification is a rational one), no justification is possible. In that postmodernism rejects (along with all its teaching) the Enlightenment's narrow stress on reason as the one really significant human faculty, its reply to the *relational question* would be a broad one; apart from the obvious difficulty that, for someone who truly consistently applies the programme of deconstruction and relativism, there will be nothing left to relate to, postmodern relating is very much more holistic, stressing the significance of feelings, or intuition, of non-rational or irrational relationships, and exploring fully the implications of culture and aesthetics and art.

Where do we go from here?

Our rapid survey of 2,400 years of the story of the concept of truth ends, then, with an admission of failure. As Hume and Nietzsche foresaw, the attempt to make human reason our ultimate authority leads to disaster – to the loss of all authority. If reason is our source of meaning, we have no meaning. If truth is to be found through reason, we can have no truth. Such is the postmodern admission.

The intriguing fact, however, is that our postmodern age has continued to function as if truth, meaning, and even authority still exist. We have to admit that there is no other way we can function; consistent relativism is unlivable.[17] Postmodern thinkers use reason to attack reason, and structured sentences in their essays of deconstruction. The world we actually live in is not the world of the postmodernist. It is a world where reason and knowledge and truth and meaning and structures do exist and function perfectly satisfactorily.

So where have we gone wrong? Are the postmodernists wrong in their rejection of modernism? Can the Enlightenment agenda of making reason the ultimate authority be rescued and made to work after all? Or do we need to go one stage further back, and rediscover the pre-Enlightenment concept of reason, where reason is not its own authority, but derives its ultimate justification from God?

These are issues contemporary thinkers have to face,[18] and we shall look at them in the third part of this book. But, meanwhile, in Part 2, we shall follow through the story of evangelicalism in an attempt to trace how that particular movement held and developed its concept of truth.

PART 2

Evangelicals and truth yesterday and today

In the past 250 years the number of evangelical Christians has grown to well over 500 million people worldwide. Some of these are philosophers; the vast majority are not. Yet they all, consciously or unconsciously, have a philosophy, a basic way of viewing the world. More specifically, they all have an epistemology, or philosophy of knowledge and truth.

In the second part of this book I attempt to analyse the epistemology of some significant figures in the story of evangelicalism. They tended to be theologians rather than philosophers, but all were well versed in philosophical thinking, and some were specifically trained in philosophy. There is variety in their approaches, but it is my hope that they will have enough in common to enable us to pick out any key features of the evangelical approach to truth.

4. The Reformation legacy

Evangelicalism has traditionally seen itself as firmly within the Protestant tradition. Our aim in this chapter is to look at four key aspects of Reformation thought that have a bearing on the subsequent development of the evangelical approach to truth. These are reason, authority, the primacy of grace, and Scripture.

Contemporary Reformation scholarship rightly stresses the richness and diversity of the ideas of the Reformers and their immediate successors. There is no one Reformation theology, or philosophy, or epistemology. The Reformation was a movement, a voyage of discovery, a developing of ideas and their application in religion and life. The sources and stimuli of those ideas were far from monochrome. We could, perhaps, distinguish three major stimuli: Renaissance humanism, reaction against scholasticism, and the rediscovery of the Scriptures. But each of these was in itself very complex. Renaissance humanism as a movement was extremely diverse; scholasticism produced a wide variety of systems, often incompatible with each other, but strongly argued by their supporters; and even the appeal to Scripture was complicated by the variety of approaches to its interpretation found among the Reformers.

The development of the Reformation was aided by the rapid spread of ideas, and by the common interests that linked all the Reformers (principally the reformation of the church through the application of the Scriptures); but there were substantial differences in approach, theology, application, and so on, from Wittenberg to Zurich, or from Geneva to Münster. So it is not possible to state a definitive Reformation line on any of these four issues. Instead, we shall look at some of the main Reformation thinking about them, aware that there were divergencies, in order to provide a background to our survey of the development of evangelical epistemology. We begin with reason.

Reason

Throughout their history, evangelicals have been accused of being anti-intellectual, whether as a result of 'enthusiasm' or obscurantism, or mere laziness. More recently, there have been those who have accused them of being excessively rationalistic; perhaps this *volte-face* reflects our postmodern reaction against rationalism. Certainly, evangelicalism's attitude to the role of reason in determining truth appears complex. The origins of that complexity lie in the Reformation.

In the early sixteenth century, scholasticism was dying as an intellectual force. In most universities and centres of learning, humanism had taken its place. Many of the Reformers were content to stand on the shoulders of the humanists, and to ignore scholastic theology and philosophy. Not so Martin Luther (1483–1546). For better or worse, his early thinking was saturated with scholasticism, and it was still a living force at Wittenberg. Before he could build a new structure, he had to get the old one out of his system. It is this that gives us the clue to Luther's attitude to reason, which has strongly influenced some aspects of Protestantism, not least evangelicalism. For, to Luther, it was the wrong use of reason that lay at the heart of scholasticism's errors.

The scholastics shared with the humanists the vision of new discoveries and new freedom for the human intellect. But for them the great new discovery was the philosophy of Aristotle, and the new freedom was the opportunity to open up Christianity to the scrutiny of reason. For them this posed no threat to Christianity, since they were convinced that the whole Christian system was rational, and its reasonableness could be clearly expounded in terms of Aristotelian philosophy. Moreover, reason was an essential tool to understand and systematize the faith, and, in particular, to harmonize its different aspects and apparent contradictions, and thus to build it into an all-embracing worldview.

Luther did not in fact reject the teachings of scholasticism wholesale, nor, despite his often quoted sayings ('Reason is the monster without whose killing man cannot live'; 'Philosophy is a practical wisdom of the flesh which is hostile to God'), did he disagree with them totally on the use of reason.[1] He agreed that reason is one of the greatest of God's gifts, to be accepted and used and followed in all the natural areas of human life. He also accepted that reason has a vital role in understanding and systematizing the faith; he described this as 'regenerate reason', directed by the Holy Spirit, leading the believer into fuller truth.[2] The aspect of scholastic rationalism he would not accept was any suggestion that unaided and unregenerate reason was sufficient either to find God or the truths of God, or to bring us to God. Whatever other truth reason may discover, the truth of God comes solely from God; whatever else reason may be able to achieve, it cannot lead us to salvation and the knowledge of God. These things are the gift of God alone.[3]

There are two ways of viewing what Luther is doing here. For some he could be seen as making a decisive break with the strongly integrated approach of scholasticism. Instead of an integrated body of truth, all aspects of which are equally open to reason, we have two types of truth: truth in the natural world, discoverable by reason; and truth in the heavenly kingdom, inaccessible to reason, and to be received through faith as the gift of God's grace through revelation. The scholastics saw an essential unity between the truths of the natural world and the truths of religion, with revelation confirming and extending those truths, while itself remaining within the jurisdiction of reason. Luther, by contrast, called for a radical dichotomy; reason and faith are for ever separated.

But a second way of understanding Luther is to see him as making no such radical division. Truth is not split. Truth is one; all truth remains God's truth. What is split is the human race. The split here is between fallen humanity and regenerate humanity. Regenerated reason, though not yet perfect and so still liable to make mistakes, has the ability to receive truth both from the world around and from God himself; since the world is God's creation, and since the God who speaks through grace is the same God who speaks through nature, the truth that the regenerate reason receives is one. But fallen, unregenerate humanity has a fallen, unregenerate reason. This does not destroy its usefulness (not even Calvin, with his concept of total depravity, wanted to say that); but it corrupts it. Our knowledge and understanding of the world, though generally reliable, are perverted by our sinfulness and self-centredness. And, in particular, our knowledge of God (and Luther does concede that unregenerate reason can have some knowledge of God), is hopelessly perverted. At best it can only be partial, inadequate, and insufficient to bring us to salvation. It is this unregenerate reason that Luther is at such pains to reject; and the philosophy he so vehemently attacks is the perverted philosophy unregenerate reason produces.

Both of these ways of interpreting Luther's attitude to reason can be traced in the development of evangelicalism. The first has at times developed into an ardent anti-intellectualism, which almost seems to deny the role of reason even in the natural world, let alone in the spiritual. But something akin to the second approach can also be traced through the history of evangelicalism. Protestantism itself has generally set a high value on the role of reason. Encouraged, no doubt, by Calvin's own approach in the *Institutes*, it soon developed its own form of scholasticism, and the rationalism inherent in such an approach was at times very attractive to some evangelicals.

Authority

The attitude of the Reformers to authority seems more clear-cut than their attitude to reason. Like the humanists, they were committed to the reformation of the church, not by means of schism, but by changing it from within. Thus authority for them could not be located in the church as it was at the time. In any case, the authority of the papacy had been eroded in the fourteenth and fifteenth centuries, not least by the bizarre events of 1409, when there were three people claiming to be pope. The scholastics gave considerable authority to reason, and appear to have felt sufficiently free from the authority of the church to develop their systems wherever reason led them. Many gave a high level of authority to the great doctors (that is, teachers), especially Aquinas and Duns Scotus.[4] But neither scholastic reason nor the doctors themselves could succeed in producing anything that was clearly recognizable as the authoritative truth. Luther, who fought hard against schism, may well have accepted the authority of a church council; but no council was held until it was too late. The cry of the humanists was *Ad fontes*, 'Back to the origins'; for them it meant going back to the writings of the Greeks and Romans from which western civilization had sprung. For the Reformers the cry was the same; if the church is to be reformed it must get back to its roots, to the early fathers, and, supremely, to the Bible.

But the cry *Sola scriptura*, 'By Scripture alone', did not bring as clear a solution to the problem of authority as some of its earliest advocates may have expected. It was soon realized that putting the Scriptures into the hands of every ploughboy[5] was not enough. Though much of the Bible appears to be clear in its teaching, much is not; and even the clear parts often become pretty complex when they are applied in real life situations. The ploughboys may have the Bible; but they also need someone to tell them how to interpret it. The more radical wing of the Reformation insisted, with some scriptural justification, that the regenerate individual needed nothing other than the guidance of the Holy Spirit to interpret the Scriptures;[6] but this was an approach the main Reformers, though they were attracted to it initially, chose to reject, fearing it would lead to anarchy. Instead, Luther saw the Holy Spirit interpreting Scripture not to the individual but rather within the whole historic people of God. Thus the appeal *Ad fontes* was to the fathers as well as to the Bible; Scripture was to be interpreted according to the mainstream teaching of the church, at any rate up to the apostasy of the Middle Ages. It is in this vein that Luther added to *sola scriptura* his catechisms, one of which had run to 100,000 copies by the time of his death. John Calvin (1509–64), for his part, placed his *Institutes of the Christian Religion* alongside the Bible to provide the key to its correct understanding.[7]

An alternative way of providing an authority to interpret Scripture was found in Zwingli's Zurich, and to an extent in Reformation England, where the role of authoritative interpreter of Scripture was vested in the state.[8]

Thus the Reformation produced a range of answers to the question of locating a source of authority for the interpretation of Scripture. In a sense they were all agreed: the authority is that of the Holy Spirit. But views on the means through which this authority was to be expressed ranged from the state to the writings of those who understood the history of the church, and to the personal heart of the individual believer.

As we have already seen in chapter 1, the concept of *sola scriptura* has been a major feature of evangelicalism. But, faced with the issue of the interpretation of the Scriptures, evangelicalism has generally, though not exclusively, departed from the mainstream Reformation tradition and adopted something akin to the radical Reformation's 'individual plus Bible plus Holy Spirit'. This has fitted well with evangelicalism's stress on the need for each individual to have a personal relationship with God, and the confidence in a high level of supernatural intervention to keep the trusting believer from making the mistakes generally attributed to those who were on the more radical wing of the Reformation.

Grace

The third element of Reformation thought that has bearing on the subsequent development of the evangelical concept of truth is that of the primacy of grace. Taking its cue from Augustine, the Reformation rediscovered that God is a God who acts, who intervenes, who comes, and who saves. Not only is this the basis of Luther's justification by faith; it is the foundation of Calvin's concept of predestination as well, and Zwingli's awareness that his life had been spared from the plague so that he might be a chosen instrument for God. God takes the first step; without him we can do nothing.

God's action in grace, then, is prior to anything we may do, whether in the sphere of salvation, or in the outworking of his purposes. And the same applies in the area of our knowledge of him and his truth. We can know him because he first comes to us and reveals himself and his truth to us. If he has not come, we cannot know him. If he does not reveal his truth, we cannot discover it.[9]

The concept of the essential primacy of God's actions was not a new one at the time of the Reformation. The scholastics, even the Pelagians, could all agree that God's action was necessarily primary, whether in creation, salvation, or revelation. The element that was new was our total powerlessness without God's prior action. For the Reformers it was not a case of our doing this and that to save ourselves, and adding in God's saving activity as an additional factor; nor of our discovering and working out this truth or that truth, and God supplementing it with revelation. Unless God takes the first step and the second step and the third step, we can never be saved. Unless God speaks, and reveals, and comes, we can never know the truth.

Though in theory committed to belief in the primacy of God's action in salvation, revelation, and so on, the Christian church has consistently tended to move the emphasis from what God does to what we do. Even the great central presentation of God's saving acts in Christ, the eucharist, tended to become something that the priest did as he offered the sacrifice of the mass. For all the stress of the Reformers, much of subsequent Protestantism tended towards deism, giving the activity of God little space in the real world; more recently, religion has tended to be looked on as 'man's search for God', rather than as God coming to us.

This is a tendency evangelicalism has sought vigorously to resist. The primacy of God's action in the world is one of its central tenets, and in some ways it has stressed it even more strongly than the Reformers. The concept of a God who acts, who takes the initiative, who becomes incarnate in Christ, who dies on the cross for the sins of the world, who comes to us through the Holy Spirit, who works in grace in our lives, who answers prayer, and whose glory will be revealed when Christ returns at the end of the age – these are all central tenets of the evangelical faith. In particular, evangelicals have stressed the primacy of God's action in revelation. While others have wrestled with the issue of our search for truth about God, evangelicals have started with the presupposition that a God of grace would not leave us in ignorance about himself, and has in fact taken the initiative and revealed himself and his truth to the world in the events recorded in the Scriptures and in the Scriptures themselves.

Integral to this concept of God's action in the world is God's contemporary action in the life and experience of the individual. In many parts of evangelicalism, the expectation of a personal encounter with God at conversion became the norm. The evangelical concept of prayer has generally made the miraculous intervention of God in human affairs a central feature. From time to time evangelicals have taught that the work of the Holy Spirit is manifested in personal experiences of God's activity, such as deep conviction of sin, a 'heart strangely warmed', or the spectacular manifestations seen in the Great Awakening and in subsequent times of revival. For many evangelicals, this kind of personal experience has been seen as the basis of their faith, and thus the guarantee of its truth.

On the issue of our inability to do anything, or to learn any of God's truth, without the prior intervention of his grace, evangelicals have shown a degree of ambivalence. In theory they have accepted this Reformation principle; in practice it has sometimes been neglected. Elements of Arminianism, salvation by believing the right doctrines, and even salvation by conforming to an evangelical lifestyle, have all crept in. Additionally, in their evangelistic zeal, many evangelicals have made much use of natural theology and evidentialism. Even so, evangelicals have consistently maintained that God's prior action in revelation is essential to our knowledge of his truth; even the use of argument and evidences has been largely with the purpose of establishing that the Bible is to be received as a revelation from God.

The Scriptures

Almost inevitably, the topic of the Scriptures has featured in each of the two last sections, as we have looked at the Reformation concepts of authority and the primacy of God's grace. As we turn to it more specifically in this final section, our interest is in exploring the ways in which the Reformers saw the Bible as truth.

We saw earlier that there was some divergence among the Reformers over the issue of how we decide which is the correct interpretation of Scripture. It was agreed that the authority to pronounce which is the right one must be that of the Holy Spirit, but there was disagreement over whether the Holy Spirit speaks directly to the individual, or through the historic church, or through the state. We noted, however, that the basic instinct of the Reformers had been to go for the first of these options; and it was largely the abuses that arose from this approach among the radicals that deterred them.

On the prior question of how we know that the Scriptures are true, there was less disagreement. Here the authority of church and state was not required, though doubtless it could have been added. Rather, as the individual reads the Scriptures, through the work of the Holy Spirit, he or she knows it is the truth of God. In the words of Calvin:

> Those whom the Holy Spirit has inwardly taught rest upon Scripture, and Scripture indeed is self-authenticated; hence, it is not right to subject it to proof or reasoning. And the certainty it deserves with us it attains by the testimony of the Spirit. For even if it wins reverence for itself by its own majesty, it seriously affects us only when it is sealed upon our hearts by the Spirit. Therefore, illumined by his power, we believe neither by our own

nor by anyone else's judgment, that Scripture is from God; but above
human judgment we affirm with utter certainty (just as if we were gazing
upon the majesty of God himself) that it has flowed to us from the very
mouth of God by the ministry of men.[10]

There has been debate over whether the Reformers saw the Scriptures as
containing the word of God, or as being the word of God, or as being the
means by which the word of God comes to us through the Holy Spirit.
Evangelicals, for the most part committed to a belief in propositional
revelation, have found no difficulty finding passages that speak of verbal
inspiration and inerrancy, such as Luther's: 'Not only the words but also the
expressions used by the Holy Spirit and Scripture are divine', or 'One letter,
even a single tittle of Scripture means more to us than heaven and earth.
Therefore we cannot permit even the most minute change.'[11] Others, who
wish to reject what they see as the literalism inherent in this approach, have
stressed that the Reformers' understanding of the truth of the Bible was of
something much more dynamic than the accuracy of its individual statements;
Calvin's primary interest, for example, was not in the minutiae of the text, but
in the illuminating work of the Holy Spirit in the individual and the church,
without which the written text of the Scriptures was barren.[12]

Since both of these approaches arise from theological and philosophical
debates that have taken place well after the Reformation, it is hardly fair on the
Reformers to interpret their claims in the light of issues they were not
concerned with. Certainly, both literalistic and dynamic elements are present
in their understanding; literalism was part of their heritage from the Catholic
Church and was virtually unchallenged in the sixteenth century; the Council
of Trent (1546), for example, claimed that both the Bible and church tradition
were dictated by the Holy Spirit.[13] A much more dynamic understanding of
the grace of God through the Holy Spirit was, as we have seen, one of the
Reformers' distinctive insights, and it was the 'coming alive' of the Scriptures
which was such a driving force in the Reformation.

It would seem reasonable to conclude that the Reformers would have been
happy to accept most if not all of our contemporary ways of understanding
that the Bible is the revelation of the truth of God, and would not have been
particularly interested in distinguishing minutely between them. The
Scriptures both contain the truth and are the truth. God speaks to us through
the Scriptures, and, equally, the words of Scripture are the words of God.
There is both revealed truth and truths of revelation. Truth is both
propositional and existential. Perhaps the successors of the Reformers would
have saved themselves much effort and not a little pain if they had refused to
let the pressures of theological and philosophical controversy force them to
take up such exclusivist positions.

5. Edwards and Wesley

The strongest roots of evangelicalism are in the Great, or Evangelical, Awakening, that started around 1740 in England, Wales, and New England. In 1735 remarkable things began to happen under the ministry of Jonathan Edwards in Northampton, Massachusetts. At Easter that same year George Whitefield ended a long period of spiritual darkness and found 'what it was truly to rejoice in God my Saviour'.[1] A few weeks later, on 18 June, the heart of the young Welshman, Howell Harris, was melted within him 'like wax before the fire';[2] and, after a long searching, three years later, John Wesley found the same experience in a room in Aldersgate Street.

Independently at first, though soon with a fair degree of working together, these and others saw the first fruits of evangelical revival, and laid the basis for the subsequent development of evangelicalism.

In this chapter, as we trace the attitude of these early evangelicals to the concept of truth, we are going to look at Edwards and Wesley, both of whom had impressive academic credentials. Jonathan Edwards (1703–58) was senior tutor at Yale and President of Princeton, and was recognized in his lifetime as America's leading philosopher. John Wesley (1707–88) was a fellow and lecturer in logic and philosophy at Lincoln College, Oxford. In other respects, there were considerable differences between them; one was a dissenter, the other an Anglican; one was a Calvinist, the other Arminian; one was the product of Puritanism, the other of reasonableness and toleration.

Jonathan Edwards

Intellectual thought in early eighteenth-century New England was dominated by Puritanism. The persecution of dissenters in England in the seventeenth century had caused tens of thousands to cross the Atlantic in search of religious freedom. Their leaders were for the most part well educated in the theology and philosophy, not just of England, but of continental Europe; many of them had fled to Europe before making their way to the New World, and Geneva, in particular, had been the inspiration of much of their thinking.

The interest of the New England Puritans was most certainly not limited to theology. Though their worldview was based very firmly on their theological presuppositions, their investigations and teaching covered all areas of knowledge: art, science, ethics, psychology, and philosophy; almost all the scientific investigations in the first hundred years of New England's history were made by clergy. For them the world was God's creation; he had written his truth in it as in a book; it is our privilege and duty to explore that book and read God's truth. Their sense of God's faithfulness, both in creation and in salvation, was very strong, a concept summed up in their doctrine of the covenant and the divine plan. The world was consistent because God was faithful; we could know truth because God was true.[3]

Indeed, in some senses, for the Puritans, knowledge of the world around was more accessible than knowledge of God himself. Their strongly Calvinistic theology stressed the omnipotence and transcendence of God; he is beyond our understanding, and the ways of the Creator are incomprehensible to the creature. Not only so, but our fallenness means that we are doubly removed from knowledge of God: by our creaturehood and the perversion of our minds and understanding through sin. Without the Scriptures and the work of the Holy Spirit our knowledge of God and truth about him would be minimal.

While the Scriptures and the Spirit helped counterbalance the results of our creaturehood and fallenness in the realm of theological truth, the New England thinkers used the concept of men and women being made in the image of God to safeguard our knowledge of the world: we can rely upon what our senses tell us because the one who created the external world has also created our minds, patterned upon his own. True, our creaturehood and fallenness often pervert the conclusions we draw from what our senses tell us; but our immediate ideas and impressions can be accepted as trustworthy.[4]

The New England Puritans, then, had explanations for the trustworthiness of our apprehension of the external world and of divine truth, and also for the possibility of error. Error was the result of our creaturehood and fallenness; truth could be known because of the faithfulness of God, the fact we are made in his image, and his grace in revelation and the Holy Spirit.

This Great Awakening, bursting in on New England Puritanism, was a time of intense religious excitement. Puritan preaching was as a rule solid, heavy, and dull. Though, as heirs of the Reformation, the Puritans believed in the reality of God's personal work in the life of the individual, they were more likely to engage in an erudite analysis of the stages of God's grace in conversion or sanctification than to lead people to expect the supernatural inbreaking of the power of God into their lives. But that was what people felt they were experiencing in the Awakening. To tens of thousands, doctrine and theology were suddenly translated into experience.

Jonathan Edwards appears to have had experiences of the nearness and reality of God from childhood on. He records one such experience which happened to him in 1737.

I had a view, that for me was extraordinary, of the glory of the Son of God, as Mediator between God and man, and his wonderful, great, full, pure and sweet grace and love, and meek and gentle condescension. This grace that appeared so calm and sweet, appeared also great above the heavens. The person of Christ appeared ineffably excellent, with an excellency great enough to swallow up all thought and conception – which continued, as near as I can judge, about an hour; which kept me the greater part of the time, in a flood of tears, and weeping aloud. I felt an ardency of soul to be, what I know not otherwise how to express, emptied and annihilated; to lie in the dust, and to be full of Christ alone; to love him with a holy and pure love; to trust in him; to live upon him; to serve and follow him; and to be perfectly sanctified and made pure, with a divine and heavenly purity. I have, several other times, had views very much of the same nature, and which have had the same effects.[5]

Those in his congregation had similar experiences. In 1735, he says, virtually every inhabitant of Northampton was subject to 'vital and experimental religion' in 'great awakenings'.

The town seemed to be full of the presence of God: it was never so full of love, nor of joy, and yet so full of distress, as it was then. There were remarkable tokens of God's presence in almost every house . . . The goings of God were then seen in his sanctuary, God's day was a delight and his tabernacles were amiable. Our public assemblies were then beautiful; the congregation was alive in God's service, every one earnestly intent on the public worship, every hearer eager to drink in the words of the minister as they came from his mouth; the assembly in general were, from time to time in tears, while the word was preached; some weeping with sorrow and distress, others with joy and love; others with pity and concern for the souls of their neighbours.[6]

The early part of the awakening, at any rate as Edwards describes it, seems relatively tame compared with the wide range of manifestations experienced by many later on, especially after the visit of George Whitefield in 1739–40. Falling, dancing, jumping, laughing, and shouting were added to weeping, and in some cases emotionalism and hysteria seem to have taken over from the experience of the presence and power of God. Many felt that the abuses of the Awakening nullified its value. Edwards repudiated the abuses, but strongly defended the Awakening as a true work of God, and as a paradigm of what true Christianity should be. In *A Treatise Concerning Religious Affections* he argued strongly that 'True religion, in great part, consists in the affections'; we are to expect our 'wills and inclinations' to be 'strongly exercised'; and 'there never is in any case whatsoever, any lively and vigorous exercise of the inclination, without some effect on the body, in some alteration of the motion of its fluids, and especially of the animal spirits'.[7]

Edwards' epistemology was profoundly influenced by Locke, but he developed Locke's thought in a direction parallel to Berkeley, without, as far as we know, being aware of any of Berkeley's teaching. In particular, Edwards' philosophy is firmly theocentric and idealistic. God alone exists in himself; everything else derives its being from God. 'Speaking most strictly there is no proper substance but God Himself.'[8] Speaking less strictly, created spirits, beings with knowledge and consciousness, can also be called real and substantial in a derivative sense. But nothing else can; all ideas and all material objects depend for their existence on the mind of God, as he expresses his eternal purposes.[9] Edwards used the analogy of a mirror; the objects in the world depend upon God as the reflections in the mirror depend upon their source; the reflections have no reality in themselves, nor do they have any independent relationship to the images which immediately precede or follow them.[10]

The external world, then, for Edwards, depends for its existence and coherence on the mind of God. Therefore, to know the external world is to know something of the mind of God. Truth is 'the consistence and agreement of our ideas, with the ideas of God' which we encounter in our experiences of the external world. Like the Puritans, Edwards bases the consistency and trustworthiness of the data of experience on the foundation of God's faithfulness; when our ideas match God's ideas as given in experience, then we have the truth.[11]

Edwards was firmly committed to both the Newtonian and Calvinistic worldviews. But each of these posed a potential threat to the immanence of God in the world. In the England of Edwards' day deism was rampant, using Newton to push God out of his universe. Much of Calvinism, too, with its inscrutible divine decrees and total determinism, threatened to leave God little or no room for immediate action in his world or in the life of the individual. Edwards' experiences of the nearness of God demanded that he reject both these tendencies, and he was able to do that with his God-centred epistemology. Just as he met personally with God and knew his heart of love and joy and holiness, so he encountered the mind of God in his experience of the world around him. Just as the experience of the living reality of God's presence was for him the heart and soul of religion, so the awareness of God's truth expressed in the created order was the heart and soul of all science.

It is interesting to note that Edwards had developed his epistemology well before the outbreak of the Great Awakening. As early as 1716 (at age thirteen) he was studying Locke at Yale, and the broad outlines of his thinking were in place by the time he left college. So it is arguable that Edwards' theocentric idealism, so far from being the result of the Awakening, was in part the basis for it, and for his continuing support of it when many of his fellow Calvinist clergy were denouncing it.

John Wesley

The religious atmosphere of England in the 1730s was very different from that in New England. The Age of Reason was in full swing. At any rate in the Church of England the prevailing tendencies were towards deism, latitudinarianism, and moderation. 'Enthusiasm', dogma and supernaturalism were out of fashion.

Very different again was the pietistic movement that flourished in Germany in the second half of the seventeenth century and spread further afield in the early decades of the eighteenth. Here the emphasis was on the religion of the heart; central was the individual's personal experience of the work of the Holy Spirit, in conversion and in each part of the Christian life. It was the Moravians' calm and joyful singing on board the *Simmonds* during the great storm of January 1736 that drew John Wesley's attention to them. Here was a knowledge of God that was real in the face of death. Here was religion that made a difference.

For two years and more Wesley struggled to find what they had for himself, until his journal for 24 May 1738 records the immortal words:

About a quarter before nine when he was describing the change which God works in the heart through faith in Christ, I felt my heart strangely warmed. I felt I did trust in Christ, Christ alone for salvation; and an assurance was given me that He had taken away *my* sins, even *mine*, and saved *me* from the law of sin and death.

'The change God works', the 'heart strangely warmed', 'assurance', and the personal experience of a God who has 'taken away *my* sins, even *mine*, and saved *me*' – all these are concepts central to evangelical experience and theology.

Again, as with Edwards, it would seem that the main structures of Wesley's philosophical and epistemological thinking were in place before his 'evangelical conversion'. The main philosophical influence on his teaching at Oxford was Cambridge Platonism,[12] with its concept of truth as eternal and divine, and its high view of men and women's ability to discover that truth through reason alone, as opposed to through the five senses. Besides showing us truth, reason would also show us morality and the will of God; when found, these would be recognized as the same as what has been given us in the Scriptures. Rejecting the harsh dogmatism of Calvinism and any form of determinism, the Platonists saw human nature as essentially free and good, able through the pursuit of reason to become more like the divine nature. But their rationalism was tempered by a mystical element. While most British rationalism was allowing empiricist and materialist concepts to push out the supernatural, the Platonists, like Edwards, embraced a form of idealism which made the divine the one true reality, one which each individual may seek and find and share in.[13]

Though modified by subsequent experience, Wesley retained many elements of this philosophy throughout his life; it undergirded much of his hostility to some aspects of Calvinism, it fuelled his reasonableness and dependence on rational argument,[14] and provided a base for his stress on our personal experience of God, and 'the grand principle of every man's right to private judgment'.

Though he never forgot his philosophy (in 1770 he stated that the three subjects he 'commonly read on horseback' were history, poetry and philosophy),[15] after 1738 Wesley's interest was primarily in evangelism. Foundational to all his preaching was the need for every person to experience conversion or the new birth. This was no small step of accepting this or that doctrine; Wesley bracketed 'Protestant' faith, which 'embraces only those truths, as necessary to salvation, which are clearly revealed in the oracles of God', with Deist, Muslim, Jewish and Roman Catholic faith as powerless to save anyone, since it was merely intellectual.[16] True saving faith has to be 'a disposition of the heart'; it is marked by 'a divine conviction of God, and the things of God',[17] and a personal trust and confidence in Christ, a 'closing with him and cleaving to him'. 'Is thine heart right?' was Wesley's question, in his sermon on 2 Kings 10:15. Never mind opinions, or modes of worship, or denominational allegiance, or form of church government, or pattern or prayer, or even doctrine of baptism and the Lord's supper;

Is thy heart right with God? . . . Dost thou 'walk by faith, not by sight' looking not at temporal things, but things eternal? Dost thou believe in the Lord Jesus Christ, 'God over all, blessed for ever'? Is he revealed in thy soul? Dost thou know Jesus Christ and him crucified? Does he dwell in thee, and thou in him? Is he formed in thy heart by faith?[18]

The new birth 'is a vast inward change, a change wrought in the soul, by the operation of the Holy Ghost; a change in the whole manner of our existence'.[19] The Holy Spirit works in the believer's heart, bringing joy, life, the knowledge of God, assurance, a new mind, and a new life of righteousness.

Here, for Wesley, is the source of true knowledge of God and of God's truth. Here is the witness of the Spirit, the witness of God himself in our spirits and in our lives; here is reality and certainty. This is not to say that he gave experience of the Spirit a higher authority than the Scriptures; in his sermon on the witness of the Spirit he calls the Bible and the Spirit 'two witnesses' which 'testify conjointly . . . While they are joined we cannot be deluded: their testimony can be depended upon. They are fit to be trusted in the highest degree, and need nothing else to prove what they assert.'[20] Where an alleged experience of the Spirit is not in accord with the Scriptures, it is to be rejected.

The high value that Wesley placed on the Bible as 'the book of God', in which he has written down the way to heaven, is evident from all his preaching and writing. 'O give me that book! At any price, give me the book of God! I have it: here is knowledge enough for me.'[21] On the issue of understanding and finding the correct interpretation of the Scriptures, he outlines four steps to be taken. First, Scripture is to be read in the presence of God: 'God is here. In his presence I open, I read his book.' Second, should 'anything appear dark and intricate' or subject to uncertainty or doubt, I must ask God for wisdom; not in a detached way, seeking the wisdom of the academic; rather 'If any be willing to do thy will, he shall know'; I seek guidance from the Spirit in order to follow the will of God. Thirdly, using 'all the attention and earnestness of which my mind is capable', I 'search after and consider other parallel passages of Scripture', meditating on them, 'comparing spiritual things with spiritual'. Finally, if still in doubt, recourse may be had to the writings of 'those who are experienced in the things of God'.[22]

Here is a significant shift of emphasis from that of the main Reformers. The individual believer studying the Scriptures in the presence of God, and expecting the direct experience of the Holy Spirit to illuminate them supernaturally, is seen as the norm; recourse to external authority is the last resort. In contrast to Luther, Wesley had considerable confidence in the immanence of the Holy Spirit in the life of each born-again believer, whether ploughboy, Kingswood miner, or Oxford graduate. This is not to say that the ploughboy would always get everything right. In a gracious passage in the introduction to his *Fifty-Three Sermons*, Wesley accepted that even he may have misunderstood the Scriptures; in that case he was eager to be corrected: 'Point me out a better way than I have yet known. Show me it is so, by plain proof of Scripture.'[23] Our understanding of Scripture and our knowledge of divine things is imperfect, and we may well make mistakes in our doctrines.

Even so, Wesley seems to teach that there is one area where even the ploughboy can be sure he has the truth: 'The children of God do not mistake as to the things essential to salvation . . . For they are "taught of God:" and the way which he teaches them, the way of holiness, is so plain, that "the wayfaring man, though a fool, need not err therein".'[24] He even goes further, and claims that 'the mighty working of his Spirit in their hearts' enables them to 'know in every circumstance of life what the Lord requireth of them, and how to keep a conscience void of offence both toward God and toward man'.[25] The Spirit-led believer, then, can be sure she or he has the truth in the practical matters of salvation and the will of God for everyday life, even if liable to be mistaken in matters of doctrine and theology.

As with the Reformers, it seems likely that if Wesley had been confronted with twentieth-century debates over what we mean when we say that the Bible is true, he would have adopted a comprehensive position. Certainly, he believed in verbal inspiration: 'He hath written it down in a book'; but for the written word to become the living word the dynamic action of the Holy Spirit was essential.

Edwards, Wesley and truth

From our survey of Edwards and Wesley we can extract five elements in the attitude to truth seen in these two leading figures in the Great Awakening and the birth of evangelicalism.

The first is *theocentricity*. The eighteenth century saw the inexorable development of the implications of the Age of Reason: God's role in the universe became smaller and smaller. No longer did he need to keep the stars in their courses, or to provide an explanation for the phenomena of the material world. Truth could be found without his help; the moral law was accessible to everyone; we could have religion without revelation. Empiricism, the philosophy which has dominated British thinking, recognized as real only what can be observed by our five senses: reality is material.

In the face of this, Edwards and Wesley both believed that reality is spiritual; God is real; material things partake of reality only as God gives it to them. The external world does not exist in itself, says Edwards; it depends totally upon the mind of God. And here is the key to knowledge and truth. Because of the nature of God, because he is faithful and true, and because we are made in his image, we can trust the data of our experiences; we can, in part, know the mind of God, the truth. Everything, truth included, is centred on God.

The second element is *immanence*. Both Edwards and Wesley were firmly opposed to deism. God must be involved in his creation, not just because without his involvement the creation would cease to be, but also because of his nature. Supremely, a personal God of love must be involved with those he has made in his own image. Wesley's years of searching for the experience of the reality of God were not just rooted in his reading of the Bible; the search was implicit in his philosophy. For both Edwards and Wesley truth had to be much more than cerebral or propositional; believing doctrines was not enough; experiencing God was essential. Perhaps each of them tended to expect their own experience of God to be the pattern for everyone else; but of one thing they were quite sure: God is not just to be known about, but known. Truth is not just doctrine; *he* is the truth.

The third element follows closely from this, and it is *the heart*. Both men were convinced of the vital role of the mind in receiving God's truth. Both accepted the vital role of reason. Edwards was firmly committed to the full Puritan dogmatic; in a latitudinarian England Wesley stood firm on the doctrines of the Reformation. But both insisted that the mind must not function in isolation. 'True religion, in great part, consists in the affections', and it will also affect the fluids of the body, claimed Edwards.[26] Faith, says Wesley, is a 'disposition of the heart'. To believe is to experience joy or conviction or peace or tears. True religion is 'vital and experimental' – vital because it is alive; experimental because we know it in our experience, and not just in our minds.

The fourth element is the need for *conversion*, not just to find salvation, but to be able to grasp God's truth. Wesley was less stringent than Edwards on the inability of the unregenerate to grasp some of God's truth; reason can convince us of the existence of God and some truths about him; but without regeneration we can have no personal knowledge of him in the sense of acquaintance with him.[27] In Edwards' sermon on 'A Divine and Supernatural Light' he contrasts the knowledge of the regenerate believer with that of the unregenerate theologian or philosopher:

This is the most excellent and divine wisdom that any creature is capable of. It is more excellent than any human learning; it is far more excellent than all the knowledge of the greatest philosophers or statesmen. Yea, the least glimpse of the glory of God in the face of Christ doth more exalt and ennoble the soul, than all the knowledge of those that have the greatest speculative understanding in divinity without grace.[28]

The fifth element is *the Bible*. Both Edwards and Wesley accepted the Bible as the authoritative revelation of God. What is plainly taught in Scripture is to be accepted as true. Though they both put considerable stress on our experience of God's grace and presence in our lives, experience was never allowed to be the ultimate authority. The one may confirm the other; but an experience unsupported by Scripture is to be rejected.

Edwards and Wesley were men of the eighteenth century; they shared its joy in learning and the many benefits that came from reason and science. They were also contemporaries of David Hume, but they did not share his empiricism or his scepticism. What clearly distinguishes their thinking from Hume's is their refusal to let reason usurp the place of God as ultimate justification for knowledge and truth, and, consequently, their recognition that we do not apprehend truth through our intellect alone. Truth for them remained objective, because rooted in God, and available to us through his grace. Though reason alone may not give us certainty, truth apprehended through the heart and the feelings can do so. Evangelicalism, then, in the century of its birth, was well equipped to resist the developing pressure of the modern period to abandon objective and holistic truth, and thus avoid the slide into relativism. In the next chapter we shall move into the nineteenth century and look at the epistemology of one of its leading evangelical theologians, Charles Hodge.

6. Charles Hodge

Charles Hodge (1797–1878) of Princeton was one of the most influential, if not *the* most influential, of American theologians of the nineteenth century. Solidly evangelical, he built Princeton Seminary into a stronghold of evangelical orthodoxy; and through his many writings (some of which are still in print today) he considerably influenced the development of evangelicalism worldwide.

The first quarter of the nineteenth century in America was the period of the second great Evangelical Awakening, a time of rapid church growth and of 'revivalist' religion, often of the more extreme kind. Typical of the period were 'camp-meetings' when many thousands would gather together for a week or so. These were characterized by physical manifestations of the presence or conviction of God, deep spiritual experiences, lots of noise, and the disparagement of the role of the intellect in religion.[1] Hodge was a Presbyterian and, though his mentor at Princeton, Archibald Alexander, had been involved in the revival movement, Presbyterians in general, with their firm roots in Reformed and Calvinist traditions, and Princeton Seminary in particular, stood firmly against the anti-intellectual element of the revival. For them religion could be a matter of both feelings and intellect, the heart and the head. It is perhaps understandable that, confronted with a form of evangelicalism that grossly overstressed the heart, Princeton found itself, in teaching and in practice, tending to stress the role of the head.

Contrary to the verdict of his contemporaries, it has recently been fashionable in some circles to write Hodge off as a theological lightweight, who failed to grapple with the epistemological issues of his day, but instead retreated into an unthinking dogmatism. The American E. R. Sandeen stated categorically that the 'Princeton professors' completely ignored the criticism of Hume and Kant, and James Barr stated that in Hodge 'no influence of Kantian thought is visible'. The impression is given that Hodge was an obscurantist, either unwilling or unable to keep abreast of the development of nineteenth-century thought, who retreated to a secure, though outdated, eighteenth-century philosophical position.[2]

This criticism is unfounded. Hodge was very well aware of the teachings of Hume and Kant and their successors. At a time when very few Americans could speak German, he learnt the language and studied for a time in Germany, mixing freely with the circle of 'mediating' theologians who had been strongly influenced by Schleiermacher,[3] and developing friendships with them which lasted for many years. Throughout his life he had books and journals sent to him regularly from Germany; his many discussions of contemporary theologians, and in particular of those who had been influenced by Kant and his successors, make it clear that he kept abreast of the development of theological ideas, without, of course, feeling obliged to accept them all.

In this chapter we shall look at two broad areas of Hodge's thought: his response to the challenge to the possibility of knowledge and truth highlighted by Hume's scepticism, and his concept of the nature of knowledge. We shall see that his response to the issues raised by Hume was quite different from that of Kant and most of his contemporaries, but that nevertheless it was a potentially fruitful one. Similarly, his insights into the nature of knowledge, forged largely in reaction to Kantianism, opened up concepts that are still very relevant today.[4]

Hodge's response to Hume

In our broad survey of the development of modernism in chapter 3, we followed the main trend by focusing on Kant's response to Hume's scepticism. This was the response that eventually won the day. But it was not the only one, nor, in the early part of the nineteenth century, was it the most popular one. Before Kant put pen to paper, Hume's fellow Scot, Thomas Reid (1710–96) had produced his response, and it was widely circulated and accepted.[5] Reid answered Hume by rejecting the theory of ideas which Hume had inherited from the British empirical tradition, and which stated that the things we perceive or think are never the objects in themselves, but only impressions or ideas of them; that is, we never perceive trees, we perceive only perceptions of trees. Hume's sceptical arguments depend, said Reid, on this theory; if we reject this theory we are saved from having to accept Hume's sceptical conclusions. So where Hume wanted to say that what we perceive is the image of a tree, Reid claimed that what we perceive is a tree. Why invent new entities ('images', 'ideas', 'impressions', 'perceptions' and the like) which, so far from helping our understanding of the world, lead us to the conclusion that we can know nothing about it? After all, no-one has ever been able to prove that these 'ideas' actually exist. Almost everyone, on the other hand, finds it impossible to doubt that trees and other objects of perception and knowledge really do exist and that we observe them directly.

Reid had to accept that it may not be possible to prove philosophically that we perceive objects directly; but he claimed that such proof was not needed. The fact is, he said, everyone believes it immediately; it is a 'self-evident truth'. He tended to use the phrase 'self-evident truth' in a number of ways. For example, he used it of the axioms of mathematics; but he can hardly be saying that the existence of the objects in the external world and the dependability of our experiences of them are self-evident in the way that the truth of a mathematical axiom is. But if he was merely saying that we are unable consistently to doubt these things, he was not saying anything that Hume had not already said; for Hume, in his more pragmatic moments, was very willing to allow that we have to accept natural beliefs as a basis for living – and that they work well. Reid in fact failed to supply an adequate answer to Hume's point that, however well they may work, philosophically speaking there is no rational justification for our confidence in them.

Reid's answer to Hume, then, was in one sense a capitulation, and in another sense a satisfying response that gave many nineteenth-century thinkers the justification they needed to continue to trust their sensations and mental experiences. In the first half of the nineteenth century, his influence, and that of the school of 'Scottish common-sense philosophy' which he founded, was phenomenal, particularly in America.[6] It was generally accepted that he had rescued human thought from Hume's scepticism, and thus that no further answer to Hume was needed.

Kant, however, was scathing about the Scottish philosophy's failure to find an adequate answer to Hume, and set out to supply his own alternative. As we have seen, he chose to accept Hume's theory of ideas, and, by means of his 'Copernican revolution', sought to build an epistemology that was consistent with it and yet avoided scepticism. He did so, however, at the price of conceding that we can never know the truth about the things-in-themselves that we believe lie behind our subjective experiences. In one sense Kant, like Reid, capitulated to Hume's scepticism, admitting that we cannot know anything about the real world as it is. In another sense, he provided an answer to Hume by giving ordinary reason a significant, though strictly limited, role in the sphere of our experience of our perceptions and thoughts, while offering hope to subsequent generations of thinkers and theologians by proposing a second, completely different, way of apprehending ultimate truth.

It is clear from his writings that Hodge was well acquainted with both Reid's and Kant's answers to Hume, and with the ways in which these had been developed by their followers. Like the whole of his generation in America, he would have been well taught in the philosophy of Thomas Reid and his school; but, unlike many, his German studies and friendship with members of the German mediating school opened him up to an awareness of the strengths of the Kantian position. It is interesting that nowhere in his writings does he engage in the extravagant praise of Reid and the Scottish school that was common in America in the first half of the nineteenth century.

Yet Hodge would have claimed that his epistemology was built neither on Reid nor on Kant. While he shared with both of them a conviction that, despite the arguments of scepticism, our beliefs and knowledge about the external world are to be treated as reliable and as a sufficient basis for action, he differed significantly from them, and so from many of his contemporaries, in one key point: he believed that the basis of true knowledge about the world as it really is had to be unashamedly God-centred rather than reason-centred. Philosophical scepticism on its own ground was unanswerable. If we are to accept the dependability of our experiences of the external world, it cannot be on the grounds of a rationally proved argument, but rather on the grounds of the nature of God, and especially of his relationship with the world; in other words, the doctrine of divine providence. 'The ultimate ground of faith and knowledge is confidence in God.'[7]

We have seen that the beginnings of modern scepticism were the result of putting reason in the place of God as ultimate justification for knowledge and truth, and that one of the forms this took for those who chose to continue to believe in Christianity was a move to a deistic concept of God, allowing him little or no part to play in the workings of the universe. Hodge's rejection of deism was vigorous and total. He described God's relationship to the world in strongly active and dynamic terms: he is 'intimately and always present with every particle of matter'; this presence is 'not of being only, but also of knowledge and power'; nothing is independent of God.[8] Because of this God is the guarantor not just of the ontological stability of the world, but also of its epistemological coherence; he not only upholds everything, but he knows everything. Additionally, he is 'the author of our nature'.[9] Humankind, made deliberately by the creator of the world, has been endowed with means of obtaining accurate information about that world, both through our own experience and investigation, and through revelation.

This strongly echoes Descartes's statement that 'The certainty and truth of all knowledge depends entirely on my awareness of the true God.'[10] Hodge would readily have accepted that his was no new insight, but rather part of the main western tradition reflected not just in Descartes, but in Bacon, Newton, and the majority of the seventeenth-century scientists with their theologically based confidence in the predictability of the natural order and the dependability of the experience of the human observer.

To what extent, then, has Hodge provided an answer to Hume's scepticism? Like Reid and Kant, he failed to produce a purely philosophical answer; unlike them, he did not claim to have done so. What he has done is to recognize, as Reid and Kant also recognized, that the basis of knowledge has to be located elsewhere than in reason. His particular insight, over against Reid and Kant, and in agreement with Descartes, was that if epistemology is going to have a solid foundation it has to be a theological one; the Age of Reason, fruitful as it was, was ultimately built not on a foundation of reason, but on Descartes's 'impossibility of God's ever deceiving me'.[11] The removal of this God, either to a deistic distance, or totally, inevitably caused the collapse of the whole system. The restoration of confidence in such a God would, Hodge felt, restore an epistemological foundation, not just for religion, but for the whole of science, philosophy and life.

Hodge, then, accepted Hume's main critique of reason, and thus, in a sense, failed to answer him. Like Reid and Kant, he conceded that the goal of sure and certain knowledge cannot be reached by reason. But while Kant avoided scepticism by concentrating on the subjective, and Reid made the knowability of the objective a necessary presupposition of perception and thought, Hodge rooted his approach to our knowledge of truth in his theology of the nature of God and his relationship with the world. And while the Kantian approach tended to produce two ways of knowing, and two types of truth, Hodge's concept of God as the guarantor of all forms of knowing enabled him to emphasize the unity of knowledge and of truth.

Hodge's theory of the nature of knowledge

Hodge strongly repudiated the tendency among those influenced by Kant to differentiate radically between different types of knowledge and truth. Dissatisfied with Kant's basic premise that knowledge and truth were limited for us to the sphere of the phenomenal, these thinkers set themselves to build on Kant's own hints that if we are to know anything about things-in-themselves it will have to be through some process other than the usual one of rational knowledge. Their way of doing this was to locate in human persons abilities or faculties that were capable of obtaining knowledge and truth but which were distinct from our intellect or understanding. This could be in the area of our feelings, as with Schleiermacher, or in the form of a 'higher reason', or something in the sphere of spirit. Thus, for these thinkers, one sort of truth – ordinary, everyday truth – could be known in one sort of way, through our intellect and ordinary reason. This sort of truth was subject to all the limitations that Hume had pointed out. But there was a different type of truth, a higher truth, known in a different way, through a higher human faculty – a knowledge of the real, the absolute, truth not subject to ordinary limitations, divine truth.

Hodge's rejection of this approach was twofold: he repudiated the concept of two types of knowledge and truth, and he rejected the division of the knowing subject into separate faculties. For him, knowledge must be integrated, truth must be one; and the knowing subject must be a whole person. For Hodge, epistemology had to be integrated.

In a number of passages Hodge declared that any act of knowing, or reaching truth, involved the whole person, 'including his understanding, heart, conscience, and experience'.[12] In a celebrated discussion over 'The Theology of the Intellect and that of the Feelings', he specifically rejected the dichotomizing of the intellectual and emotive apprehension of truth. The two for him were 'inseparably connected'; they always work together; 'neither the cognition without the feeling, nor the feeling without the cognition'.[13] The intellect, the feelings, and the will are not to be sharply distinguished; they are not different substances or faculties; they are integral parts of 'the whole soul', and in most if not all of our acts and experiences they are working as a complex whole.[14] Where Coleridge[15] distinguished sharply between the Understanding and the Reason, and Schleiermacher taught that 'perception, feeling, and activity' operated in clearly differentiated spheres ('scientific', religious, and 'practical'/'moral' respectively), Hodge insisted 'that the soul is a unit; that its activity is one life. The one rational soul apprehends, feels and determines.' None of these 'faculties' is 'independent' or 'distinct'.[16]

Linked closely with this concept of the integration of the person was Hodge's view of the integration of knowledge itself. Though he was aware of the difference between personal knowledge and propositional knowledge, it was not his habit to differentiate the two clearly. For him, knowing facts about a person was all part of knowing that person. Further, in contrast to the Kantians, no radical distinctions were to be made in the objects of knowledge. There are not several types of truth; truth is one. Any given truth must cohere with any other truth. The ultimate nature of things is concord, not contradiction; all truth fits together as an integrated whole. In particular, for Hodge, it was not necessary to make a radical division between theological and non-theological truth, as those influenced by Kant did. For him, both 'philosophy' (in its widest sense of human thought and experience) and 'theology' (based on revelation) 'assume to teach what is true concerning God, man and the world' and so, as 'two great sources of knowledge' they must be ultimately 'consistent in their valid teachings'.[17] This was not an easy position for Hodge to maintain in the third quarter of the century when the conflict between science and the Bible was at its height. But he stuck firmly to it, with the strongest of commitments to both science and the Bible, convinced that true science, and the Bible rightly understood, would never be in conflict.

Again, the basis for Hodge's position here is his conviction that ultimate justification is to be found in God rather than in reason. Truth is one because truth is rooted in God, and God is one. The same God who is 'the author of our nature and the maker of heaven and earth' is the source of revelation and theology. Such a God cannot be inconsistent. For him, truth cannot be anything other than one; and such is his nature and the nature of his relationship to human beings 'made in his image' that truth can be one for us as it is for him. Hodge does not appear to explore the issues involved here very fully, and it is significant that some of his successors in the Calvinistic tradition have criticized him strongly at this point. But it would appear that his strong view of the image of God in human persons (so strong that at one place he is able to say, 'If man was made in his image, God is like man')[18] is a foundational element in his thinking here.

Hodge was aware that for his contemporaries, making God the foundation for knowledge raised the issue of the foundation for this foundation, the guaranteeing of God. At times, influenced by his generation, and by Princeton's tendency to stress the head over against the revivalists' heart, he slipped into using reason to provide this ultimate justification, setting a trend which was increasingly followed by his successors at Princeton. But there was a very definite strand in his thinking which provided an alternative answer, one not very different from that of the Schleiermacherians, and in keeping with that of the Reformation and the evangelical tradition. It was that our experience of God (which is an experience of him revealing himself to the whole person, intellect as well as feeling) is self-authenticating; or, rather, God himself gives the authentication.

He referred to this non-rational experience in a number of ways and at a number of levels. In its most diluted form it is an innate intuition shared by all, a 'sense of dependence', a 'consciousness of responsibility', 'aspirations after fellowship with some Being higher than ourselves'. At a rather higher level it is the encountering of God in the revealed truth of the Word, whether written in the Bible or preached; for Hodge this was certainly not just a rational process; revelation and the receiving of revealed truth came not by reason but 'by a supernatural intervention of God by the Spirit'. At a third level Hodge spoke of our experience of God as he gives himself to the individual in saving grace. This experience is 'altogether mysterious'; it cannot be explained rationally; it is not based on 'external evidence' or 'argument' or 'historical or philosophical proof'; it is solely 'the exercise of omnipotence'. Our 'communion with the infinite God' is something we of ourselves cannot produce; it is 'the gift of God's Spirit'.[19]

It is this self-authenticating experience of God that formed the foundation for Hodge's theology, which in turn provided the base for his confidence in reason and our ability to know truth. At this point Hodge is continuing the Reformation tradition, and is close to Schleiermacher and other post-Kantians who put the experience of God central in their systems. He differed strongly from them, however, in insisting on the objectivity of the God experienced, and on the fact that the initiative for the experience rested with God and not with the human person.

Hodge, then, faced with Kantianism, chose to retain a firmly objective concept of truth.[20] He did this by keeping God as ultimate justification, and viewing him as one who gives us truth through the Holy Spirit. We receive truth not just with the intellect, but with the whole person, and this enables us to have confidence in it.

So far Hodge's approach is close to that of Edwards and Wesley. But there are two related elements in Hodge which, though perhaps minor in themselves, began to move away from the position of the eighteenth-century evangelicals, and set a trend developed by some of his successors at Princeton and beyond. The first was his confidence in reason. Developed in opposition to the revivalists' anti-intellectualism and the Kantians' refusal to allow ordinary reason any place in theology, in the fires of controversy it showed signs of becoming his final court of appeal. The second was a tendency to move the emphasis from Christianity as experiential to Christianity as doctrinal. The eighteenth-century evangelicals had accepted, of course, that it is both, and Hodge would readily have agreed. But, again in the fires of doctrinal controversy, and aware of the excesses of revivalism, Hodge tended to put less emphasis on the experiential than did his evangelical predecessors. This can be seen in the very concept of a systematic theology, something none of the previous evangelicals had attempted. Systematizing theology was, of course, a favourite preoccupation of the Calvinists and Puritans; but Edwards consciously reacted against the dryness of the Puritans, and Wesley, like the Cambridge Platonists, was implacably opposed to the Calvinists. For all his writings on the primacy of grace and the work of the Spirit, and for all the warmth of his preaching, the burning heart, the hallmark of the eighteenth-century evangelicals, is not so apparent in Hodge. For all his insistence on the sovereignty and power of God, Hodge, especially in his later years, would have sat uncomfortably with the dramatic experiences of supernatural power familiar to Edwards and Wesley.

7. Warfield, Machen and fundamentalism

The publication of Hodge's *Systematic Theology* stands at the mid-point between the beginnings of evangelicalism and the present day. Our survey of the concept of truth underlying the movement in the first half of its history has necessarily been very limited, but we have seen sufficient to identify a number of key elements.

We have surveyed in the Reformation the background to evangelicalism's attitude to reason, authority, the primacy of grace, and the centrality of Scripture. The evangelical stance in these areas, though at times complex, is an integrated and consistent one. The strong conviction of the primacy of God's grace has provided a firm base for a belief in a God-given revelation in the Bible, which is to be received as truth by our God-given reason empowered by the Holy Spirit. But, for the evangelicals, doubtless as a result of the heart-warming experiences of the first and second Evangelical Awakenings, such a revelation was more than just factual truth or dry doctrine. It was essentially a personal experience of the living God, something that affected every part of us, our feelings as well as our intellect, our heart as well as our head. Knowledge is knowing God; he is the truth.

We summarized the significant elements we traced in Edwards and Wesley as *theocentricity*, recognizing God as the key to all knowledge and truth; the *immanence* and personal knowability of God; the centrality of *the heart*; the need for *conversion*; and the foundational role of *the Bible*. Each of these themes recurs again and again in Hodge, who, in the face of trends in nineteenth-century theology, also stressed the integration of truth, and the integration of the knowing subject.

At the end of the previous chapter we noted the twin tendencies in Hodge to put increasing emphasis on reason, and to stress the doctrinal nature of Christian truth at the expense of experiential truth. We turn now to two of Hodge's successors at Princeton seminary who furthered these tendencies, and to the movement that arose from them, fundamentalism.

Fundamentalism

Evangelicals have frequently been branded as fundamentalists. Doubtless, some evangelicals are fundamentalists, and many fundamentalists are evangelicals, but the large majority of evangelicals, while claiming they hold to the fundamental doctrines of the Christian faith, would reject the title 'fundamentalist', limiting its use to a relatively small party within evangelicalism. George Marsden, the leading contemporary historian of fundamentalism, claims that even at the height of the 'heresy trial' era in the United States most ordinary American evangelicals were virtually untouched by the issues, and many conservative leaders 'declined to take hard lines'.[1] It is probable that the proportion of fundamentalists to evangelicals in the United States has never been more than one in ten; the figure in the United Kingdom would be considerably smaller.

Derek Tidball, citing John Stott, lists eight significant differences between fundamentalists and evangelicals:

1. Fundamentalists are suspicious of scholarship while evangelicals are open to it.
2. Fundamentalists deny, while evangelicals recognize, the human and cultural dimensions of the Bible.
3. Fundamentalists revere the Authorized (King James) Version of the Bible, while evangelicals believe there are more accurate translations.
4. Fundamentalists interpret the Bible considerably more literally than do evangelicals.
5. Fundamentalists are strongly separatist, while evangelicals are more open to other Christians.
6. Evangelicals are more critically aware that their beliefs are influenced by their culture than are fundamentalists.
7. Fundamentalists tend to be more politically right-wing and less concerned about the social implications of the gospel than evangelicals.
8. Fundamentalists insist on premillennial views of the second coming, while evangelicals hold a variety of views.[2]

Various attempts have been made to analyse fundamentalism in socio-logical, cultural or political terms. Some have argued that the key to understanding it is to see a specific doctrine of the millennium as its central feature. Others have categorized it as essentially a reactionary movement, anti-evolution, anti-modern theology, anti-intellectual, anti-ecumenical, anti-feminist, and so on. One of its hallmarks has been its militancy, which has led it to adopt an aggressive and confrontational style in expressing its views. This style has all too often been reflected in those who argue against it; it is only since the mid-1980s that serious attempts have been made to come to an unbiased understanding of evangelical fundamentalism as a religious phenom-enon and to provide a scholarly analysis of it without engaging in controversy for or against it.

As with many movements, those who have been looked on as the fountainheads of fundamentalism would not necessarily have identified themselves as fundamentalists or accepted all the stances adopted by their successors. This is true of B. B. Warfield and J. Gresham Machen, and of several of the writers of *The Fundamentals*, the series of twelve publications that appeared between 1910 and 1915, and which gave the movement its name.[3]

B. B. Warfield

Benjamin B. Warfield (1851–1921) was Professor of Didactic and Polemic Theology at Princeton Seminary from 1887 until his death. Like his predecessor, Charles Hodge, he was committed to Princeton's Calvinistic Presbyterianism. But while Hodge had at least flirted with post-Kantian concepts, by Warfield's day Princeton tended to look on the epistemology of Kant and his successors as the source of much of the evil in liberal and modernist reinterpretations of Christianity. Warfield saw himself as an apologist for orthodoxy, and as such appears to put more confidence in rational argument than Hodge had done.[4] In the fires of controversy he was pushed to a more extreme position than Hodge had chosen to take.

Warfield saw his task as the defence of orthodox Christianity in an anti-supernaturalistic age. For him, Christianity was in essence a supernaturalistic religion, but, 'immersed in an anti-supernaturalistic world atmosphere, Christian thinking tends to become as anti-supernaturalistic as is possible to it'. A 'supernatural God', who acts 'in a supernatural mode' in creation, redemption, revelation and through the Holy Spirit, was for him 'the core of the Christian profession', and the basis of all his theology.[5]

Such a supernatural God, if he exists, must, for Warfield, exist objectively, and his actions and revelations must be fully objective. Against those who held a subjective view of theological truth, Warfield insisted on its objectivity. Theology, for him, was a science.[6] Scientists still, in his day, and for several decades after, universally believed they were dealing with objective fact; they were describing the world as it really is; their findings were not the creations of their own minds, but discoveries (one might almost say revelations) of things as they really are. Truth was objective and absolute. Further, said Warfield:

> For the very existence of any science, three things are presupposed: (1) the reality of its subject matter; (2) the capacity of the human mind to apprehend, receive into itself, and rationalize this subject matter; and (3) some medium of communication by which the subject matter is brought before the mind and presented to it for apprehension.[7]

He cited astronomy as an example. Astronomy presupposes the objective existence of heavenly bodies, of means by which we may observe them, and of minds that do not just apprehend them, but make sense of what they apprehend, rationalizing and combining the data into a correlated system.

In clear contrast to the post-Kantian thought of his day, Warfield argued that theology, like other areas of knowledge, or like the sciences,

> . . . presupposes the objective reality of the subject matter with which it deals; the subjective capacity of the human mind so far to understand this subject matter as to be able to subsume it under the forms of its thinking and to rationalize it into not only a comprehensive, but also a comprehensible whole; and the existence of trustworthy media of communication by which the subject matter is brought to the mind and presented before it for perception and understanding.[8]

The task of the theologian, for Warfield, was not the subjective one, followed by many of his contemporaries, of considering human concepts of God and his relationship with the world. Rather, it was to accept that there is objective, absolute truth about an objective God which God himself has made available to us through an objective revelation and which we are able to apprehend and to some extent understand.[9] This truth the theologian must establish and defend, not (stresses Warfield) as an end in itself, but as a means to the one true end of enabling others to come to know God in the fullest evangelical sense, 'that vital knowledge of God which engages the whole man',[10] which moves them 'to love God with all their heart and their neighbour as themselves; to choose their portion with the Saviour of their souls; to find and hold him precious; and to recognize and yield to the sweet influences of the Holy Spirit'.[11] Thus no theologian may handle the subject 'in a cold and merely scientific spirit', but rather living close to God, 'having a full, rich, and deep religious experience', 'filled at all times with the manifest influences of the Holy Spirit'.[12]

Though he came very near to it, Warfield did not want to say that our subjective experience of God is finally dependent on theology, any more than that theology is dependent on our experience of God. Rather, both theology and religious experience arise from the one source, 'the truth of God'.[13] This truth is not merely rational or merely existential. Warfield sees the operation of faith, reason, and 'the heart' as all essential to the reception of this truth; he pictures a 'triangle of truth'[14] whose sides are authority (God's revelation received by faith), intellect (rational acceptance), and the heart (religious experience). All three are essential, and the relative neglect of any of the three will make both our religious experience and our theology 'one-sided and deformed'.[15] In particular, neglect of the objective element of authoritative revelation and an over-stress on religious experience will cause us to 'discard Christianity and revert to natural religion'.[16] In his article on 'The Deity of Christ' in *The Fundamentals*, Warfield stated that the evidence of Scripture and 'the impression Jesus has left upon the world' were both valid evidences for Christ's divinity. Towards the end of the article he appears to give experience precedence over Scripture: 'The supreme proof to every Christian of the deity of his Lord is then his own inner experience of the transforming power of his Lord upon the heart and life.'[17]

Like Hodge, and in accordance with the evangelical tradition, Warfield believed that personal knowledge and experience of God are of greater importance than the intellectual knowledge of doctrine. But he refused to let this soften his insistence on the existence of objective truth about God, and on an objective God-given revelation which is essential to our knowledge about God, and so, in effect, to our knowledge of him. Without revelation we cannot know the truth about God; unless we have a trustworthy revelation, we have no sure basis for our faith or test for our religious experience. Warfield cited with approval Adolphe Monod's words: 'If faith has not for its basis a testimony of God to which we must submit, as to an authority exterior to our personal judgment, and independent of it, then faith is no faith.'[18]

Revelation, for Warfield, was supremely revelation in the Scriptures. He accepted that God reveals himself and his truth in many ways, but, in an age which largely rejected the concept of biblical revelation, he felt that 'the task has come to be to distinguish between God's general and God's special revelations, to prove the possibility and actuality of the latter alongside the former, and to vindicate for it a supernaturalness of a more immediate order than that which is freely attributed to all the thought of man concerning divine things'.[19] For Warfield, the Bible was 'a divine-human book, in which every word is at once divine and human';[20] he strongly rejected any concept of dictation or mechanical inspiration.[21] But, again, in an age that over-stressed the Bible's humanness, he saw an urgent need to emphasize its supernatural nature. This he did in article after article, arguing for divine inspiration of every part – every word – of the Scriptures. And if every word is divinely given, then every word must be completely trustworthy and so true, objectively true, corresponding to God's objective truth.

The Princetonians' strong heritage of doctrinal and credal formulations of the faith, confronted with liberal theology's apparent sellout of the traditional doctrines of the church in favour of subjective experience, pushed Warfield as apologist to stress the objective nature of Christian truth, and, in particular, its doctrinal and propositional nature. Despite his ready acceptance that theology is both subjective and objective – of the feelings as well as of the intellect – and that truth can be personal as well as propositional, the thrust of most of his apologetic is that God's truth is objective, doctrinal, and propositional. And, as the 'battle for the Bible' went on, it was on this element that the attention of his fundamentalist successors was almost exclusively fixed.

J. Gresham Machen

J. Gresham Machen (1881–1937) was a student of Warfield at Princeton, and served on the staff there from 1906 until 1929, when he and some of his more conservative colleagues withdrew to found Westminster Theological Seminary. From then until his death he was a controversial champion of conservative orthodoxy against liberalism. In the typical spirit of fundamentalism, he argued that liberalism was not Christianity, and that therefore liberals and conservatives could not coexist in churches or denominations. Expelled by the Presbyterian Church in 1936, Machen joined with others in founding a new denomination, now known as the Orthodox Presbyterian Church, which vigorously defends the truths of historic Christianity and the Westminster Confession of Faith.

Machen disliked being called a fundamentalist, and in his scholarship and rejection of premillennialism he differed from the mainstream of fundamentalism.[22] Nevertheless, he felt a great affinity with the fundamentalists, and was looked on by them as one of their champions.

The basis of his epistemology was a belief in objective truth, in facts, 'the objectivity of truth'.[23] Where his opponents saw experience as primary, Machen believed that facts underlay experience.

Whatever may be true of religion in general, the *Christian* religion is most emphatically dependent on facts – facts in the external world, facts with which 'science' in the true sense of the word certainly has a right to deal . . . The Bible is quite useless unless it is a record of facts.[24]

These facts are independent of us; they would still be true even if no-one on earth believed them; they would still be 'facts for God'. And they are eternal: 'They are facts now and they will remain facts beyond the end of time.'[25] It is fashionable to trace this concern for facts back to Scottish common-sense realism;[26] but we have already seen that this concept of fact goes back well beyond Thomas Reid; it is a restatement of the western concept of truth dominant since Plato. Such a concept of objective fact was still central to the sciences in the first half of this century, but it was a concept that the post-Kantians had all but removed from religion, and that was already under serious attack in the field of historical studies. Marsden cites the case of Carl Becker, who, in a presidential address to the American Historical Society in 1931, entitled 'Everyman His Own Historian', argued that though events in the past occurred, we can now only ever have ideas, memories, or interpretations of them; the event itself is lost to us for ever; the belief that we can discover 'facts of history' is false; there are no facts, only interpretations.[27] Machen had been well taught in (and very impressed by) the latest ideas in historical consciousness and higher criticism during his studies in Marburg in 1905–6, and was convinced that such a rejection of fact would remove the heart from Christianity.

Machen was quite willing to admit that he could not give a philosophical answer to all the criticisms of his belief that we can know objective facts as well as ideas and interpretations,[28] though theologically he would have answered them, as Hodge and Warfield had done, with a Cartesian 'God would not let us be deceived'. But for him the issue was very straightforward: either we say that truth can never be attained, and so lose truth altogether and be forced into 'pragmatic scepticism', or we hold that some truth can be attained, and so accept that objective truth does exist.[29]

Given that Christianity deals with facts in the external world, with which 'science' has a right to deal, for Machen it followed that Christianity must necessarily lay claim to truth for all such facts, and must not content itself with claiming truth in the 'religious' sphere alone. 'It is a poor religion', he wrote, 'that can abandon to science the whole realm of objective truth.'[30] The results of Christ's death upon the cross, or of his resurrection, depend on the facts of his death and his resurrection; these are 'facts in the external world'. The Bible, then, as God's authoritative revelation, must be completely trustworthy in matters of science and history, as well as in matters of 'religion'.[31] Truth, for Machen, must be one, consistent over all the disciplines. 'A thing cannot possibly be true in religion and false in philosophy or in science.'[32]

Like Warfield, Machen saw supernaturalism as of the essence of

Christianity. Liberal theology's avowed aim was, for him, to remove the miraculous, the supernatural, from the Bible. But to remove the supernatural is to remove everything:

> The outstanding result of a hundred years of effort to separate the natural from the supernatural in the early Christian view of Jesus is that the thing cannot be done. The two are inseparable. The very earliest Christian account of Jesus is found to be supernaturalistic to the core.[33]

Machen believed it was as valid for him to start from supernaturalistic presuppositions in his approach to Christianity as it was for his opponents to start from anti-supernaturalistic presuppositions. Indeed, he went a stage further, and claimed to show that only on his presuppositions could Christianity be understood or consistently held.

Machen rejected religious experience as a source of truth on the grounds that it is 'endlessly diverse', and so, on it own, a very poor guide. It may confirm the truth, but it is not a source of truth.[34] Nor, for Machen, would it do to say (as his opponents did) that Jesus, or 'the spirit of Jesus', is a sufficient source of truth. He saw liberalism as reconstructing Jesus to suit contemporary thought, and thus, while claiming to make Jesus the source of truth, in effect creating both Jesus and truth according to its own presuppositions. In reply to those who claimed that a 'present experience of Christ in the heart' could make us independent of the Christ of the Bible, he replied: 'It is vain to speak of reposing trust in the Person without believing the message', and 'Christian experience depends absolutely upon an event', and so upon the truth of the New Testament record.[35] Religious truth, including truth about Jesus, must come by God-given revelation: and though some truth may be revealed in creation and through 'the moral law', God's definitive revelation is to be found only in the Scriptures.[36] 'We make the Bible, and the Bible only, the test of truth and life.'[37]

Given the presupposition that there is a God who can communicate truth to us, it seemed reasonable to Machen that he would do so, and that he would do so in a form that was completely trustworthy:

> The Bible not only is an account of important things, but that account itself is true, the writers having been so preserved from error, despite a full maintenance of their habits of thought and expression, that the resulting Book is the 'infallible rule of faith and practice'.[38]

Like Warfield, Machen firmly rejected any suggestion of 'mechanical' inspiration.[39] He found no problems in the idea of God speaking through human personalities in a wide variety of cultures and situations, and yet at the same time speaking truly, giving us a Bible that is 'completely true in matters of fact'.[40] Convinced that this was what in fact had happened, Machen devoted considerable energy to arguing the case for the supernatural inspiration of the Bible, 'the reasoned defence of the truth of the Bible'.[41]

Machen's epistemology is parallel to that of Warfield and Hodge, but, perhaps as a result of the pressures of controversy, it is possible to trace a distinct narrowing of emphasis if not of substance. Where Hodge had insisted that all truth must be both existential and cognitive, and Warfield that experience is needed as well as the intellect, Machen's distrust of religious experience, even experience of Christ, led him in effect to say that the Scriptures are the sole source of truth, and thus that truth is only verbal, in words and propositions.

Fundamentalist epistemology

The story of the development of American fundamentalism is a complex one; many of the analyses that have been attempted have been far too simplistic. The movement was not, for example, an anti-intellectual backlash. However much its detractors pictured it as such, its leading proponents were scholars and intellectuals. Charges of anti-intellectualism were flung from both sides in the conflict largely because the two sides differed radically in their presuppositions and found it difficult to conceive of any intelligent person failing to agree with their conclusions.[42] Nor was it basically anti-evolutionary or premillennial; more than one article in *The Fundamentals* was willing to accept some form of theistic evolution (as was Warfield), and the only article on eschatology accepted that divergence of views over the millennium was quite acceptable provided we retain the basic truth of Christ's personal return preceded by the preaching of the gospel to all nations.[43] *The Fundamentals* in places also accepted biblical criticism, including 'higher criticism'.[44] Even the subsequent militancy of fundamentalism is largely absent in *The Fundamentals*.

Nevertheless, it is possible to isolate four elements that appear to be basic to the fundamentalist movement and which are relevant to our consideration of their epistemology.

Foundational is their insistence upon the presupposition of *supernaturalism*. For them, the Christian God was by definition supernatural; exclude all supernatural elements from Christianity, and what is left ceases to be distinctively Christian. Retain it, and doctrines such as the deity of Christ, the incarnation, the virgin birth, miracles, and special revelation all become tenable. Even evolution can be adopted in a modified form if God is allowed to intervene in the process by 'special acts';[45] and 'higher criticism' can be accepted provided it is not conducted from anti-supernaturalistic presuppositions.

It was certainly not the case that all the opponents of fundamentalism had consciously adopted naturalism and were embarked on a wholesale programme of ridding Christianity of every supernaturalistic element. Many who were embarrassed at the idea of miracle or special revelation still retained a concept of God that allowed him to be involved in special acts of creation and grace in the individual. But undoubtedly the ethos of the age was to eradicate as many elements of supernaturalism from Christianity as possible. The presupposition of all the sciences, including the newer sciences such as psychology, was that all explanations should be naturalistic; we should never need to resort to the supernatural. The fundamentalists saw this principle being applied to theology, as well as to evolution and ethics and the like, and were determined to resist it.

A second distinctive element in fundamentalism was the belief in *objective truth in religion and history* as well as in science. Their opponents still largely accepted the possibility of objective truth in science, but had long since applied the Kantian concept of the unknowability of things-in-themselves to religion, and were working at applying it to history. For them, God or his truth could not be known; all we have is our ideas of God and of religion. Theology is thus not the study of God or information about God, but the study of our ideas about God and religion. Similarly, events in the past are forever lost to us; the proper object of historical study is our current ideas and interpretations of the past.

By contrast, fundamentalists retained the traditional western view of truth, applying it to religion and history as well as to science: truth does exist objectively and it can be known. If all we have to go on is human ideas and interpretations, then we shall never be able to know anything at all. But there is final truth, an absolute, a yardstick by which we can and must test our ideas and interpretations.

Allied to this point is a third element in the fundamentalist concept of truth: *the integration of all forms of truth*. It is being increasingly recognized that the idea that evangelical religion and science are in conflict or at war originated from those who were opposed to Christianity, not from those who retained traditional Christian beliefs. True, fundamentalists, especially the anti-evolutionists, mocked many of the claims of the scientists, but they by no means rejected the scientific enterprise as such. A. C. Dixon, executive secretary and editor of the first five volumes of *The Fundamentals*, confidently claimed: 'I am a Christian because I am a thinker . . . a rationalist . . . a scientist.'[46] Again and again the fundamentalists claimed that true science and Christianity were not, and would never be, in conflict.

There is not, and never has been, any real conflict between Religion and Science. There may be conflicts between interpretations of

Scripture and interpretations of the facts of Nature; but what God has written in His Word never conflicts with what God has written in His creation.[47]

Truth is one; whether we are exploring God's handiwork in creation or studying his revelation in Scripture, he will not contradict himself.

A fourth basic fundamentalist belief, and the one which has received most attention, was their concept of *special revelation*. The fundamentalists still retained a fair amount of the rationalism and evidentialism of the Enlightenment tradition; one writer in *The Fundamentals* spent his whole article arguing for the truth of Christianity without once mentioning the authority of the Bible.[48] But, surrounded as they were with increasing pluralism in philosophy and theology, they had no difficulty in accepting that in many areas, if ultimate truth is to be known, then it must be revealed to us by God. Given their concept of a supernatural God who can intervene in history, become incarnate, do miracles, and so on, it did not seem at all strange to them that he should be able to inspire individuals to write his truth in a book, such that, textual corruptions and the like apart, that book can be claimed to be wholly and perfectly true.

> The Bible as we now have it, in its various translations and revisions, when freed from all errors and mistakes of translators, copyists and printers [is] the very word of God, and consequently without error.[49]

Their opponents, starting from the presupposition that the Bible is not the Word of God, but a record of men and women's religious ideas and experiences, found this belief incredible, especially in the light of what they saw as glaring mistakes and obvious falsehoods in the Bible. Undeterred, the fundamentalists leapt to the defence of the Scriptures, seeking to explain the 'mistakes' and harmonize the apparent contradictions, and claiming that the evident power of the Bible to change people's lives and bring them face to face with God, along with its internal claim to be God's revelation, were sufficient to establish it as the very Word of God.

This claim, for most fundamentalists, necessarily entailed inerrancy,[50] a doctrine which they felt was implicit in the mainstream of Christian orthodoxy, but which they refined and made especially their own. Just what is meant by inerrancy has been a matter of debate; an attempt at a definitive statement on it, 'The Chicago Statement on Biblical Inerrancy' (1978), affirmed that 'Scripture in its entirety is inerrant, being free from all falsehood, fraud, or deceit', but accepted that 'we must pay the most careful attention to its claims and character as a human production'. Thus

History must be treated as history, poetry as poetry, hyperbole and metaphor as hyperbole and metaphor, generalization and approximation as what they are, and so forth. Differences between literary conventions in Bible times and in ours must be observed: since, for instance, non-chronological narration and imprecise citation were conventional and acceptable and violated no expectations in those days, we must not regard these things as faults when we find them in Bible writers. When total precision of a particular kind was not expected nor aimed at, it is no error not to have achieved it. Scripture is inerrant, not in the sense of being absolutely precise by modern standards, but in the sense of making good its claims and achieving that measure of focused truth at which its authors aimed.[51]

Inerrancy does not preclude hermeneutics; the inerrant truth of God given in Scripture still requires at least an element of correct interpretation. But this must 'stay within the bounds of the analogy of Scripture', allowing authority to Scripture rather than to 'independent reason'.[52]

Each of these four themes of fundamentalism – supernaturalism, the objectivity of truth, the oneness of truth, and the God-given truth in the Scriptures – is familiar from the general history of evangelicalism. A degree of development can be traced, moving the main emphasis away from truth as something to be experienced as well as believed, towards verbal and doctrinal truth in the Scriptures. Yet the element of the heart was not totally lost; fundamentalists continued to hold that the supernatural work of the Spirit in the individual is essential. It is, again, a case of controversy causing a strong emphasis to be placed on a concept that is under threat, at the expense of another equally valid one.

8. Forsyth and Denney

The clash of conflicting ideas, whether ideological, political, or academic, should ideally lead to each side learning from the other, and to an enriching of understanding. Sadly, this does not always happen; arguing their case in a situation of conflict can push people to unbalanced or extreme positions. We have seen elements of this in the previous chapter, and may feel that a parallel, though different, mistake was made on the other side of the Atlantic, as we turn to two leading British evangelicals who were contemporaries of Warfield.

P. T. Forsyth

P. T. Forsyth (1848–1921) was a convert from liberalism to evangelicalism. He studied under Ritschl at Göttingen, and served for twenty-five years in various pastorates in England. It was the demands of pastoral ministry, and a personal revelation of the holiness and grace of God, that turned him 'from a Christian to a believer, from a lover of love to an object of grace'.[1] From 1901 he was Principal of the Congregationalist College in Hackney. His many publications ranged over cultural, social and ethical issues, as well as more specifically doctrinal; his key works were on Christ and the cross.

Once he had abandoned liberalism, he became its firm opponent:

The greatest issue for the moment is within the Christian pale; it is not between Christianity and the world. It is the issue between theological liberalism (which is practically unitarian) and a free but positive theology, which is essentially evangelical.[2]

Nevertheless, though he rejected the theology of his liberal period, he does not appear to have abandoned its philosophy. As a result, his epistemological framework in places contrasted with that of, say, Warfield and Machen, and enabled him to build up a theology that was thoroughly evangelical, yet in certain respects differed from theirs.

There are six basic elements in his epistemology. The first is its theological starting point, its *theocentricity*. In deliberate contrast to liberalism, Forsyth insisted that Christianity, theology, philosophy, indeed everything, must start and end with God. The liberals started with their own understanding, their ideas, their experiences, their reason. Evangelical Christianity, said Forsyth, starts with the revelation of God in Christ.

> The one begins with man, the other with God, the one with science or sentiment, the other with the Gospel, the one with the healthy heart and its satisfaction, the other with the ruined conscience and its redemption. The one begins with the world (as I say), the other with the Word. But in practice, we find this – that to begin with the world is to become dubious about the Word; whereas to begin with the Word is to become sure about the world. A philosophy can bring us to no security of a revelation; but a revelation develops a philosophy, or a view of the world.[3]

The God Forsyth began with was supremely a holy God: the 'holiness of God is the real foundation of religion'.[4] And he was a God of grace: the 'miracle of revelation, of grace' is that 'the unapproachable approaches, enters, tarries, lives, dies, conquers among us and in us, knows us into our only knowledge of itself, subdues all things to its sanctity, and establishes its good and blessed self in us and on us all'.[5]

Arising from his concept of theocentricity comes the second element in Forsyth's epistemology: his belief in *the objective reality of God*, and so of God's acts in the world and of his revelation. 'For a religion the first requisite is an objective reality.'[6] 'Christian faith has never found the ground of its certainty in itself, but always in Christ.'[7]

This leads to Forsyth's third foundational concept, that *truth is given*.

> The more we fix our attention on the object of our certitude, the more we humbly realise that it is something *given*. Its source is not in us. It is of grace. The men of discovery, of inspiration, tell the same tale. Truth

finds them, not they it . . . It is given us. We do not make it, we have to yield to it.[8]

Forsyth spoke of 'the effectual primacy of the given', expressed both in terms of historical fact, as opposed to subjective ideas or experience, and in terms of grace, 'a gift to our poverty', not something we invent. There is an 'Apostolic Gospel', a revelation which is 'final and absolute' and universal.[9]

Fourthly, *the given is not primarily an experience or a doctrine or a book, but God himself.* 'What he gives us first in this donation is . . . Himself, His holy self.'[10] The Bible and experience have their place; but, in essence, revelation, for Forsyth, was action: 'the free, final and effective act of God's self-communication in Jesus Christ for man's redemption'.[11] The 'element' of revelation is not truth but action,[12] redemption, not illumination, God acting in holiness and grace to redeem and save. It is Christ we need, not just words about Christ.

After the Reformation, Protestantism replaced the church with the Bible as the infallible source of pure doctrine. This meant, says Forsyth, that 'the ruling notion of religion was then truth', and led to a logical scholasticism that was flat, stiff, and inhuman.[13] Christ, on the other hand, 'does not give us a programme of history or a compendium of doctrine, as the Catholic and old-Protestant theory of a book-revelation is. He gives us a power of God, a certainty of faith, a quality of life, a finality of destiny, in contact with him.'[14]

The Scriptures, then, for Forsyth, must never be an end in themselves. Christianity is Christ,[15] and what is revealed is Christ, not the Scriptures. Inspiration and infallibility belong to the gospel rather than to the book;[16] though, while Forsyth rejected the concept of verbal inspiration, he encouraged preachers to find the words and phrases of the Bible so full of spiritual food that they would have difficulty in not believing in it.[17] The Bible 'preaches Christ to the world' and gives us 'Christ's own interpretation of himself'. Its writers 'were and are the only authentic interpreters of Christ'. So the Bible is authoritative, an essential part of the total revelation: 'the apostles are gone but the book remains, to prolong their supernatural vision, and exercise their authority in the church'.[18] Similarly, experience, even experience of God in Christ, must never be an end in itself; it must be an experience of *Christ*, never an *experience* of Christ.

Fifthly, *reality, truth, revelation, God in Christ himself, are encountered immediately by the individual, not through the understanding or intellect, but through the will.*

There is such a thing, then, as a religious *a priori* in us, though it is not an authority but the power to own authority. It is not a passivity, but a receptivity, a loyalty, an obedience. Revelation does not come to us as if we were blank paper, dead matter, or blind forces. It finds something to appeal to, to stir, to evoke. But this *prius* resides in the will and its power, not in the reason and its truth. It is a voluntarist *prius*, and not a noetic.[19]

This capacity to receive revelation is itself God-given; it is 'set up by God though His act of Grace, in the moral soul, in the soul as guilty, in the new and holy Humanity, in the experience of faith'.[20] It is not demonstrable, only realizable. Forsyth appears to have viewed this capacity as similar to Kant's moral imperative, and did not attempt to explain how God plants it in us, any more than Kant explained the existence of the moral imperative.

This brings us, finally, to Forsyth's concept of *the relationship and relative priority of the will, the reason, the heart, experience, and theology*. Forsyth was a Congregationalist, and he traced his ecclesiological roots back through Independency to both Puritanism and Anabaptism, with a clear bias towards the latter. The welcome legacy of Anabaptism was, for him, a 'religion of souls . . . rooted in a positive and experimental soil – in the evangelical experience' which gave the theology inherited from Calvinism 'a living soul', personal, passionate, with wine in the bottles and sap in the veins. 'The machine became an organism. The system became vital.'[21] Thus 'our theology is not a fixed system we must accept but a gracious experience which we must declare, not the mould, but the image of the Church's spiritual life'.[22]

Both theology and experience are essential; experience must be checked by a God-given theology. 'What we need is a theology that creates an obedient experience rather than experience that creates an interpretive theology.'[23] Experience alone is too small, too narrow, too variable, too impure. The key thing is not our experience, but that which lies behind the experience, the object of our faith, the revelation to which we respond. In the same way, our theology can never be final or an end in itself; we cannot do without dogma, but the focus of interest must never be in the dogma or the theology, but in that to which they point. Nothing, however good it may be, must be allowed to usurp the place of the holy God.

Confronted with God, our primary response is not in the region of the intellect, but of the will. The intellect is not irrelevant; 'our response to Christ is not a blind one'.[24] Forsyth would have agreed with Hodge that we cannot respond to something of which we have no understanding at all. But he refused to give priority to our rational judgment. 'It is not a prior condition of faith'; 'we do not review God's claims and then admit him as we are satisfied'. We do not assent and then trust; we taste and then see.[25] Forsyth contrasted religious belief with scientific belief; in science the facts compel us to believe; in religion the facts – or rather the fact, God's revelation of himself – have a 'constraining' but not a compelling power.

In the face of the religious fact we are free. We are free to believe or not believe, trust or not trust, as in science we are not free, as we are not free with any theoretic knowledge of a mere object. Religion, faith, is not simply a fresh experience following necessarily on the stimulus.[26]

It is a choice, a commitment, a moral response of obedience, trust and worship, not a rational one of criticism and legitimation.[27]

In Forsyth, then, in contrast to much of what was happening among the evangelicals on the other side of the Atlantic, the basic evangelical emphasis, seen so clearly in Edwards and Wesley, on the supernatural activity of God in grace and salvation received by us through the response of faith, is brought prominently to the fore. Where Warfield and Machen and their successors faced liberalism by stressing doctrinal and propositional truth, Forsyth answered it with action, a God who acts. 'Christianity does not peddle ideas; it does things.'[28] Again we can ask whether, in the fires of controversy, Forsyth overstated his case, as perhaps the Americans did theirs. Do we have to affirm *either* action *or* ideas? Can revelation not be both personal and verbal? We can accept that God 'is the only Authority we have in the end';[29] but even Forsyth was willing to admit that he can communicate that authority through more than one channel.

Forsyth's thinking was undoubtedly influenced by the post-Kantian philosophy he embraced as a student, particularly in his stress on the personal, the experiential, action and the will. But, in keeping with his often repeated principle, he was never willing to give it ultimate authority; philosophy was to be judged by God's revelatory act, not vice versa. Of the six points we have looked at above, the foundational first three – theocentricity, the objectivity of God, and the givenness of truth – all had their roots firmly in the evangelical tradition and ran counter to the mainstream of post-Kantian thinking. Forsyth was very well aware of his philosophical roots, and was as capable of criticizing them as he was of the theology they had produced. Just about all his references to Hegel and German idealism were negative; and he was discerning in the way he used the insights of Kant and the neo-Kantians. It is much more a case of his philosophical background enriching and developing his evangelical insights than providing the sole basis for his theology.

As we have seen, Kant had taught that God and God's truth were beyond rational knowledge; but his removal of theology out of the sphere of ordinary reason opened up the possibility that there could be other ways of apprehending God and his truth, apart from our normal ways of knowing. His followers worked hard at exploiting this possibility, seeking to analyse the 'faculty' we use in religion. But Forsyth rejected the division of the person into different faculties. He, like Hodge, declared that he wanted integrated knowledge by an integrated person;[30] therefore he was not able to solve the problem of God's inaccessibility in the way the post-Kantians did. So he solved it in true evangelical fashion by his concept of a supernatural God taking the initiative in grace and revealing himself directly to us. True, his description of the 'religious *a priori* in us' sounds reminiscent of the post-Kantians' religious faculties. But he could have defended it by insisting that it was 'receptivity, a loyalty, an obedience',[31] while their faculties, following Kant, were something much more active: they did not receive God; in effect they created him.

Here is a point of contact and a point of contrast with the American tradition we have been looking at in the last two chapters. Both approaches answered Kant by saying that God has so made us that he can reveal himself and his truth directly to the individual. But, though each side claimed that the individual is the whole integrated person (mind, will, feelings, and so on), the stress in Forsyth was on the will, while for the Americans it came to be increasingly on the intellect.

The retention of elements of post-Kantianism in his thinking, then, gave impetus to specific aspects of Forsyth's understanding of evangelicalism, just as their 'common-sense' background influenced the Princetonians. The heart of evangelicalism does not have to be tied into any one specific epistemology; it was strong enough to survive being adapted to, and adapting, modified forms of post-Kantianism and 'common sense'. Indeed, to put it more positively, evangelicalism is rich enough to adapt itself and be enhanced by the varying approaches of the various philosophies.

James Denney

Forsyth called his younger contemporary, James Denney (1856–1917), 'the theological prophet', and 'the greatest thinker, we have upon our side'.[32] Graduating with a first in classics and philosophy from Glasgow University, he spent fourteen years in pastoral ministry, and then twenty years as Professor and later Principal of Glasgow Free Church College. Like Forsyth, and in the true spirit of evangelicalism, Denney had a passion to preach the gospel, and made the cross the centre of his theology. Basically a biblical theologian, he was less involved in frontline apologetics than Machen or Forsyth, though he had battles to fight over Scottish social and ecclesiological issues. Wide-ranging in his interests, he was as comfortable lecturing on Benvenuto Cellini as on the second coming, and he was able to recite by heart not just the Greek New Testament, but all the tragedies of Shakespeare.[33]

Like Forsyth, Denney started his pastoral ministry with considerable leanings towards liberalism, a position reflected in his first published work, a review of Henry Drummond's *Natural Law in the Spiritual World* in 1885. His close friend W. Robertson Nicoll claimed that it was reading the sermons of

C. H. Spurgeon, together with the influence of his wife, that led him into 'a more pronounced evangelical creed', and the decision to make 'the Atoning Death of the Lord Jesus Christ' his central theme.[34]

Foundational to his epistemology was his insistence on *the integration of all forms of knowledge and truth*. In an age which increasingly put the historical and the spiritual, or the theological and the scientific, into two totally unrelated categories,[35] Denney refused to put religious convictions in one compartment and other beliefs somewhere else.[36]

> *All* that man knows – of God and the world – must be capable of being constructed into one coherent intellectual whole. All that any one of us knows, as a Christian, or as a student of science, physical, historical, anthropological, archaeological, must be capable of such a construction; and our doctrine of God, instead of being defiantly indifferent here, must involve the principles on which this construction shall proceed . . . The world is all of a piece; man's mind is all of a piece; and those easy and tempting solutions of our hardest problems, which either arrange the world or the activities of the mind in compartments having no communication with each other, are simply to be rejected.[37]

Whatever the post-Kantians may say, 'the mind will inevitably revolt against this schism in its life'. If we think at all, we must integrate history with faith, theology with philosophy, religion with science. There is only one kind of truth and all truth is one. 'All knowledge is one, all intelligence is one; and it belongs to theology, above every science, not to dissolve, but in the very name of God, to maintain and interpret that unity.'[38]

Secondly, Denney was convinced of *the existence of objective realities that lay behind all forms of knowledge*. 'Reality' was 'his favourite, or most characteristic word'.[39] The whole purpose of his great study *Jesus and the Gospel* was to assert the realities of the historical Christ in an age when many theologians were declaring it was irrelevant whether there was any historical reality behind the biblical stories or not. 'What we have to do', he declares, 'is to get at the facts.'[40] Our religious convictions must have 'an objective value which is as real as that of our scientific convictions, and quite capable of being wrought into one intelligible whole with them'.[41] His studies in atonement and reconciliation were built on a historical incarnation and crucifixion: 'There is certainly no reconciliation but through the historical Christ.'[42] Writing about the resurrection, he accepted that many started with the dogma that such an event was quite impossible, and he conceded that 'it is vain to controvert such a dogma by argument'. However, he added, 'it may be demolished by collision with facts'.[43]

That brings us to a third element in his epistemology: *the presupposition of supernaturalism.* As suggested above, he did not spend time arguing this; he felt he was as justified in taking it as a presupposition as others were in denying it. For him, the resurrection was 'the supreme miracle', the supreme act of God in redemption in vindication of his Son.[44] If that was historical fact, as he was convinced it was, then any supernatural act of God was possible. The supernatural must act in nature and in history: 'both nature and history may really be made [God's] instruments'; in both 'there may be events and facts the whole character of which is this, that they are embodiments of divine truth, or manifestations of divine love and power'.[45]

Fourthly, for all his stress on historical facts, Denney was as committed as Forsyth was to *the centrality of the individual's personal experience of the grace and revelation and redemption of God.* True faith is faith in a person, not in articles.[46] However vital the historical may be, saving truth is not only in the past.

> It is *here*, in the living Christ and the experience of Christians. It has its foundation laid in historical facts, no doubt; but it has at the same time its witness in itself, for the consciences of sinful men, needing and seeking God. It is the combination of the historical fact in the past with its Divine meaning and relevance in the present, in which the whole weight of the evidence lies.[47]

Even more strongly, in his discussion of reconciliation, he was able to claim that 'the basis of all theological doctrine is experience, and experience is always of the present'.[48] Denney is not claiming here that the source of doctrine is subjective experience; rather that until a person has experienced the reality which the doctrine is speaking of, he or she cannot truly believe that doctrine. 'The material with which the theologian deals can only be certified to him through religious experience; in other words, only a living Christian is competent to look at the subject.' 'No doctrine has any value except as it is based on experience.'[49]

This brings us, fifthly, to his concept of *the truth of the Scriptures.* For Denney, the personal principle of experience first and doctrine second applied to the Bible as much as to any aspect of Christianity. It is not a case of accepting the authority or inspiration of the Bible, and as a result experiencing its power; rather, it is because we experience its power that we grasp its inspiration.

> The Bible is, in the first instance, a means of grace; it is *the* means through which God communicates with man, making him know what is in His heart towards him. It must be known and experienced in this character before we can form a doctrine concerning it. We cannot *first* define its qualities, and *then* use it accordingly; we cannot start with its

inspiration, and then discover its use for faith or practice. It is through an experience of its power that words like inspiration come to have any meaning, and when we define them apart from such experience we are only playing with empty sounds.[50]

Denney rejected inerrancy, though he accepted the concept of infallibility in the sense that the Scriptures infallibly bring us to God and salvation.

Even though in any number of cases . . . the *gospels* should be proved in error, the *gospel* is untouched; the word of God, the revelation of God to the soul in Christ, attested by the Spirit, lives and abides. Revelation is ultimately personal, as personal as faith. It is to Christ we give our trust, and as long as the gospels make us sure of what He is, they serve God's purpose and our need.[51]

Denney was concerned, like Forsyth, to locate ultimate truth not in the Bible but in God. Undoubtedly, he says, we find truth in the Bible, and therefore we prize it; 'but the truth does not derive its authority from the Scriptures, or from those who penned them. On the contrary, the Scriptures are prized by the Church because through them the soul is brought into contact with this truth.'[52]

Denney and Forsyth were repeating a central evangelical insight when they stressed that ultimate truth is to be found in our experience of the living God, an emphasis Warfield and Machen failed to make so clearly. But we may feel that this emphasis does not necessarily entail a lessening of confidence in the Scriptures as God-given truth, the insight particularly stressed by the Americans. Both insights are true to the evangelical tradition, and both can be held together.

Britain and America

Denney's views on Scripture were delivered as a lecture in Chicago Theological Seminary in 1894, in a series subsequently published as *Studies in Theology*. In the preface to the book Denney comments that the lectures were published as given, with the exception of the one on Scripture, 'which excited considerable discussion' and was subsequently rewritten, not to change its basic content, but to avoid misunderstanding. Undoubtedly, his epistemology, with its application to the Bible, did not commend itself to all his American hearers, though, being British, he could probably get away with more than an American theologian would have been allowed. Though it had many forms, including at times strong expressions of fundamentalism, British evangelicalism in the main took a different course from American in the first few decades of the twentieth century. In particular, issues of the infallibility or inerrancy of the Bible were much less to the fore; most British evangelical writers in the first half of the twentieth century gave a very high place to the Scriptures as trustworthy and generally accurate, but refused to call them inerrant.[53] It is noteworthy that T. C. Hammond's *In Understanding be Men*, originally published in 1936 and used as a handbook of evangelical orthodoxy by generations of students linked to the Inter-Varsity Fellowship, while happy to speak of revelation 'in the form of a Person and a Book', and of 'verbal inspiration' (albeit qualified), mentions neither infallibility nor inerrancy.[54]

There may be a number of reasons for this. There can be little doubt that the battle for the Bible in America, rightly or wrongly, was more than an issue of inspiration and inerrancy. For those involved in it, it was a battle for America. For a substantial part of the nineteenth century, evangelicalism had dominated the religion and culture of the country, and effectively controlled higher education. Its vision of a Christian America was virtually within its grasp. The attack on the Bible threatened this ascendancy, and, worse still, sought to remove all traces of Christianity from American national life. Big issues were at stake, and battle lines were drawn very clearly, and maintained very rigidly. The situation in Britain was quite different. If any religious grouping could claim the nation it was the Church of England, a denomination that has always been mixed theologically, and one that was not predisposed to fight for Britain in the way many American evangelicals fought for America.

A second reason may be the simple fact that Britain is nearer to Europe than America is, and the British temperament is different from the American. Certainly, British evangelicalism was more generally open to acceptance of the findings of German biblical criticism; and, being for the most part open to some form of theistic biological evolution, British evangelicals did not find it too difficult to accept concepts of progressive revelation. Perhaps, too, the British love of compromise led them to a greater openness to alternative views than that shown by Americans, who had been brought up in the 'either in or out, lost or saved, true or false' revivalist tradition.

There is a third factor, and for our purposes the most significant. We have traced in chapters 2 and 3 the crucial shift from God to reason as the ultimate justification of knowledge and truth. Evangelicals, perhaps more than any other group, resisted this shift; but they were not immune to its influence. On the whole, American evangelicals appear to have been more strongly influenced by it than British, perhaps because of the influence of the philosophy that had been developed from the Scottish common-sense school and that dominated American learning. Both American and British evangelicals, if challenged, would have insisted that their epistemology was

God-centred; but the tendency on the one side was to make this God a God of reason, and on the other a God of experience. Warfield's statement that 'We believe in Christ because it is rational to believe in Him' was as unacceptable to Forsyth or Denney as Forsyth's statement that 'Our theology is not a fixed system we must accept but a gracious experience we must declare', or Denney's, that 'The basis of all theological doctrine is experience', was to Warfield.

9. Carl Henry

The Reformation principle of the primacy of God's grace has been held firmly by evangelicals, not just in their theology of salvation, but in their epistemology. Our knowledge of truth depends on God's prior action in revelation, whether existential or verbal. But this lays them open to the objection that any purported revelation can be challenged: what grounds have we for holding that it is true? If God is to be the ultimate justification for truth, how do we justify our beliefs about God?

Carl F. H. Henry (1913–), named by *Time* magazine in 1978 evangelicalism's 'leading theologian', has been a central figure in American 'new evangelicalism' (a post-war reaction to the narrowness of fundamentalism which nevertheless retained fundamentalism's very high view of the Bible). He has held posts in the philosophy of religion at Northern Baptist Seminary and Fuller Theological Seminary, a college specifically founded to enable evangelicals to engage with contemporary scholarship. A prolific writer, in 1946 and 1947 he published *Remaking the Modern Mind* and *The Uneasy Conscience of Modern Fundamentalism*, calling on evangelicals to reshape their thinking, and, in particular, to develop a comprehensive worldview that rejects the narrowness and separatism of the fundamentalists and applies the Christian message to all areas of life, including the social, ethical, and political.

His most significant work, *God, Revelation, and Authority* (six volumes, 1976–82), runs to about a million and a half words, and includes discussions of a wide range of issues in philosophical theology. Its main goal is to set out and defend Henry's epistemology, one he has consistently championed in half a century of publishing. He defines his position as 'rational presuppositionalism', and it can be summarized in nine points.

Worldview, reason, revelation and faith

First, Henry sets out to supply *a comprehensive and integrated Christian worldview*. In a relativistic age in 'crisis of truth and word'[1] he offers a 'metaphysical view that professes to make sense of all reality and life and involves a universal truth claim'.[2] He is confident of his right to do this, despite the vetoes or restrictions of alternative worldviews.[3] Equally, he asserts the possibility of an integrated and unified system; all truth has a common source in God, and so is ultimately one.[4]

Secondly, such a worldview is based on *the objectivity of God and his revealed truth*. 'The Christian's primary ontological axiom is the one living God, and his primary epistemological axiom is divine revelation.'[5] God's 'reality and objectivity' are foundational and unequivocal; he 'exists forever in a self-specified condition free of external determination; his reality, purpose, and activity are not contingent upon the universe'.[6] This God has freely chosen to give us 'a deliberate disclosure of his reality'[7] that enables us to know ultimate, factual, fixed truth and live according to 'fixed epistemic and ethical controls'.[8]

Again, thirdly, Henry emphasizes *the supernatural nature of God and his activity*. In the face of the naturalistic worldviews that have resulted from the Enlightenment, and, particularly, the attempts of liberal theologians to desupernaturalize Christianity,[9] Henry argues for 'historic Christian super-naturalism'[10] expressed in 'the evangelical insistence on a sovereign super-natural deity and on transcendent truth'.[11]

Fourthly, *reason, logic, meaning and truth are rooted in 'God's intellectual attributes'*.[12] 'The Christian knows God to be the source of all truth; truth is what God thinks and says. Christianity has never been embarrassed by the centrality of the *Logos* in the Trinity; *Logos* and Wisdom are intrinsic to the Godhead.'[13] Reason and the laws of logic are the expression of God's mind; he is the author of all meaning; truth is truth because he thinks and wills it.[14] 'God's mind and will are the source of all truth, of mathematics, of logic, of law, and of cosmic order.'[15]

Fifthly, Henry's central thesis is that *God reveals and speaks*. There is no reason why we should limit God to one form of revelation (through either a person or a book, through either encounter or concept). God reveals and speaks in a number of ways, in his creation, in general revelation, and supremely in Christ, the incarnate Word. But, additionally and foundationally, he is able to formulate and communicate truth in an epistemic word, in which he articulates truth verbally through 'intelligible disclosure';[16] and this, in sovereign grace, he has chosen to do. 'Revelation in the Bible is essentially a mental conception; God's disclosure is rational and intelligible communication.'[17]

Sixthly, *God has created human persons such that they can receive divine communication*; all, whether Christian or not, have a 'noetic structure' sufficient to understand and receive it. Henry accepts that there are various aspects of the 'image of God' in human persons,[18] but 'the rational or cognitive aspect has logical priority'; a person without reason, for example, would not be able to distinguish right from wrong, so the rational aspect must be logically prior to the moral.[19] The image of God in us gives us a basic awareness of some truths: 'Through the *imago Dei* given at creation, every human person gains an ineradicable awareness that God exists and that other selves and the external world exist.'[20] The image also enables us to receive truth through the Bible, as it is illuminated and interpreted by the Holy Spirit.[21]

Seventhly, Henry's approach to truth is *credo ut intelligam* – 'I believe in order to understand.' He considers this a middle position between fideism (seen, for example, in Barth) and the empiricism/evidentialism which he believes is widespread among American evangelicals. For fideism, 'the existence of God is a matter of sheer faith contrary to reason'; finite, sinful reason has no right to test the validity or truth of divine revelation.[22] But, for Henry, setting faith and reason over against each other in this way is quite unacceptable; since both are aspects of God's creation, they should not be opposed to each other, but rather work together in harmony.

At the other end of the scale, Henry criticizes empiricism, typified for him by Aquinas and contemporary evidentialists, both for giving an unjustifiable priority to reason, and for failing to produce adequate results. The empirical approach, based on what we can observe through our five senses, deals only with the finite and phenomenal, and so cannot give us ultimate truth about God. At best, it only ever gives probabilities, never certainties. Even if we extend empiricism to allow us to accept religious experience as valid, we still have the problem of interpreting and authenticating our experiences.[23] Henry accepts that proofs or evidences for the existence of God[24] or the fact of the resurrection[25] may serve to remove obstacles to unbelief, but they are never sufficient to engender faith. In the last analysis, basing our faith on anything other than God's revealed truth, whether it is evidences or arguments or experiences, is going to be inadequate.[26]

As his middle way between fideism and empiricism/evidentialism, Henry puts forward what he sees as an Augustinian position, one followed broadly by Anselm, Luther and Calvin, which emphasizes both the priority of faith and the necessity of reason. 'Faith is a step on the way to understanding.'[27] We believe in order to understand; without belief we shall not understand. 'The revelation of the living God is the precondition and starting point for human understanding; it supplies the framework and corrective for natural reason.' Reason's task is a vital one, but it is on the foundation and within the climate of faith.[28] This is true, says Henry, not just of evangelical Christianity; the principle applies in all areas of knowledge. Even the scientist and the Christian evidentialist have to start from basic presuppositions which they are unable to prove, and so have to hold by faith; every philosophy starts with a worldview, adopted without proof, which reason then applies to particular situations in the world.[29]

Axioms and special revelation

This brings us to our eighth point: Henry's concept of axioms or *presuppositions*, and their relation to reason. 'Throughout its long history,' he declares, 'philosophy has always recognized the legitimacy of assuming without proof a philosophical axiom or postulational principle as an initial basis of reasoning.' So we have every right to take the existence of God as a basic first principle 'even in the absence of empirical proof'.[30] We are as intellectually justified in adopting supernaturalistic first principles for our theistic worldview as those who adopt naturalistic ones.[31]

But the axioms the evangelical adopts, says Henry, are not (or should not be) arbitrary. 'The Christian believer knows assuredly that his postulates and control beliefs are not conjecturally grounded, but are anchored in the triune God's self-existence and self-disclosure'; as such, they are 'basic to human noetic structure'.[32] This assured knowledge is not the result of reasoned proof, but rather of 'rational intuition', by which 'all men possess certain underived *a priori* truths without any process of inference whereby these truths are derived'.[33] Following Augustine and Calvin, Henry includes in these truths not just the laws of logic and mathematics, but also 'epistemic relationships to God, the world, and other selves'.[34] God has so made us that, as thinking beings, we intuitively know that we exist, the world exists, other minds exist, and that the 'immutable and eternal' exists. These beliefs are universal and constant, necessary structures of our thinking. Henry sees them as parallel to Kant's categories of thought, but differing from them in that they arise from external reality, and are not based, like Kant's categories, simply on our subjective experience.[35]

Henry, then, is prepared to talk of at least some of his axioms as intuitively known and therefore indubitable. But he is fully aware that this will hardly convince the sceptic, who is capable of doubting the existence not just of the immutable and eternal, but of other minds and the external world as well. So he has a further line of defence. Every worldview has to have a foundation of certain presuppositions or axioms adopted by faith; though we cannot use reason and argument to establish the foundation, we can use them to show that what is built on the foundation is sound. Our task, then, is to show that 'the Christian world-life view' is 'an all-inclusive explanation of reality which answers the most problems and leaves the smallest residue of unsolved problems'.[36] Every worldview starts with faith; the Christian's task is to go on to demonstrate that his or her faith is not mere fideism or 'nonrational belief',[37] but the basis for the best explanation of the world as we know it, giving 'a more consistent, more comprehensive and more satisfactory explanation of the meaning and worth of life than do other views'.[38]

In such a task, says Henry, the primary tool is logical consistency: is the worldview free from internal self-contradiction? Logical inconsistency in a worldview is sufficient to make it implausible. Logical consistency in a worldview is not final proof of its validity, though it helps to confirm it for those who adopt its presuppositions by faith.[39]

Without the law of contradiction we can neither think nor have truth; among the competing worldviews only one can be correct.[40] Christians, who are convinced that their worldview is the correct one, must unmask the inconsistencies of other views and demonstrate the rational consistency of their alternative. By 'persuasive rational evidence' they can then demonstrate that alternative views lack the intellectual compulsion of the Christian view.[41] Henry admits that this is a lengthy task, and accepts that life is too short to examine every conceivable alternative to the Christian worldview. But we can investigate the plausibility of its most cogent rivals, and meanwhile do what we can to 'systematize, deepen, and apply' our own presuppositions in order to test them for explanatory power and logical consistency.[42]

Logical consistency is not the only test for truth. Henry is willing to accept that explanatory power that covers the full range of our experience (from scientific empirical experience to mystical experience) can play a role; but he insists it is a subsidiary role, since experience can never give us certainty. True to his heritage in American evangelicalism of the first half of this century, Henry is deeply suspicious of any move to build Christianity on experience: 'to make religious experience – whether the feelings, or volition, or moral sentiment, or even empirical arguments from the world – the rationale for Judeo-Christian beliefs leads invariably and inevitably to a dilution of the biblical view'.[43]

Henry defends himself against the charge of rationalism by pointing out that his rationalistic test for truth is dependent on the acceptance of foundational presuppositions by faith, and is not the basis for them. Reason, he insists, has no normative or creative role in respect to truth;[44] and what it does offer us is strictly limited: it can never give us 'infallible truth about ultimate reality'.[45] But, equally, his position is not fideistic, in that he stresses faith without rejecting reason,[46] and refuses to set the one over against the other: 'reason is the ally and not the enemy of divine revelation'; evangelicals have 'no cause to shun logic', and need have nothing to fear from 'public reason'.[47]

On the issue of certainty, while attacking empiricism for giving us at best only probabilities, Henry admits that, even though the test of logical consistency may help to confirm it, the truth of his approach cannot be logically proved. But that does not mean we cannot be certain. Certainty has no necessary connection with truth. We may be certain that vinegar causes warts; certainty 'can be more emotional or volitional than cognitive'. The source of Christian certainty is spiritual:

> The Christian faith offers not mathematical or speculative certainty, but rather spiritual assurance. Divine authority eliminates the rational gap between probability and certainty. Such assurance is grounded not in empirical probabilities but in a supernatural witness of the Holy Spirit that individually enlivens objectively inspired Scripture. The Spirit uses truth as an instrument of persuasion, truth attested by Scripture and testable for logical consistency.[48]

This brings us, finally, to Henry's view of *God's special revelation in the Bible*. Though he is specifically concerned to defend the concepts of propositional revelation, verbal inspiration and inerrancy, he by no means limits his theology of revelation to the Bible. For him, revelation is to be defined in terms of 'the living God who shows himself and speaks for himself'.[49] In presenting fifteen theses on revelation, he does not get specifically to verbal biblical revelation until the tenth. Priority is given to God's revelation in Christ: 'The climax of God's special revelation is Jesus of Nazareth, the personal incarnation of God in the flesh; in Jesus Christ the source and content of revelation converge and coincide.'[50]

Given the presupposition of a God who can communicate intelligibly to rational creatures he has made, and who has chosen to do so, Henry sees no reason why we should not accept that he has done this in a propositional, verbal, and completely trustworthy way. Against the fundamentalists, however, he argues for a critical and historical approach to the Scriptures, insisting that we do not impose on them concepts of verbal precision that are appropriate only to the twentieth century. We should not expect 'modern technological precision' in statistics or measurements, in citations of Old Testament passages, parable, poetry, proverb, hyperbole and exaggeration.[51] Though Henry resists the pressure by the fundamentalists to make inerrancy a test of evangelical orthodoxy, he thus accepts a qualified concept of verbal inspiration and inerrancy.[52]

This, then, is Henry's rational presuppositionalism. It is rational, because reason plays a crucial role in God, in revelation, and in our response to revelation;[53] and presuppositional, because, like every worldview, it is built on axioms which are accepted without proof. These are principally Henry's two foundational axioms, the fact of God and the fact of his revelation, with, additionally, his further presuppositions such as the rationality of God and the ability of human persons to receive divine communication.

The key factor in Henry's approach is his stress on what we might call the direction of movement in the area of truth. It is most definitely from God to us, and not from us to God. We do not start with the not-God (that is, ourselves and the world) and move from there to God. Rather, God starts with himself, and moves from there to us, whether in the incarnation, or in the creation, or in the work of the Holy Spirit imparting both factual information and certainty.[54] This emphasis is illustrated by his insistence, in contrast to many of his fellow evangelicals, that we do not formulate a doctrine of the inspiration of the Bible on the basis of our investigations into its teaching, effect, claims about itself, and so on.[55] Our first act is to accept: God speaks and we listen. Investigations come later, and help to confirm (or destroy) our initial faith.

Closely linked to this is Henry's stress on basic presuppositions, notably of a God who takes the initiative in revelation – presuppositions which have to be received by faith, though they can be partially confirmed (or destroyed) by subsequent reason. Significant here is Henry's acceptance that rational certainty is not possible. Fundamentalism tended to assume that the rational arguments for the truth of Christianity could be so presented that any reasonable man or woman would necessarily be convinced; the case would be proven, and our knowledge could thus be rationally certain. Henry rejects this, pointing out that the kind of certainty he wishes to claim is spiritual rather than rational.

Henry, then, can be seen as building his epistemology on the principle of the primacy of God's grace.[56] In our next chapter we shall look at another evangelical theologian who sought to stress this same principle, with rather different results.

10. Helmut Thielicke

In 1963 Helmut Thielicke (1908–86) toured the USA, preaching, lecturing, and engaging in public dialogue and informal conversation with theologians, ministers and students of all theological backgrounds, but especially evangelicals and fundamentalists.[1] His critique of aspects of fundamentalism was strident, but his own evangelical zeal won him a fair hearing; the fundamentalists listened best, he recalled, if they had first heard him preach.

Born into a Lutheran family, Thielicke was educated for the Lutheran ministry in four German universities, picking up two doctorates on the way. He was Professor of Systematic Theology and later Rector at Tübingen, and then Dean of the theological faculty and also Rector at the University of Hamburg. He was a gifted preacher and church leader, who began his first multi-volume work, on ethics, while he personally was struggling with the issues raised by living as a Christian under the Nazi regime.

Rather bravely, but graciously, he was able to point out to his fundamentalist audiences that America had never passed through a period of critical theological 'Enlightenment' as Germany had. American Christians had been able to receive and pass on their rich traditions of evangelical Christianity with comparative ease, each generation following the one before, enjoying its spiritual capital, questioning very little, shut off from the outside world, and, in the process, becoming 'frozen'.[2] In Germany such peace was impossible; the Enlightenment

. . . relentlessly and systematically posed the question of how one can accept faith in the absolute in the midst of the relativity of the historical and how the truth of reason and truth of history are related to each other. This kind of searching cross-examination put so many difficulties in the way of all naïve and self-confident orthodoxy that it simply could not go on pursuing the even tenor of its way but had to come to grips with its assailants.[3]

Our interest in this chapter is how Thielicke responded to this challenge. We shall consider this under seven headings.

The primacy of God

Foundational is Thielicke's rejection of human autonomy in favour of theonomy, the rule or authority of God. He analysed the philosophy of Descartes as the crucial turning-point in the West's concept of knowledge and truth, the point at which we exchanged objectivity for subjectivity, God and the world for the self. Before Descartes, said Thielicke, neither the thinking subject nor the act of thought was considered of primary importance. What *is* (being) and, very especially, the fact of a creator God were seen as foundational – basic even to the concept of the self. 'The nature of the self cannot be abstracted from the fact that it is created by God, that it has guiltily broken free from him, and that it is visited and redeemed by him. We are those who have a history with God.'[4] This history constitutes our being, so our being can be defined only relationally. We know who we are only as we know who God is; and we learn who God is through his revelation in Christ.

Descartes rejected such an approach. Where Luther had believed that I must know who God is to know who I am, Descartes said that I must know that and who I am to know who and what God is. Luther started with 'God is' and 'God says'. Descartes started with 'I'. In Descartes, then, the focal point of interest shifted from the objective to the subjective.[5] Doubt (and doubt is the 'red thread' that is the key to understanding the development of thought in the eighteenth and nineteenth centuries)[6] removed objective being – God and the world – from the centre of the stage, and put the 'I', the doubting subject, there instead. *Cogito, ergo sum*, 'I think, therefore I am', 'stands on the threshold of modern thought. One might call it the initial thesis of secularization.'[7] Out of this revolution has come not just the Enlightenment, but the Enlightenment's distinctive way of doing theology, one that starts with the subject. All the great modern theologies have been characterized by 'subjectivity'.[8]

By contrast, Thielicke claims to offer an approach to theology that refuses to allow the self to claim a monopoly of truth, one that is based not on the self and its reason, feeling, or experience, but on 'the authority of traditional revelation founded on the Bible'.[9] It does not deny all rights to the subjective, any more than the subjective approaches ignore totally the objective. But its thrust is 'towards the historically concrete'.[10] It rejects the strident claims made for human autonomy that followed Descartes's revolution.

Our relationship to the truth

Thielicke thus insisted on the objectivity of God, revelation, and truth. But his engagement with the German tradition made it impossible for him to leave the matter there. However objective the truth may be, the self, the subject, must be involved in receiving it. We are not blank slates; the truth has to be appropriated, and for us it is not truth until it is appropriated. 'The slate has a hand in what is written on it.'[11]

For Thielicke, then, though God and truth are in themselves absolute and objective, it is a mistake for us to 'absolutize' or objectify truth. Truth has to be something we relate to, and relationship involves the subjective. Thielicke used the illustration of a camera film; it is able to produce accurate photographic reproductions because it is coated with light-sensitive substances which relate specifically to the images projected on to it. Without light sensitivity it could not capture the images, any more than we can capture sunlight in a sack.[12]

So truth is historical and verbal, but never just historical or verbal. Objectified history is not truth, nor is an objectified message or objectified dogma. Firmly in the tradition of Kant and Kierkegaard at this point, Thielicke insisted that it must be a matter of a personal relationship between the individual and the truth, whether that truth is God himself, God's revelation in history, in Jesus, or in the preached or written word.[13]

But Thielicke parted company with Kant and the Cartesian tradition by insisting very firmly that the relationship is not something we create, but something that is created in us by God. He contrasted Kant with Luther. The Kantians, he says, approximate God to themselves. They are the fixed point; God is a 'mere predicate of anthropology', an object constituted by the exercise of faith. In Luther, by contrast, God accommodates himself to us, condescends to us in love, comes to us in the incarnation, speaks our language, and refuses to be 'a timeless God in himself who is not in relation to us'.[14]

Failure to retain this foundational insight of Luther, claimed Thielicke, has been the great mistake of the subjective Cartesian tradition. The autonomous self can never find the truth. Descartes, Locke and the empiricists gave autonomy to the reason, but, as Hume and Kant demonstrated, there are inevitable limits to the powers of reason. Though ultimately objective, God is way beyond reason's power to objectify.[15] Additionally, reason in particular, and the self in general, can never know God because of the fall, in which creation was disrupted and the human race was alienated from God, putting itself in a position of bondage, of darkening, of being given up, and so existing in a permanent state of suppressing the truth (Rom. 1:19ff.). Even within its limited sphere, then, reason will oppose the concept of God.[16] The Kantian tradition, though it accepted the limitations of reason, still failed to dethrone the self. Schleiermacher, for example, replaced reason with feeling, but it was still the feeling self.

Revelation

If one of the 'two authorities that claim a monopoly of truth'[17] fails, we have every justification to turn to the other. Instead of starting with the self as our authority, we shall allow God to start with himself, and give us his revelation as our authority. The direction of movement is to be reversed. 'Something comes to man from without . . . he can only receive it . . . he does not himself produce it.'[18] This is grace; this is the love and wisdom of God achieving what for us would be impossible.

But how do we know that this revelation is truly God coming to us? How do we escape from the abyss that sees our experience of God revealing himself to us as nothing more than *our* experience, and never allows us to move from the subjective to the objective behind it? Thielicke could not allow reason or any other manifestation of the self to stand in judgment over the revelation; that would mean restoring the self's ultimate autonomy. So it must be God who authenticates the revelation.

Revelation is God coming to us. He comes in the events of salvation history and in the exposition of the Scriptures, but supremely in Jesus Christ, the incarnate Word. In essence, revelation is 'participation in the divine self-knowledge'.[19] It is more than supernatural inspiration or invasion;[20] it is the 'miracle of the divine self-disclosure' of a God who is qualitatively distinct and objectively inaccessible, who 'alone can know what is in God' (1 Cor. 2:11).[21] So it is redemption as well as revelation; the key to revelation is the salvation event; the Word of revelation not only discloses itself to the hearer, but actually creates the hearer, 'bringing him to being in the truth'.[22] The old Cartesian self has to die; it has to cease to serve as the point of reference.[23] But out of this death comes a resurrection in which the autonomous self is replaced by life in Christ.[24] No longer, therefore, do we seek to control or manipulate the truth; now we are in the truth, we hear the voice of him who is the truth, and we let the truth work on us and shape our lives.[25]

Without this salvation event in which God comes to us, doctrinal orthodoxy and even the Scriptures are empty. At the beginning of the third volume of *The Evangelical Faith* Thielicke quotes C. H. Spurgeon, the nineteenth-century Baptist preacher whom he greatly admired: 'When the Spirit of God departs, then even the truth itself becomes an iceberg.'[26] Revelation is God revealing; it is alive and active because God is alive and active. Once we lock it up in dogmas we have killed it. 'There are no timeless theological statements and no perennial theology.'[27] The living God can never be static, fixed once and for all. Even the truths of salvation history and the teaching of the Bible must never be looked on as mere history or doctrine; they are living history, the living encounter of living people with the living God. 'Here we are dealing with the history of a living heart.'[28]

The Bible

In this context Thielicke rejected the verbal inspiration of the Bible. Practically, his rejection was the result of his wholesale acceptance of the critical approach to the Scriptures.[29] Theologically, he argued that it entailed both the Holy Spirit in 'mechanically directing a process of writing',[30] and 'the levelling down of all biblical statements', so that the empirical (statements about the world) and the transcendent (statements about God) 'merge epistemologically'.[31] Additionally, in his view, a verbally inspired Bible would remove any possibility of faith as trust, and result in 'a very slavish obedience . . . which would be totally mechanical and indiscriminate', instead of a living relationship with God.[32] Further, viewing the Scriptures as the Word of God, for Thielicke, erases the difference between God the Word incarnate in Jesus Christ, and the human testimony to it.[33]

The unregenerate and the truth

Thielicke pressed his emphasis on God revealing truth to us, as opposed to our discovering truth about God, to its full conclusion, in the spheres of both doctrine and practice. In and of ourselves we have no possibility of accepting the truth; we can only suppress it. Knowledge of the truth is fundamentally closed to someone who is 'being in untruth', who has not yet been re-created or regenerated or 'integrated into the salvation event'.[34] So the unregenerate can neither understand nor accept God's truth.[35] True, they can believe 'the facts of religious history, even the history of the Christian religion'.[36] What they cannot believe or receive is 'the divine truth manifested in these facts'. It is in this context that Thielicke was able to say dogmatically that there is no such thing as natural theology.[37] The unregenerate person may understand or accept, say, the arguments for the existence of God. But such arguments are not theology; their interest is not the true God, the God who comes to us in active and creative grace and regenerates us so that we can receive his truth. Here, again, Thielicke reflected the Kantian division between theological truth, known only to those who have put to death their rationalistic 'Cartesian' self, and other forms of truth, historical, philosophical or whatever, which are open to both the regenerate and the unregenerate.

Preaching

The means that the Holy Spirit uses to accomplish this active and creative revelation is preaching. Faith comes by hearing. Preaching is not merely the rehearsing of doctrines or the proclamation of the mighty acts of God; it is the opening of deaf ears, the creative miracle in which faith is given, Christ is present, and the Spirit of God grants participation in the self-knowledge of God.[38] Apart from accepting that the New Testament, as the earliest and original Christian testimony, has a 'normative function in relation to all later forms of proclamation', providing a criterion, focus, and place of appeal, Thielicke readily put preaching on a level with the New Testament Scriptures. 'Both share the promise that in their Word no less and no other than God's Word is proclaimed and the Kyrios links his own ongoing presence with this proclamation (Mt. 18.20).'[39] Thielicke's central concern here was not to elevate preaching or to minimize the New Testament, but to draw a clear distinction between the incarnate Word and other ways in which the Word comes to us.[40]

Faith

The response to preaching is faith. Faith is not *fides quae creditur*, the acceptance of a message, even of the sayings of Jesus.[41] It is not even something we do. It is what God does in us as he comes to us in preaching. If we exercised faith, faith would be a work;[42] instead, it is God's work in us. 'It is engendered by the Word and by the creative work of the Spirit within it.'[43] Nevertheless, as we would expect, Thielicke did not picture faith as wholly passive. It requires an affirmation, against appearance, experience, and the trend of natural knowledge.[44] We are free to exercise faith; it is a response, not to theological statements that compel belief, but to the creative and effectual power of the Word that works within us as we encounter it in proclamation.[45]

Perhaps the most significant thing about Thielicke's epistemology is the radical discontinuity in his thinking between theological truth and other truth.[46] In keeping with his Kantian heritage, he could not allow any mixing between ordinary truth and divine truth, between the scientific, historical or factual and the transcendent. Just as his *The Evangelical Faith* has no section on creation, though it constantly refers to God's work in the new creation, so his interest when dealing with knowledge and truth is almost exclusively in dealing with the knowledge of transcendent truth.[47] Though he accepted the historical reliability of the New Testament, he refused to make its historical truth the basis of theology or faith. Even theological truth itself has in a sense constantly to be rejected; once our experience of God becomes truth to be set alongside other truth, it ceases to be true theology.

In Thielicke we have a man of true evangelical spirit, whose theology vibrates with the life and creative power of the God who saves and brings about the miracle of the new birth. Here is the primacy of the grace of God; here is Christ exalted and encountered; here is preaching that changes lives. Here too is reverence for the Scriptures, though it is a reverence that arises because Christ is to be found through them, not for the Scriptures as an end in themselves. Apologizing for his bluntness, Thielicke told his fundamentalist audience that his interest (perhaps in contrast to theirs) was not primarily in the Bible at all. 'I am interested only in the Lord Jesus Christ. The Holy Scripture is only the ship in which he sleeps. And because *he* is sleeping in it, I am *then* also interested in the ship.'[48]

What is missing in Thielicke is a 'high' concept of the inspiration and trustworthiness of the Scriptures. For some this would disqualify him from the title 'evangelical'; for others the fact that he has maintained the warmth and heart of the evangelical gospel, as Forsyth did, shows he is clearly evangelical, even if something of an enigma. Thielicke himself would take a third position: the fact that he does not hold to what might be called the traditional evangelical view of Scripture, so far from disqualifying him, in fact releases him to be truly evangelical. The heart of the evangelical gospel and the evangelical experience is Christ, the living personal Christ, encountered and known by the individual now. Replacing the living Christ by the Scriptures, doctrinal formulations, or a Christ in a book, takes the heart from evangelicalism and destroys it.

To these issues we shall return later in this book.

11. Reformed epistemology

We saw in chapter 9 how Carl Henry developed a presuppositionalist epistemology as the basis of his approach to evangelical theology. All worldviews, he argued, have to start with basic presuppositions. So it is as acceptable for a Christian to posit theistic presuppositions as for an atheist to posit naturalistic ones. We do not have to produce empirical proof before we can take the existence of God as a basic first principle. But that is not to say that these presuppositions are not open to, and in need of some form of, justification. Henry held that for the Christian, the chief justification is the individual's conviction that they have been personally revealed to him or her by God. But in the public arena, justification will need to take the form of demonstrating that the adopting of the theistic presuppositions gives 'a more consistent, more comprehensive and more satisfactory explanation of the meaning and worth of life than do other views'.[1]

Throughout the history of evangelicalism, there has always been a tendency among thinking evangelicals to capitulate to the demands of the Enlightenment and to seek to justify their beliefs by the use of reason. In an age that insisted that only what was rational could be real, and used reason to attack the claims of Christianity, it was natural for them, in their apologetic and evangelistic zeal, to seek to show that Christianity was rational and could stand up to and answer any amount of rational investigation and critique. From such rational apologetics it was not too difficult to slip into saying that reason and argument were able to provide a sufficient basis for accepting the truth of

Christianity, effectively moving from claiming that the foundations of Christianity are rational or reasonable to saying that rationality or reason is the foundation of Christianity.

The demonstration of the truth of Christianity through the use of reason alone, or through reason aided by experience, was, of course, the goal of seventeenth-century rationalism, and the warm-hearted evangelicalism of Wesley was in a sense a reaction against it. Even so, evangelical apologists were often at the forefront of attempts to prove the existence of God, and their defence of the Bible was frequently based on rational arguments. Norman Geisler, for example, claimed that his version of the cosmological argument, if not 'rationally inescapable', was 'existentially undeniable',[2] and set it out in the form of a logical proof.[3]

It would hardly be fair to these evangelical apologists, however, to give the impression that for them the presenting of rational arguments for the existence of God or the truth of the Christian message is the whole of the story. Faithful to their evangelical heritage, they would want to insist that there is all the difference in the world between convincing someone on the basis of rational arguments that God exists and that the message of the Bible is true, and making that person a Christian. The arguments can affect a person's intellectual beliefs, they would claim; but it takes the supernatural work of the Holy Spirit to change his or her life, to make him or her a new person, a true Christian. So the work of convincing the mind, with the help of rational arguments, is only a preliminary stage; it is bringing the person to the point where he or she is open to the really significant thing – the work of divine grace and power in true evangelical conversion.

Evangelical rationalism, then, could never be total. But at times it has been strong, and the *credo ut intelligam* we saw in Carl Henry has often been muted. This emphasis has, however, been a major feature of one strand of evangelical thought, the one broadly known as Reformed epistemology. To explore it we shall look briefly at the work of two virtually contemporary Dutchmen, one of whom worked in Holland and the other in the United States: Herman Dooyeweerd and Cornelius Van Til. After a survey of one of Van Til's best-known followers, Francis Schaeffer, we shall consider the more specifically philosophical presentation of the approach by a group of evangelicals led by two of America's leading philosophers, Alvin Plantinga and Nicholas Wolterstorff.

Herman Dooyeweerd

Dooyeweerd (1894–1977) was Professor at the Free University of Amsterdam from 1929 to 1965. The Free University had been founded in 1879 by

Abraham Kuyper (theologian, philosopher, and Dutch Prime Minister) as a means by which the vigorous tradition of Dutch Calvinism could counter the spread of secularism and liberal theology, and put into practice one of its basic convictions: that Christian beliefs should be developed to form a holistic system, a Christian worldview that covered every area of life. Dooyeweerd developed such a system, with a complexity of detail (and of style) that challenges the comprehension of most readers. But the basic structures of his approach are straightforward, and it is those that concern us here.

Foundational to Dooyeweerd's approach is a total rejection of the concept that we can find truth apart from God. He vigorously repudiated 'the pretended autonomy of philosophical thought', and 'the belief in human theoretical reason as the ultimate judge in matters of truth and falsehood'.[4] This pretended autonomy is seen in the development of European thought based on Greek philosophy, and especially in the Enlightenment's concept of the ultimate authority of human reason. In particular, the modern secular world and the liberal theologians start from this false premise that our thinking is neutral and autonomous: reason unaided by God can give us truth. It cannot, said Dooyeweerd; we cannot start with unbiased, neutral, objective reason; we can only start with the human heart. The heart is neither neutral nor simply rational; it is religious, and as such it is either in tune with God or hostile to him. The heart that is hostile to God cannot understand the world because it is out of gear with the Creator, who alone gives meaning to all things; therefore it cannot have a true understanding of the world. The heart that is in tune with God, illuminated by the Holy Spirit and helped by the revealed Word of God in the Scriptures, is able to read the Book of Nature and come to a true understanding of the world.

> Since the fall and the promise of the coming Redeemer, there are two central main springs operative in the heart of human existence. The first is the dynamis of the Holy Ghost, which by the moving power of God's Word, incarnated in Jesus Christ, re-directs to its Creator the creation that had apostatized in the fall from its true Origin. This dynamis brings man into the relationship of sonship to the Divine Father. Its religious ground-motive is that of the Divine Word-Revelation, which is the key to the understanding of Holy Scripture: the motive of *creation, fall, and redemption by Jesus Christ in the communion of the Holy Ghost*.
>
> The second central main spring is that of the spirit of apostasy from the true God. As religious dynamis (power), it leads the human heart in an apostate direction, and is the source of all deification of the creature. It is the source of all absolutizing of the relative even in the theoretical attitude of thought. By virtue of its idolatrous character, its religious ground-motive can receive very diverse contents.[5]

All thinking and living, then, is according to a 'religious ground-motive', founded on a 'starting-point' or 'Archimedian point'[6] from which all else arises. This is more than a philosophical presupposition (though it certainly includes that); it is a religious stance; it is the heart, the whole being, adopting a position in relationship to the Creator and so to the creation. Our relationship to God (positive or negative) will determine our worldview, our philosophy, our presuppositions, and all other aspects of life.

In Dooyeweerd's system, a Christian does not need to establish the authenticity of her or his starting-point in terms that are acceptable to those who adopt different starting-points; indeed, it would be an impossible task, since the very concept of an Archimedian starting-point is that it is outside of the system to which it gives rise. Here, then, is a form of presuppositionalism which results in a complex philosophical system, and yet which at base claims to be a matter of the heart and of our relationship to God.

Cornelius Van Til

There are several parallels to Dooyeweerd's thinking in the approach of his fellow Dutch Calvinist, Cornelius Van Til (1895–1987), whose family emigrated from Holland to the United States when he was a boy. After training for the ministry, he taught briefly at Princeton Seminary, and then joined Machen at the new Westminster Theological Seminary where he was on the staff from 1929 to 1975.

Like Dooyeweerd's, Van Til's approach was unashamedly presuppositionalistic. He distinguished sharply between Christian and non-Christian epistemologies (and was quite prepared to put all apparently Christian epistemologies that did not follow his method into the latter category). There can be no compromise between the Christian and the non-Christian approach; they are 'two mutually exclusive visions'.[7] The heart of the Christian epistemology is its presupposition of the triune God of the Bible, along with the biblical doctrines of creation, providence, and redemption. This presupposition is the starting-point from which all else can be understood. The non-Christian rejects this starting-point and chooses some other, principally empirical facts or the laws of logic. But, said Van Til, neither facts nor logic can provide an adequate starting-point, since in both cases we can justifiably question what lies behind the facts and the laws; neither of them can be absolute, giving us an ultimate authority. Only God, the source of facts and of laws, can do that.

> Every fact and law in the created universe is brought into existence by God's creation. Every fact and every law in the created universe

continues to exist by virtue of the providence of God. Every fact and every law in the created universe accomplishes what it does accomplish by virtue of the plan or purpose of God.[8]

Thus true knowledge of facts is open only to the person who begins with the presupposition of the triune God of the Bible and submits to the authority of the Scriptures. 'The very contention of theism is that a fact, to be known truly, must be known as a theistic fact . . . Without the light of Scripture no fact can be known truly'.[9] Van Til accepted that it was very unfashionable to introduce concepts of authority into philosophical discussions. But he was convinced that 'Christianity is, for better or worse, a religion of authority',[10] and pointed out that his opponents equally, though perhaps unknowingly, chose to submit to an authority, that of 'the facts' or of the laws of logic. 'We have chosen to follow fully-fledged Christianity at all costs, while they have chosen to follow the "scientific method" at all costs.'[11]

Like Dooyeweerd, Van Til held that we are not required to justify our belief in the authority or truth of the Bible in empirical or rationalistic terms. That would require the Christian to move out of the biblical worldview and adopt the presuppositions of a non-Christian worldview, something we cannot do. Perhaps a little inconsistently, however, Van Til, like Henry, allowed that in apologetics we can seek to demonstrate the superiority of the Christian worldview to all others by showing how well it fits with the whole of experience.

Francis A. Schaeffer

The stress on the radical difference between worldviews built on Christian and non-Christian presuppositions was continued by one of Van Til's best-known followers, Francis A. Schaeffer (1912–84).[12] At heart an evangelist, he spent a significant part of his life seeking to persuade thinking people of the truth of Christianity, and in so doing he developed and applied Van Til's apologetic approach.

Christians and non-Christians alike, says Schaeffer, start consciously or unconsciously from presuppositions, prior postulates, beliefs or theories on which their worldview is built.[13] Of all the possible sets of presuppositions, those of the Christian worldview alone enable us to build up a consistent and true picture of the world.

> *The truth of Christianity is that it is true to what is there.* You can go to the end of the world and you never need be afraid, like the ancients, that you will fall off the end and the dragons will eat you up. You can carry

out your intellectual discussion to the end of the game because Christianity is not only true to the dogmas, it is not only true to what God has said in the Bible, but it is also true to what is there, and you will never fall off the end of the world. It is not just an approximate model, it really is true to what is there . . . This is what truth is from the Christian viewpoint and as God sets it forth in the Scripture.[14]

If the biblical worldview is true, says Schaeffer, any other worldview that contradicts it cannot be true. Schaeffer was strongly committed to arguing within the laws of logic, which he defined as 'the science of correct reasoning', the 'predictable and inevitable consequence of rational analysis' and, in particular, the law that ' "A" cannot equal "non-A" '.[15]

So Schaeffer's apologetic method sought to do two things. First, it attempted to show that all non-Christian worldviews are ultimately untenable if they are truly consistent with their presuppositions. 'No non-Christian can be consistent to the logic of his presuppositions.'[16] No-one, for example, who believes that everything is the result of chance can consistently live out that belief. Someone who denies a personal origin to the universe cannot consistently live as a personal moral being in the world, since personhood and morality are logically inconsistent with his or her worldview, and, according to Schaeffer, no-one can live impersonally and amorally.[17]

Secondly, Schaeffer's apologetic method endeavoured to demonstrate that a worldview built on the presupposition of an infinite, personal God who works in the world and speaks to us in a 'verbalised, propositional factual revelation'[18] in the Bible provides a full and consistent and livable answer to all the questions we have to face, both concerning the world around us and concerning ourselves. In *He is There and He is Not Silent*, Schaeffer explored three key issues: the question of why anything exists at all, the 'dilemma of man', and the problem of knowledge and truth, arguing that the Christian answer to each of these is sufficient and satisfying.

Schaeffer spent a good deal of his time arguing the truth of the evangelical faith with students and intellectuals. In so doing he helped to convince his fellow evangelicals, many of whom were tending to retreat into anti-intellectualism, that the rational case for Christianity is strong; there is no need to abandon the intellect when adopting the evangelical faith.[19] But Schaeffer would have been the first to deny that his approach was rationalistic. His apologetic used arguments that were rational; they had to be to convince those he was arguing with. Like Henry, he defended Christianity on the grounds of its consistency:

The Christian system is consistent as no other system that has ever been. It is beautiful beyond words, because it has that quality that no other system completely has – you begin at the beginning and you can go to the end. It is as simple as that. *And every part and portion of the system can be related back to the beginning.* Whatever you discuss, to understand it properly, you just go back to the beginning and the whole thing is in its place. The beginning is simply that God exists, and that He is the personal-infinite God.[20]

Schaeffer's thorough commitment to the use of logic in his argument and apologetic gave a strongly rationalistic feel to his approach. But his system as a whole was not rationalistic in at least three significant ways. First, as the above quotation illustrates, it was still at heart presuppositionalistic. Despite a style and method of presentation that seem to suggest it, Schaeffer was not in fact using reason to show that Christianity is true, thus subjecting it to the test of reason. He was using reason to show that if we adopt the presupposition of the Christian God, our resulting worldview will pass the test of reason with flying colours.

Secondly, Schaeffer constantly demonstrated a breadth of outlook that went far beyond the merely rational. His writings are full of references to art and music and culture; his concept of what makes us human stresses our personal and moral aspects every bit as much as our reason. Personality, he declared, is central.[21] At a time when many evangelicals were failing to engage with social and cultural issues, Schaeffer was issuing a clear call to a holistic approach to life and the world, involving not just spirit or intellect, but heart, emotions, art, personal involvement and social action.[22]

Thirdly, in the true evangelical tradition, Schaeffer readily accepted that no argument would ever make a person a Christian; nor could the accepting of the rationality of an argument be equated with receiving the truth. Both believing the truth and becoming a Christian were the result of the work of the Holy Spirit. Schaeffer's apologetic was merely clearing the ground, helping the person come to a place where God could reveal himself and his truth.

Plantinga and Wolterstorff

In 1983 Alvin Plantinga and Nicholas Wolterstorff, both recognized as leading American philosophers, edited a collection of essays written by a group of American evangelicals as a part of a project linked to Calvin College, 'Toward a Reformed View of Faith and Reason'. The book was called *Faith and Rationality*, and was quickly recognized as making a key contribution to the debate on epistemology both within the theistic tradition and further afield. Both Wolterstorff and Plantinga have played leading roles in the continuing debate. Plantinga's lengthy study of 'warrant', for example, which considers the grounds on which a belief may rightly be accepted as knowledge or truth, has been called 'one of the major accomplishments of twentieth-century epistemology'.[23]

Faith and Rationality is written from the standpoint of what Wolterstorff calls 'the Continental Reformed (Calvinist) tradition' or 'Reformed epistemology',[24] that is, the tradition exemplified in Dooyeweerd and Van Til, and traceable in many of its elements back to Calvin. This tradition has a number of insights that the writers see as relevant to our current situation. We shall briefly consider two of them.

First, it rejects the view that 'belief in God is rationally acceptable only if there is evidence for it', a view that Plantinga calls 'the evidentialist objection to belief in God'.[25] Plantinga uses Aquinas as an example of this view, even though it was the Enlightenment, with its emphasis that everything should be subject to the test of reason, that stressed it most strongly, claiming that we should believe in God only if it can be shown that it is reasonable to believe in him; and that we demonstrate that it is reasonable to do so through argument and 'sufficient evidence'. If evidence is insufficient, then we have no grounds for belief in God.[26] Summarizing his discussion of Calvin's opposition to this approach, which he sees as implicit in his rejection of natural theology, Plantinga writes:

> The Christian does not *need* natural theology, either as the source of his confidence or to justify his belief. Furthermore, the Christian *ought* not to believe on the basis of argument: if he does, his faith is likely to be 'unstable and wavering', the 'subject of perpetual doubt'. If my belief in God is based on argument, then if I am to be properly rational, epistemically responsible, I shall have to keep checking the philosophical journals to see whether, say, Antony Flew has finally come up with a good objection to my favorite argument. This could be bothersome and time-consuming; and what do I do if someone does find a flaw in my argument? Stop going to church? From Calvin's point of view believing in the existence of God on the basis of rational argument is like believing in the existence of our spouse on the basis of the analogical argument for other minds – whimsical at best and unlikely to delight the person concerned.[27]

Following its rejection of evidentialism, a second emphasis of the approach of Reformed epistemology is to take belief in God as properly basic, that is, as a belief we start with rather than as one we arrive at as the result of a process of reasoning. Calvin, says Plantinga, claims that 'God has created us in such a way that we have a strong tendency or inclination toward belief in him'; granted, this tendency has been overlaid or suppressed by sin, but it is still 'universally present'.[28] Once we are freed from the evidentialist demand that belief in God must be rationally justified before we can start to hold it, we are at liberty to say that the presupposition of the existence of God can be the basis of our noetic structure or approach to understanding the world.

Plantinga makes it clear that in claiming that belief in God is 'properly basic', he is not claiming that it is groundless.[29] He uses the parallel of perceiving a tree; we believe the tree exists not on the basis of other beliefs, but directly; it is a basic belief. But it is not a groundless belief; we are able to produce grounds for holding it – we are walking in a wood, we see a tree-like shape, we hear the sound of the wind in its branches, feel the texture of its bark, and so on. The same is true of belief in God; Plantinga cites our experiences of God and the existence of the world around us as such grounds. He also accepts that belief in God – like any basic belief – can be accepted as basic without its entailing the kind of dogmatism that refuses to countenance any contrary evidence or arguments.[30] Just as a person may take the belief 'This is a tree' as properly basic, and subsequently discover that he is suffering from a brain disorder which makes him think he is seeing trees when he is not, so someone who takes the existence of God as properly basic will be open to allowing counter-evidence or arguments to show him or her that that belief was in fact mistaken.

The debate over Reformed epistemology continues,[31] often at a technical level in the philosophical journals. Modifications and refinements of the Reformed position will no doubt arise out of the discussions, but there are no signs as yet that the approach has been shown to be untenable.

In the Reformed tradition, then, we have a presuppositionalism that stands midway between rationalism and fideism. The truth of its beliefs does not depend on reason or evidences; it is something that is assumed, adopted by faith. But it is most certainly not an anti-rational or irrational faith. It is one for which we have adequate grounds, which provides sufficient warrant for our holding those beliefs, even if it does not provide the kind of proof that enables us to have logical certainty: it is always possible that we may one day decide that our believing of the presupposition is not warranted, after all.

Perhaps it is significant that Wolterstorff refers to this tradition as 'Continental', and that its recent roots lie in Holland. It may be even more significant that its central concern (one that has tended to be pushed out by the philosophical debate that has followed) is to be holistic, to develop a Christian worldview that covers not just the philosophical but the personal, the moral, the political, the cultural, and so on. Dooyerweerd started with the heart, not the mind, and, in so doing sounded a note that was key to evangelicalism, and that some had come near to losing.

12. The quiet revolution

One of the most significant movements over the last two or three decades in philosophy, and subsequently in theology, has been the development of hermeneutics. Though the subject matter of hermeneutics (a term derived from a Greek word meaning 'interpretation') was originally the interpretation of texts, and especially biblical texts, philosophical hermeneutics has broadened the area of interest to the interpretation of all data. One of the key figures here was Hans–Georg Gadamer, a German philosopher, who explored the extent to which the individual's understanding and interpretation of data are influenced or controlled by such factors as his or her history, language, presuppositions, and the like. He concluded that such factors, which he called the knower's 'horizon', have a profound effect in shaping what comes to be knowledge. Indeed, such a horizon is essential to knowledge; the individual cannot begin to know any truth until he or she has a horizon and fits the data into place within that horizon. But, said Gadamer, equally, the object or text we are trying to grasp has a horizon of its own; the individual seeking to interpret the data does not have total control. The data work on the individual as well as the individual on the data. There is a dialogue, an interaction. It is out of this dialogue that truth comes; and it comes when the two horizons are fused together. Truth here, then, is not something purely objective, static, fixed, rational or propositional. It is something much more open; something the individual is involved in creating; the outcome of a process; the merging together of any number of differing factors; an event.

Theologians and biblical scholars soon realized that the principles and insights gained as a result of broadening the scope of hermeneutical enquiry had much to say when applied back to our interpretation of biblical texts and the doctrinal formulations of the Christian faith. In a very short time theological hermeneutics took on a whole new dynamic and dimension, and many evangelicals, whose interest in the biblical texts and doctrines is second to none, have shared wholeheartedly in the search for a satisfactory contemporary hermeneutic. Inevitably, this has had repercussions on their understanding of the nature of truth.

The traditional evangelical approach to hermeneutics has been based on Luther's doctrine of the perspicuity of Scripture. This was not a claim that the meaning of every part of the Bible is immediately obvious to all who read it; Luther and the Reformers would not have spent so much time expounding and commenting on the Scriptures if they had really believed this. But it was an epistemological claim that, after due study and understanding, we can clearly know the truth of the Bible's teaching, which thus gives us a firm basis on which we can confidently act. The task of the scholar, then, is to seek to understand precisely what each part of Scripture is saying, interpreting Scripture by Scripture, and extracting the truths God has put there for us to find. This presupposes a basic givenness: there is objective, God-given truth in the Scriptures that the Christian scholar, or the Christian ploughboy guided by the scholar, can dig out, and which would continue to be there even if no-one ever came with pick and shovel.

But alongside this belief in objective given truth in the Scriptures was the Reformers' doctrine that the work of the Holy Spirit is needed to enable us to know that truth. It is not only the unregenerate person who is unable to receive God's truth; even the Christian cannot receive it without the illuminating work of the Holy Spirit. 'Whatever is not illuminated by his Spirit is wholly darkness.'[1] As we have seen, this emphasis was sometimes lost, especially as the growing confidence in human reason infiltrated the church. But its loss was an aberration, not the norm, and those who are open to the accusation of ignoring it would generally have wanted to insist that they believed in it. Thus, for example, Charles Hodge, who has often been branded a rationalist,[2] very explicitly stated that the 'influence of the Spirit is required to prepare the minds of men for the reception of the truth'.[3]

The truth, then, is there in the Scriptures to be quarried, and we have pick and shovel for the task. But the rock-face turns out to be too hard for our puny tools. Some dynamite is needed – the *dynamis* of the Holy Spirit – to loosen the rock and make it quarryable.

But the quiet hermeneutical revolution of the past few years requires us to take the metaphor one stage further. Traditional evangelicals, even when they have paid due attention to the necessity of the work of the Holy Spirit, have tended to assume that once the rock-face has been blasted, the rocks that have been loosened by the explosion simply have to be picked up and used. The Holy Spirit illumines the Scripture, and we can then take it and apply it. But in recent years, evangelicals have increasingly recognized that this is too simplistic. Picking up the rocks and using them turns out to be a far from simple task. Many complex questions arise. Why do we choose this rock rather than that one? When we have chosen it, we get to work shaping it; why do we shape it as we do? Then we use it; but how and why do we select the particular task for which we choose to use it? Why do we use this rock for that task in the way we do?

Thus many evangelicals have come to recognize that hermeneutics is more than a straightforward matter of the Holy Spirit illuminating God-given truth. We ourselves have a significant hermeneutical role to play. The truth God has given us in the Scriptures is necessarily shaped and moulded by us as interpreters. Just what this entails, and the extent to which we do it, continue to be a matter of debate. But there is one issue on which evangelicals would want to remain firm. However much, or little, we are able to shape the truth by our hermeneutic, there still remains an irreducible God-given core. However much we may select and shape the individual rocks, what we are quarrying is still _rock_. Whatever influence we, our culture or our situation may have over it, that is something we cannot change; we can never make it into cheese.

Again, our interest here is in only a limited (though central) element of the hermeneutical revolution: its epistemological implications. To what extent have evangelicals had to change their concept of the nature of truth in order to take on board their new understanding of the hermeneutical process? What implications does the admission that we at least partly shape the truth have for the traditional concept of fixed, unchanging, God-given truth?

We shall start our survey in the United States with Bernard Ramm. We shall then briefly examine the more conservative response of those involved in the Chicago International Council on Biblical Inerrancy. Then we shall move to Britain and consider the approach of an evangelical who is recognized as a leader in the whole field of hermeneutics, Anthony Thiselton. We shall end the chapter by looking at two other British evangelical scholars, Peter Cotterell and Max Turner.

Bernard Ramm

Bernard Ramm (1916–92) came from a fundamentalist background, but, through his books and teaching at a number of (mostly Baptist) American evangelical colleges, he soon established himself as one of the United States's leading post-fundamentalist thinkers. His postgraduate study was largely in philosophy, and he was interested in hermeneutics from the start of his career. He produced *Protestant Biblical Interpretation* in 1950; it soon became a standard textbook and ran to three editions, the third being produced in 1970. In it he wrote:

> The whole system of Conservative Protestant Christianity rests unreservedly on special revelation and the divine inspiration of Scripture. In that the message of God has meaning only when interpreted, it is ever incumbent upon the church to reflect and inquire if she has rightly interpreted the Word of God. A system of hermeneutics is crucial to our theology.[4]

For Ramm 'the most acute theological problem today is to assess to what extent or degree culture determines the character of Scripture'.[5] Any revelation from God must come in and through a cultural form, and cannot be isolated from it; a revelation in a vacuum would be meaningless.[6] And yet, said Ramm, traditional American evangelicalism, and especially fundamentalism, has failed to take the cultural element in the Bible seriously. Their approach for him was typified in Charles Hodge. Hodge held that the human authors of the Bible were children of their times and were ignorant of modern astronomy, physics, biology, and so on; but when they did speak of factual or scientific matters they were supernaturally protected from error, and so made true statements in these matters. Ramm was happy to accept the first part of this view, but saw the second as untenable on the grounds that culture and worldview cannot be separated from a text. Every statement, whether in Scripture or out of it, is to a greater or lesser degree conditioned by the culture and background of the person making it.[7]

> World views, world pictures, views of causation, and the interconnection of things are deeply embedded in the text of Scripture, which makes Hodge's theory very difficult to execute. Every single text that seems to affirm some element of an ancient world view or world picture (*Weltbild*) cannot be allowed to stand, for it would admit error in the text. All evangelicals who follow Hodge's solution have a solution that the modern sciences of cultural anthropology and linguistics would say is impossible.[8]

This, says Ramm, if true, has profound implications for the traditional evangelical view of Scripture and for the evangelical hermeneutic. Evangelicals have to accept that all the statements of the Bible are culturally conditioned, and that the culture in question was in error about all sorts of matters of fact.

Thus, there is no escaping the conclusion that the Bible contains culturally conditioned errors of astronomy, physics, biology, and the like – a conclusion fatal for traditional fundamentalism, which had taken its stand firmly on the principle that a book inspired by a perfect God must be flawless. Establish one proven error, and its claim to be God's book falls, and the whole of the Christian message falls with it.

For Ramm, therefore, the basic need for American evangelicalism was a new paradigm.[9] The old paradigm is inadequate both in itself, and in its confrontation with contemporary culture and understanding and with the developments in biblical research and theology. It has failed to keep pace with and engage with modern thought, and thus has become irrelevant to many thinking moderns. Ramm saw fundamentalism as functioning with a basically pre-Enlightenment paradigm.[10] He maintained that a new paradigm is needed which remains thoroughly evangelical, but is also thoroughly modern. In his search he turned to Europe. *After Fundamentalism* put forward the thesis that Karl Barth may be the one who can best set us on the way to a new paradigm.[11] Ramm saw Barth's theology as fully 'evangelical', though he made it clear there were elements in it he was personally unwilling to accept. But the new paradigm did not necessarily have to come from Barth; it just so happened that Ramm studied under Barth and was profoundly influenced by him; so Barth was his starting-point. But he also acknowledged a debt to P. T. Forsyth and Abraham Kuyper,[12] and specifically suggested that Thielicke was one who could provide an alternative paradigm to Barth's.[13] Here, then, are four strands of European evangelicalism from four different European countries, any one of which, according to Ramm, could hold the key that will release traditional American evangelicalism from its cage.

The criterion for the new paradigm is that it should take both the humanity and the divinity of the Scriptures seriously. Developments in scholarship and research demand that we revise our traditional concept of the extent to which the Bible's humanness has influenced its content. Ramm's analysis of the primary problem was: 'There is no genuine, valid working hypothesis for most evangelicals to interact with the humanity of Scripture in general and biblical criticism in particular.'[14] But the days for retreating into obscurantism are over; evangelicalism must face the issues and find a way of taking them on board without throwing out its foundational insights, and, in particular, without destroying its belief in the 'divinity' or divine origin of the Scriptures.

The great attraction of Barth for Ramm was that his approach to Scripture was able to take full account of the historical-critical developments that the fundamentalists were so sure would destroy both the Bible and the whole of Christianity, and emerge not just with Christianity intact, but with a concept of revelation that in many ways was more powerful and alive than that of the fundamentalists. Where the fundamentalists have reduced the Word of God

'literally to a book that one can carry around in one's pocket',[15] Barth retained
the 'spiritual dimension' of the Word of God, without, in Ramm's view, in
any way detracting from 'the divinity' of the Scriptures,[16] or the central
teachings of orthodox Christianity.[17] Ramm rejected the persistent criticism
that Barth's theology is existential and subjective, with no necessary
foundation in objective revelation; it was an issue he raised personally with
Barth on more than one occasion, and the answers he was given were such
that he was able to conclude that 'it is clear that Barth believes in both an
objective doctrine of the divine inspiration of Scripture and a propositional
element in revelation'.[18]

Whether or not he was right in seeking to persuade his fellow evangelicals
that this was indeed Barth's position, it is clear that Ramm believed that the
new evangelical paradigm should retain these two elements and combine them
with a dynamic Christocentric emphasis such as that in Barth's doctrine of
revelation. This would allow us, he felt, to approach Scripture with an
awareness of its humanness, its cultural conditioning, and the like, but also, by
using the tools of contemporary scholarship, to get behind the human writings
to the core revelation that God has given us there, a revelation which is one
with God's contemporary revelation of himself to us in Christ through the
work of the Holy Spirit.

This entails the rejection of a purely verbalist concept of inspiration and
revelation. The truth is not the words in the book, but the Word which the
Spirit communicates to us and to which the God-given words bear witness.
This, with its implication that the written words of Scripture may in some
sense be false, was hard for many of Ramm's fellow evangelicals to swallow.

The Chicago Statement on Biblical Hermeneutics

In 1982 a number of leading conservatives who were in agreement with the
1978 Chicago Statement on Biblical Inerrancy produced a further manifesto:
The Chicago Statement on Biblical Hermeneutics.[19] Starting with the foundational
presuppositions that God is the author of the Scriptures (article 1), and that he
can express and has expressed his truth inerrantly in them, just as he expressed
himself sinlessly in Jesus Christ (article 2), the statement accepted that
'technical study of Scripture by biblical scholars' was acceptable provided that
such study starts with 'preunderstandings' which are 'in harmony with
scriptural teaching and subject to correction by it' (articles 24 and 19). It was
confident, however, that such study will never establish the errancy of any part
of Scripture. 'Since God is the author of all truth, all truths, biblical and

extrabiblical, are consistent and cohere.' 'The Bible speaks truth when it touches on matters pertaining to nature, history, or anything else' (article 20). No genuine scientific fact is 'inconsistent with the true meaning of any passage of Scripture' (article 21). On the nature of truth it asserted:

> We affirm that the Bible expresses God's truth in propositional statements, and we declare that biblical truth is both objective and absolute. We further affirm that a statement is true if it represents matters as they actually are, but is an error if it misrepresents the facts (article 6).

The original Chicago statement had implied that scholarship has a vital part to play in, say, deciding which biblical statements are to be treated as poetry, hyperbole, metaphor, and the like, and in locating biblical literary conventions that differ from ours, such as imprecise quotation and non-chronological narration. The later statement makes it clear that this is acceptable only if the research is that of scholars who accept the presupposition of inerrancy. This provides a strong base for their hermeneutic, but is open to the criticism that it appears unwilling to listen to contemporary scholarship when that scholarship appears to challenge its basic presupposition.

This brings us face to face with one of the foundational epistemological issues confronting evangelicals: can anything be allowed to challenge their basic belief that God has revealed his truth to us in the Bible? The Chicago statement seems to answer 'No'. Such an answer, however, seems out of step with the general evangelical tradition, including that of the Princetonians. This tradition has been so secure in its conviction that its presuppositions are correct that it has been perfectly willing to open them up to the fullest examination. We saw Wesley doing this, and Hodge, and Thielicke, respectively allowing theology, reason, and historical-critical enquiry to put evangelical beliefs under the spotlight.

Anthony Thiselton

Whatever resistance there has been in the United States to allowing evangelical presuppositions to be challenged by the new developments in hermeneutics, the evangelicals of the United Kingdom appear for the most part to have accepted their implications without much difficulty. Perhaps this process was helped by the fact that Anthony Thiselton, a leading figure in the development of hermeneutics in Britain, is an evangelical. His two books, *The Two Horizons* and *New Horizons in Hermeneutics*, are widely accepted as magisterial.

In the middle decades of this century the focus of philosophical interest tended to move from questions of truth to questions of meaning. Many philosophers had reached the conclusion that truth as traditionally understood was unattainable. So they had to face the question: if we are not communicating truth when we use words and propositions, what are we doing? A number of theories were developed that explained language in functional or emotive terms; all of them tended to minimize or ignore the objective content of statements, and focus attention on their subjective element.

Thiselton shares with these thinkers an interest in meaning rather than simply in truth. But he starts from a belief in the objective nature of truth, and, specifically, in the possibility of our hearing God speaking to us in the Scriptures. The Bible, he holds, is more than a mere record of ancient religious beliefs and aspirations, or a 'trigger designed to spark off premature "applications" of men's own devising'.[20] Rather, 'God speaks through the Bible today'.[21] Our concern, then, is to hear what God is saying. Traditionally, in order to do this, we simply need to understand what the text was saying, using linguistic and historical study to unlock its message.

> Traditionally hermeneutics entailed the formulation of rules for the understanding of an ancient text, especially in linguistic and historical terms. The interpreter was urged to begin with the language of the text, including its grammar, vocabulary, and style. He examined its linguistic, literary, and historical context.[22]

But contemporary hermeneutical theory, which Thiselton follows, stresses that recognition of the historical conditioning of the biblical texts is not enough; we need to recognize that we, the interpreters, also stand in a given historical context and tradition.[23] There are 'two sets of variables',[24] and both have to be taken into account. We have to understand the text within its 'horizon', and we also have to be aware of our own 'horizon' and of how this affects our reading of the text and hearing what God is saying to us in it.

Does this mean that it is impossible to reach purely objective truth? In a sense, says Thiselton, yes. We never can free ourselves totally from the influences of our horizon, and make full allowance for the Bible writers' horizons, so as to be sure that we have reached the naked truth behind the Bible accounts. But, in fact, failure to do this is no problem; truth divested of all context, of every trace of a horizon, would be a poor, thin thing – so thin as to be non-existent. Even the truth of God has to be clothed in some context to be significant. Our aim is not to isolate truth completely from its cultural context, whether in the form of the historical horizon or our contemporary one. Rather, it is to be able to look at it in those contexts, and to make due allowance for them, and so come as near as possible to the basic core truth.

The more carefully and thoroughly we do our research and investigations, the more confident we can be that we are getting close to hearing what God is saying. In particular, the horizon of the ancient text is to be fully explored so that it may speak authentically. No holds are barred; in addition to traditional linguistic and historical enquiry, Thiselton accepts that 'critical historical enquiry remains indispensable in the interpretation of ancient text'.[25]

Besides saying that an effective hermeneutic is one which takes due account of both horizons, the ancient and the contemporary, Thiselton insists that it must pay due attention to both the subjective and objective elements in each horizon. Here he takes issue with the existentialists, who, he claims, have given us perfectly valid insights into the key role of the observing subject, but have developed these insights in an unacceptably one-sided way. Bultmann, for example, has done a great deal to develop our understanding of some biblical concepts and passages by his application of the existentialist approach to them. But he is quite wrong to limit the use of language to the existential or subjective and to claim, as he does, that the objective content of the biblical text must be removed altogether.[26]

In contrast to the existentialists (and others) who have over-emphasized the role of the subjective, Thiselton seeks to combine the subjective and the objective in his version of what is known as the 'speech-act theory'.[27] This locates meaning not in isolated words but in the broader experience of communication, the speech-act, which will include not just words but the whole context of the utterance (or the writing): why it was spoken, how it was spoken, what effect it has had, the presuppositions that give it its significance, and so on. In particular, says Thiselton, many speech-acts have at least a partial *performative* element to them, as well as a descriptive one.[28] 'The cat is on the mat' may be purely factual or descriptive. But 'Pass the salt', 'Thank you', and 'I name this ship the *QE2*' are more than factual. They are doing things; to reduce them to the merely factual robs them of much of their meaning. It is possible to think of ways in which even 'The cat is on the mat' may have a meaning that is more than descriptive. We may have a house rule, for instance, that cats should not be allowed on mats; so the statement has moral and practical force: 'The cat ought not to be on the mat'; 'Do something to get the cat off the mat.'

So it is, says Thiselton, with many of the statements in the Bible, and, in a sense, with the Bible itself. They are not to be understood merely as descriptive and factual, statements of the way things were or are. Their meaning is something more than the purely descriptive; it is *performative*; it does things. Thiselton quotes a useful illustration[29] to highlight the difference between performative speech-acts and straightforward descriptive statements.

Envisage a person who goes shopping, and is followed by a detective.

The shopper has a list of words written on a slip of paper: 'butter, eggs, bread, bacon . . .' His or her aim is so to transact the task as *to make the world of reality match the words* on the list. The transference of goods *changes the extra-linguistic world in accordance with the words* which embody *instructions, promises, or intentions*. The detective, on the other hand, does the converse. He carefully observes and notes down what takes place, i.e. describes the world as it is. The purpose of his list is to provide a *descriptive report in words which match the reality of the world*.[30]

The two lists will look the same; they will have the same propositional content. But their *force* or *direction* is different. The shopper's list consists of words which perform or do something; they change the world, or those bits of the world that were on the supermarket shelves and are now in the shopper's kitchen. The detective's list is purely descriptive; in his case the world shapes the words.[31]

Thiselton sees both of these emphases or directions in the biblical writings. Some passages, of course, appear to be just descriptive; but others are clearly performative. God's promises are an obvious example. So is a statement like 'I love you, O LORD, my strength' (Ps. 18:1), where the psalmist is not so much giving a factual description of his emotional state as actually performing an act of love.[32]

Thiselton is concerned that we keep both the descriptive and the performative elements in our interpretation of the Scriptures. Interpreting the Bible merely as descriptive, as providing objective factual truth, is inadequate. But a stress on the subjective performative element that rejects the descriptive objective one is equally inadequate. Indeed, the two are inseparable; the self-involving language presupposes the descriptive language with its truth claims;[33] it is in fact logically dependent on it. The self-involving nature of the statement 'Jesus is Lord' ('I am his slave; I obey and trust him') is meaningful only if there is such a thing as an objective Jesus who *in fact* has been raised from the dead and designated as Lord by God.[34]

All this might appear to take us a long way from Luther's concept of the perspicuity of Scripture, and even further from the concept that each word of Scripture is the word – and so the truth – of God. Where now are evangelicals to locate the truth of the Scriptures? In the author's intention? In the author's words? In the author's words interpreted in the context of his horizon? In the words interpreted in the context of the original readers' horizon?[35] In the words interpreted in the context of the present-day readers' horizons? In a combination of two or more of these? And what sort of truth is it when located? Is it objective and final? Is it to a greater or lesser extent determined by the reader? If so, does this mean it is outside of any objective control? Or does the reader have only limited power to shape it? Could it be that objective truth remains intact even after subjective interpretation has done its task? If so, how do we separate this objective truth from its subjective overlay? And can we ever be certain that we have actually done this, and have arrived at the whole truth and nothing but the truth?

Cotterell and Turner

The fact that evangelicals in Britain are actively exploring these and other related issues is, in a sense, more significant than the specific answers they are developing. For it presupposes that at least some British evangelicals have accepted that it is not adequate to claim simply that the locus of truth is the written word or words of the Scriptures. If a given passage of Scripture is open to a number of interpretations, it is valid to ask if all of these interpretations are true, and, if not, how we know whether any specific interpretation is true or false. The weight of the evangelical epistemological tradition makes it virtually impossible to concede that all interpretations are equally valid; so the development of adequate criteria to decide which interpretation gives us the truth and which does not has become a pressing need for British evangelicals.

Thus two leading British evangelical scholars, Peter Cotterell and Max Turner (in their book *Linguistics and Biblical Interpretation*, 1989), starting with the conviction that the Bible is the inspired revelation of God, seek to apply contemporary insights in semantics and linguistics to the task of deciding which interpretation of the Scriptures we should adopt. They do this on the basis of their understanding of inspiration (one in keeping with traditional evangelicalism) as 'complementary authorship': the Scriptures are the work of both human and divine authors; 'God was in some way sovereign over the otherwise ordinary, human, and intentional act of authorship.'[36] Though, they say, we cannot rule out the possibility of a *sensus plenior* (fuller meaning), the belief that, say, Paul is a divinely inspired writer enables us to affirm that 'the main lines of his teaching in 1 Corinthians are also what God intended to be said to the Corinthian situation, and that God speaks to other parallel situations through what is said to Corinth'.[37]

Given this, they conclude, the closer our understanding of the meaning of 1 Corinthians gets to that of Paul when he wrote it and the Corinthians when they received it, the closer we shall get to the truth of God that he is revealing to us in the letter. Therefore all means – grammatical, historical, literary, linguistic, and so on – are to be used to get as near as possible to the original meaning. Cotterell and Turner advocate two distinct steps in the hermeneutical process:

1. The determination of what we will call the Discourse Meaning of the

text, that meaning which can be arrived at by competent judges with sufficiently extensive knowledge of the *linguistic context*, the *discourse cotext* (the contribution of all the other parts of the text to that part under immediate consideration) and the *situational context* shared by the writer and his intended readers. This is what we mean by *exegesis*. Exegesis is the bringing to expression of an interpreter's understanding of an author's intended meaning (or, more precisely, though they are very closely related, of the discourse meaning) of the text.

2. The interpreting of the text. That is the bringing to expression of the interpreter's understanding of the significance for his own world of the discourse meaning of the text.[38]

Will we know with compelling certainty when we have truly determined the discourse meaning of a specific part of the Scriptures, or found the correct interpretation for our own situation? Probably not, say Cotterell and Turner. It is often hard enough to be certain of the meaning of something written by a colleague whom we know; how much harder, then, to be sure we have got the right understanding when separated by a gulf of time, language, culture and presuppositions.[39] But the inability to achieve certainty should not mean that we abandon the attempt, or allow equal validity to all interpretations, but rather that we work all the harder at getting as near to the truth as possible. But we should do this with 'appropriate caution':

We need fully to recognize that *our* reading of the letter to Philemon (or whatever), however certain we may feel it is what Paul meant, *is actually only a hypothesis* – our *hypothesis* – *about the discourse meaning*. It is the result of seeing certain aspects of the text and of providing what *we understand* to be the meaning that provides coherence to the evidence . . . We all need, perhaps daily, to take to heart the message expressed so admirably by Oliver Cromwell in a letter to the General Assembly of the Church of Scotland (3rd August 1650), 'I beseech you, in the bowels of Christ, think it possible you may be mistaken!'[40]

Cotterell and Turner do not address the issue of the illumination of the Holy Spirit, and would appear to hold that the task of exegesis, if not that of interpretation, can be done as well by the unregenerate scholar as by the regenerate. Thiselton has little time for those who suggest that the work of the Holy Spirit can provide a short-cut to our knowledge of the truth and thus make the task of hermeneutics unnecessary.[41] There is no 'esoteric gnostic route to knowledge'; the Holy Spirit works '*through* human understanding' and does not 'short-circuit the problem of hermeneutics'.[42]

If, then, there is no esoteric route to knowledge through the illumination of the Holy Spirit or the like,[43] and our investigations into the biblical texts can only ever give us provisional conclusions, do we have to abandon claims to truth in theology? The answer appears to be yes, if by 'truth' we mean something that is established by meticulous scholarship and invincible argument beyond all possible doubt. But perhaps that is not what we mean by truth.

13. The contemporary scene

We are coming to the end of our survey of the history of evangelicals and truth. Inevitably it has been incomplete, but I hope that it has been sufficient to highlight the significant issues of the nature of truth, the basis of truth, the role of reason, the place of revelation, the role of the Holy Spirit, the 'head' and the 'heart', and interpretation. The third section of this book will draw these elements together as we explore to what extent the insights which evangelicals have developed over the past 250 years can serve us as we face the implications of the collapse of the traditional western concept of truth. Before we do that, we shall take one further look at evangelicalism as it actually is, and pick out three significant features of the contemporary evangelical scene.

The three features I have selected are my own personal choice, and I am aware that other observers would choose differently. There has recently been a spate of books by American evangelicals, for example, pointing out the prevailing anti-intellectualism among evangelicals.[1] But these books are set very much in the North American scene, sometimes ignoring completely the existence of evangelicals elsewhere in the world. But, despite the statistic that evangelicals are the largest single group of religious Americans, the fact is that the large majority of evangelicals live outside of North America, and especially in the non-western world. The proportion of non-western evangelicals is growing steadily and is anticipated to be 77% in the year 2000.[2] Though much of the growth is among the poor and uneducated, it is unfair to assume that they all share the anti-intellectualism that appears to be the heritage of American fundamentalism.

The pentecostal and charismatic movement

For me, the most significant feature of evangelicalism at present is the growth of the pentecostal and charismatic movement. David Barrett's figure for pentecostals/charismatics for the year 2000 is 619 million,[3] one tenth of the world's population. Many of these will not be in traditional evangelical groupings, but it is fair to say that where the movement has spread (say, in indigenous pentecostal groups or among Roman Catholics), it has almost always developed features that are similar to those of evangelicalism. Additionally, the movement has in many cases had significant influence on evangelicals who would not see themselves as part of it.

Two key elements of the movement are supernaturalism and the role of experience. They are closely linked. The Age of Reason had tended to make Christianity a matter of the head, of right beliefs and right doctrines. Especially among Protestants, worship became predominantly verbal; the saying, hearing or singing of propositional truths. Faith tended to be acceptance of doctrines. Contact with God was made in prayer or through the preaching of the Word, again a largely verbal and cerebral activity. All of this tended to minimize the scope for God's activity; liturgy, structures, and the influence of the naturalistic mindset of the age put the focus of religion very much more on what *we* do than on what God does.

In reaction to this, some started to look for a more dynamic form of Christianity, more in keeping with the accounts in the gospels and the Acts of the Apostles, and with times of spiritual renewal like the eighteenth-century Evangelical Awakening and the Welsh Revival of 1904–5. The key, they felt, was the supernatural work of the Holy Spirit and a willingness to let God work in his way in the church. They set themselves to pray for the supernatural power of God in the outpouring or infilling of the Spirit; and in many cases their prayer was answered. The result was a swing from a largely cerebral form of Christianity to a largely experiential one. Foundational was a dynamic inner experience of encounter with God – his presence, power, love or holiness, experienced sometimes individually and sometimes corporately. Following on from this were external manifestations, which were seen as the result of the encounter: prostration, gifts of the Holy Spirit (especially speaking in tongues), expressions of emotion like crying or laughing, and bodily healings. A pattern of worship and of living developed which moved away from the cerebral towards something more holistic: participatory congregational worship, excitement, joy, expressions of worship through hand-clapping, arm movements, dancing, and a concern for each other and for the practical implications of the faith.[4]

Here then is a rapidly growing form of Christianity which adheres to the central tenets of evangelicalism but which has renewed the stress on the primacy of God and made our response to him a matter of the whole person, including the body and the emotions, and not just the mind. If we were to return to our four questions outlined in chapter 2, we could say that they would give a positive answer to the *certainty question*, thanks to the supernatural work of God. In common with evangelicalism as a whole, they have retained religious truth as firmly *objective* and rooted in God, but they have diverged from those forms of evangelicalism which have tended to give a central role to reason in answer to the *relational question* and the *ultimate justification question*. We relate to God's truth, they would say, with the whole person, not just with the mind; and ultimate justification is most definitely something God does, not the achievement of a process of human reasoning.

The most rapid growth of pentecostalism has been in non-western countries which have not been subjected to the process of the Enlightenment. In a sense it can be seen as a pre-Enlightenment movement. Though there are some signs of an 'intellectualizing' of the pentecostal experience,[5] it may be that it will be spared being subjected to the whole force of western modern rationalism.[6]

The charismatic movement was a second wave of the pentecostal movement which has had considerable influence on churches of the main Christian traditions. Though a lot of new charismatic groupings have sprung up, many charismatics have remained in their traditional denominations, resulting in a very wide dissemination of the movement's ideas. Even in churches which could not be called charismatic, the movement has focused attention on the supernatural and on the response of the whole person to our encounter with God. Though the beginnings of the charismatic movement pre-date the general acceptance of the postmodern approach, there can be little doubt that postmodernism has helped to provide a climate in which charismatic phenomena are more readily accepted.

Openness

The second significant feature of contemporary evangelicalism is its increasingly open texture. Though there are exceptions, the phase of obscurantism and refusal to face up to the implications of modern scholarship and contemporary culture is passing. Perhaps because of its growth, the movement is less defensive and less afraid to subject its beliefs to academic scrutiny. Two key institutions, London Bible College in Britain, and Fuller Theological

Seminary in the United States, were founded in the 1940s for just this purpose;[7] these two colleges alone have produced hundreds of evangelical scholars, many of them of the first rank. Even the current attacks on anti-intellectualism among American evangelicals can be seen as part of this process. They are in fact a call to evangelicals to come out of the ghetto and engage the whole of their being, including their mind, with the contemporary world; and the call is not being made from outside the movement, but from within, by today's leading evangelicals.[8] The flock may be dragging its feet, but the shepherds are leading it in a very positive direction.

We have seen this process in operation in the areas of philosophy and hermeneutics, and it is very noticeable in the field of biblical studies.[9] An illustration of it can be seen in the specific area of epistemology. In 1982 IVP, perhaps the publishing house that is most clearly committed to evangelical principles, published David Wolfe's *Epistemology: The Justification of Belief*. The book faces squarely the arguments for epistemological scepticism and relativism, and accepts that it has no conclusive answer to them; we cannot ultimately justify our Christian web of beliefs in the traditional sense of showing that they are true. Wolfe then goes on to suggest a revised criterion of justification or warrant:

> One is warranted, insofar as any warrant is possible, in believing that an interpretive scheme is true provided that it withstands the criticism to which it continually remains open . . . Only to the extent that a scheme remains open to continued testing is it able to display its credentials. Only then can it show the strength of its internal structure and its ability to illuminate experience. Far from being a favor, to protect one's interpretive scheme from criticism is to rob it of the only way it can display its claims to truth. I mention this because it is sometimes considered a virtue to insulate one's scheme from criticism. Some Christians, some Communists and some Freudians, among others, share this view. The criticisms of opponents are effectively neutralized by appeals to sinful unbelief, class membership or subconscious resistance, all of which make it unnecessary to take the arguments of the critics seriously. This may neutralize the opposition, but it also trivializes the truth claims of the protected position. Criticisms must be faced squarely.[10]

Wolfe's criterion rests on the awareness that a set of beliefs can be conclusively falsified, but never conclusively verified. So a set of beliefs that has never been tested is less likely to be true than one that has survived a long series of attempted falsification; or, perhaps more accurately, we are more justified in believing that a well-tested set of beliefs is true than in believing that an untested set is true.

There are two significant issues here. One is the admission that logical or rational certainty in the holding of beliefs is not possible. We always have to live with the possibility that we may be wrong. This does not imply that we think that we *are* wrong; but any belief, however strongly held, 'is compatible with admitting that falsifying conditions are imaginable . . . It is logically possible that my belief is in error'.[11] Here is a note of openness to the possibility of error that we heard sounding clearly from Wesley, but which has been somewhat obscured in certain parts of subsequent evangelicalism.

The second significant issue is the call to evangelicals to encourage criticism of their set of beliefs. If evangelicals are right, they have nothing to fear from criticisms of their beliefs and principles; if they are wrong, the sooner they are shown this, the better. This is not to say that evangelicalism should be open to the kind of piecemeal criticism that, for example, attacks its concept of prayer from, say, naturalistic or deistic premises. On naturalistic premises, supernatural answers to prayer are of course impossible. So the debate over prayer has to move to a different level; that of the debate between supernaturalistic and naturalistic presuppositions. Openness to criticism effectively means the continuing testing of the whole system, and that is a big task.

Holism

My third feature of contemporary evangelicalism is the movement towards a holistic approach, something we have already come across several times in this chapter. It is expressed in two main ways: the recognition of the wholeness of human personhood, and the desire to engage the beliefs and principles of evangelicalism with the whole of life. In our survey above we noticed the broadening of the expectation that encounter with God would be not just cerebral, but something that affects the whole person, the feelings, the emotions, and the body. Evangelicalism has not found it easy to keep a satisfactory balance between the heart and the head, or between the spiritual and the psychological and their physical expressions; the movement has been vigorously attacked for both 'enthusiasm' and rationalism. But it has, for the most part, continued to believe that each aspect of human personhood is created by God and significant both in our relationship to him and in our life in the world. It may well be that the current postmodern swing away from concentration on the rational has helped evangelicalism to return to a more holistic concept of the person; but it is a concept that has never been completely lost.

Similarly, evangelicals have at times wavered over their commitment to a holistic approach to the relationship between faith and life in the world. There are plenty of examples of pietistic withdrawal and ghetto defensiveness, especially in the earlier part of this century. Yet we have also, for example, traced in the Dutch Reformed tradition a strong desire to embrace and relate to the whole of life and of the world, and we have seen this call reflected in recent American publications. It is expressed in the growth of concern for social, cultural and political issues. In the United Kingdom we can note the founding of organizations such as the relief organization TEAR Fund (1968),[12] the Christian arts festival Greenbelt (1974), the magazine *Third Way* (1977),[13] and CARE (Christian Action Research and Education, 1983). These are just a few among a mass of new structures and organizations that have arisen in the last thirty years, expressing British evangelicals' determinism to relate their faith to the whole of life.[14]

This current holistic emphasis is not new to evangelicalism. It was at its heart from its inception until about the 1920s, when, for a number of reasons, it was submerged.[15] It was seen, for instance, in Wesley's deep concern for social justice.[16] It was especially apparent in the widespread social concern and action of the Victorian era. Derek Tidball writes:

> In 1884, the Earl of Shaftesbury told his biographer, 'I am essentially and from deep-rooted conviction an Evangelical of the Evangelicals. I have worked with them constantly, and I am satisfied that most great philanthropic movements of the century have sprung from them.' It is a judgment from which no serious historian would dissent. Evangelical faith became the mainspring of what we now, misleadingly, call 'humanitarian action' . . . Kathleen Heasman estimates that 'three-quarters of the total number of voluntary charitable organisations (in Britain) in the second half of the century can be regarded as evangelical in character and control'. Ian Bradley gives an insight into what this would mean in saying that, since the Clapham Society started the 'Bettering Society' in 1798, six new charitable societies were started each year. By mid-century there were 500 of them, and they continued to grow! It is the extent of the evangelical philanthropic empire which is truly staggering. In addition to the work of the churches and of missions, like the Salvation Army, evangelicals involved themselves in relief, reform and improvement work in every area where social evil was to be found.[17]

The relatively brief period, then, when much of evangelicalism was marked by an exclusive stress on the spiritual, and by a withdrawal from engagement with a full range of social and cultural issues, can be seen as an aberration rather than as typical. Personal conversion and experience of God may be foundational to evangelicalism; but on that foundation are built a total lifestyle and a developing, distinctive response to each aspect of the society and world around us. Current evangelicals are increasingly willing to recognize this.

Evangelicals and truth today

We can pick out six elements from this survey of three significant aspects of contemporary evangelicalism that have bearing on the issue of truth. The first two arise from the renewed emphasis on the supernatural. Fundamentalism has been criticized as being essentially Bible-centred at the expense of everything else.[18] Neither evangelicals nor fundamentalists would want to admit that their interest in the Bible is anything other than a means to knowing God; but the renewed stress on God, his supernatural activity, and our direct experience of him, has helped to make it clear that God himself is the focus of our faith, worship and life, and that the locus of truth is primarily in him, and only derivatively in the Bible.

Allied to this is the development of a broader understanding of revelation and communication from God. A specific interest of the pentecostal/ charismatic tradition has been in the area of God communicating with us, whether verbally through 'tongues', 'prophecy', or various other forms of inspired utterance, or through experiences, feelings, bodily manifestations, pictures, symbolic actions, and other non-verbal forms. A few evangelicals have reacted to this and insisted that the only way that God communicates is through the Scriptures to the human intellect, but the majority today would hold that communication (and so truth) from God can take many forms, of which the cerebral and verbal, though essential, is only one.

A third element, also arising from the pentecostal/charismatic movement, but familiar throughout evangelicalism, is the central role of experience. Knowing truths about God on its own is nothing; personally experiencing and truly knowing God is everything.

The fourth element is closely linked to these last two. It is the awareness of the holistic nature of human personhood. There is considerably more to us than the rational; there is the heart as well as the head, the spiritual, the emotional, the volitional and the practical as well as the cerebral. So we can relate to the truth with more than just our minds.

A fifth element arises from evangelicalism's current openness. Evangelicals are sounding a muted note on certainty; they are willing to be open to the possibility they may be wrong. There is less dogmaticism in their claims, whether in the area of hermeneutics or in the admission that their presuppositions cannot be finally established. This is not necessarily, of course, evidence of loss of confidence in the evangelical position. Indeed, it may be the opposite: evangelicals may be more willing to submit their worldview and its implications to scrutiny simply because they are increasingly confident of its viability or truthfulness. But it acknowledges that arriving at the truth is not as straightforward or as conclusive as some may have suggested.

Finally, the increasing interest of evangelicals in issues beyond the specifically spiritual or doctrinal means that their system has to be a broad one, a true *world*view. Here current evangelicalism stands in strong contrast to the Kantian and Wittgensteinian traditions that allow no engagement between theological truth and, say, scientific truth. For evangelicals, a call to engage with the world necessarily means a call to engage theologically, to integrate their theological understanding and beliefs with everything else.

PART 3

Evangelicals and truth tomorrow

Billy Graham in his autobiography records a conversation with Winston Churchill. 'I am a man without hope,' said the Prime Minister. 'Do you have any real hope?' Quite a cue for Billy Graham!

The enormous growth of evangelicalism can at least partly be explained by its offer of hope, something that gives new beginning and meaning to life in a world that has lost its way. In the third part of this book we shall explore what evangelicalism might have to offer in the face of the collapse of our concept of truth.

14. Interlude

The traditional western concept of truth has collapsed. For nearly two thousand years it offered a structure by which we could understand, know, and live with ourselves and the world around us. It did this by stressing objectivity and locating ultimate truth and justification in God. It collapsed because the locus of truth and the means of justification were moved from God to reason, and reason proved to be inadequate for the task.

Its collapse opened the way for postmodernism and, in particular, for relativism. The structure that enabled us to think, know, and relate to the world around us has been lost. All metanarratives have been abandoned. Truth can no longer be something outside of the individual, something public, discoverable and testable, and able to be discovered, debated and agreed. Rather, truth is subjective, something we each create for ourselves, truth-for-me. Objective truth is impossible.

Faced with this collapse, we have perhaps four options. We can accept it, and accept relativism as its inevitable result. Secondly, we can do what the vast majority of thinking people are doing: we can accept it but continue to live as though it had not happened. Thirdly, we can accept it but try to find a new concept of truth to replace what we have lost. Fourthly, we can refuse to accept its collapse as final; we can rake around in the wreckage and try to find something we can salvage.

In the third part of this book we shall work on the third and fourth of these options. But before we start we ought to take a look at the first two.

The arguments for accepting epistemological relativism are very strong. The traditional one, which we came across in chapter 3, is that we can never know anything other than our own individual 'impressions and ideas', and so can never know anything about the external world. Then there is a group of sceptical arguments which point out that once we admit we may be mistaken in one of our beliefs, we have to accept that any or all of our beliefs may be mistaken. In addition, there is the issue of justification; any claim to be truth needs to be verified or justified; to do this we need some basic principle of verification or justification; but we can always ask 'Is this principle true?' If we answer by providing a justification for that principle, we can still ask 'Is this justification true?' So, says the argument, we are launched on an infinite regress with no hope of finding a fixed point on which the truth of all else can depend.

Nevertheless, despite the strength of its arguments, and the fact that it has been so widely and rapidly accepted in the West, relativism is untenable. There are two arguments against it; the first is powerful though not absolutely conclusive, and the second makes it completely untenable.

The first argument against relativism is that it cannot state its case without being inconsistent with it. The relativist says there is no absolute truth; all so-called truth is relative. But 'There is no absolute truth' and 'All so-called truth is relative' are both statements that, to mean anything at all, have to be taken as true – statements of absolute truth. Relativism cannot be stated without self-contradiction.

Relativisits, however, have a possible way of replying to this argument. They may accept that they cannot consistently state their position; therefore they do not attempt to state it; they simply continue to hold it. Alternatively, they may claim that, in that they reject reason, they are not required to be rational or consistent in holding or stating their position. This response brings us to our second argument against relativism.

Suppose Mandy, a relativist, says, 'The cat is on the mat.' I look at an empty mat and say, 'There is no cat on the mat.' For Mandy that is no problem. It is true for her that the cat is on the mat, and it is true for me that the mat is empty. But, since she has said 'The cat is on the mat', I find it hard to leave it at that. I want to know what she means by 'The cat is on the mat'. Perhaps she is thinking of a mat in the next room. No, she assures me; it is *this* mat. Perhaps she means that the words 'The cat' have been written on the mat, probably with invisible ink. No, she says; it is a real, four-legged, tailed, feline cat. Maybe there is something wrong with my eyes; so I get down on my knees and run my hand over the mat to see if I encounter a furry body. But I don't. And so on. I do all I can to extract some meaning from her statement; but in the end I have to give up. However much 'The cat is on the mat' may be true-for-her, for me it is not just untrue; it is meaningless. When she says 'The cat is on the mat', no meaning is transmitted, no communication takes place. She may as well speak gobbledegook, or, alternatively, say nothing. Relativism destroys meaning and makes communication impossible. In the relativists' world there is no meaning; no person can communicate with any other person. Not only is that unlivable; we all know beyond any doubt that there is such a thing as meaning, and that communication does happen. So relativism must be false.

What, then, about the second option (the one in fact followed by almost all thinking people in the West today), that of accepting postmodernism and relativism, but refusing to accept their implications and carrying on as though nothing has happened? Scientists reject the concept of objective truth, but go on making discoveries and writing books about the atmosphere of Jupiter, and global warming, and the behaviour of cancer cells. Postmodernists attack all structures, using the highly developed structure of language to do so. Powerful arguments are put forward defending the abandonment of reason and argument.

However inconsistent such procedures may seem, they are, of course, inevitable. Apart from total solipsism, even the relativist cannot operate in the world without utilizing the concept of objective truth, since it is foundational to meaning and communication and to the simplest acts of living. Even if I have no wish to communicate it, there seems a certain inflexibility in, say, the proposition 'I can walk through brick walls'. I may be totally convinced that this is true-for-me, but every time I try to put it into practice I get a sore nose. We all have to assume objectivity in order to live. Further, when others try walking through walls they too get sore noses; objective elements in my experience are confirmed by objective elements in others' experiences.

Some may be prepared to accept that this interesting state of affairs is so, and ask no further questions. Those who are truly committed to the postmodern presupposition 'There are no metanarratives' will point out that asking the question why this state of affairs should be so presupposes an answer which entails a metanarrative; so they would naturally be disinclined to ask the question. This is a procedure exactly parallel to that taken by those who refuse to allow the question 'What caused the Big Bang?', since the answer inevitably takes us outside of their purely naturalistic worldview.

Others may accept that there is a need to justify such a procedure, and do so pragmatically: it is justified because it works. This is a major step forward; but we can still ask the questions 'Why does it work?' and 'Why does the fact that it works justify our following it?'

So we find ourselves asking questions. And however strong our commitment to postmodernism and relativism may be, we have to admit that the asking and answering of questions is foundational to human life as we know it. Exploring the world around us, and ourselves, and our relationships to each other, and the meaning of things, and concepts like beauty, truth, value and goodness, did not start with the Enlightenment; these things are an essential part of what it means to be human. To veto the asking of questions is to deny our humanity.

But is not asking questions a return to rationalism, to the mistakes of the Enlightenment and the modern period? Is not postermodernism right in its insistence that reason has simply failed to answer the questions, at least the big ones, and so we are justified in giving up the attempt? My answer is that reason in the modern period has been found wanting, but that is not necessarily because reason in itself is flawed; it may be because of the way the modern period has used it. Here, indeed, is the central mistake of postmodernism: it gives us an extreme either/or: either reason as used by the modern period, or no reason at all; if we reject the first we must go for the second. But this does not follow at all; we are quite at liberty to reject the first and find an alternative to the second.

So we come to the third and fourth of our options: to develop an alternative concept of truth, either something radically new and different, or something salvaged from the collapse of the old one. This we shall attempt to do by examining some of the distinctive insights of evangelicalism, particularly in the light of the current situation, but also taking what we can from the thinking of past ages.

A number of factors in evangelicalism help set the scene for such a programme. First, as we have seen, evangelicals have for the most part rejected the Kantian option of subjectivizing and compartmentalizing truth. Thus they have resisted the shift away from objectivity and the isolation of theology from the everyday world, and the subsequent tendency to reshape religion 'from below', thus losing its traditional distinctives. More broadly, they have resisted the post-Kantian tendency towards a fragmented universe, where truths have become increasingly isolated from each other.

Secondly, evangelicals for the most part have kept central in their thinking the concept that religion is primarily the story of God taking the initiative in the affairs of planet Earth, rather than a record of the human race's search for God. This concept is expressed in their holding firmly to the traditional doctrines of creation, providence, and God's action in the world in revelation, incarnation, salvation, miracle, the Holy Spirit, and the second coming.

Linked in with this is a belief, often tempered but rarely lost totally, that the very acceptance of the existence of a God of this sort opens up our concept of the created order to any number of possibilities. With apologies to Dostoevsky, if there is a God, anything is possible. The evangelical God is big enough, in theory at any rate, not just to do miracles and become incarnate, but to solve philosophical problems and provide a working basis for epistemology.

Fourthly, there are elements in the evangelical theological understanding of

God and his nature that are significant for their epistemology. Chief among these is their stress on a God who communicates, and who is able to do so in ways that are readily accessible to human creatures. Another element is their concept of God's immanence in the world, a concept highlighted by the centrality of the believer's personal relationship with him. Linked with this is God's care and concern for women and men, and his faithfulness and dependability: he would not deceive us, and would not want us to be deceived.

Finally, the evangelical doctrine of the nature of men and women, especially as made in the image of God (however that may be interpreted), has tended to provide a firm bridge between the divine and the human, the infinite and the finite, which is able to take a great deal of weight, epistemological and otherwise.

These factors, then, offer the possibility of developing a distinctive evangelical epistemology. True, the very contemplation of such an exercise in a 'post-Christian' age may seem to some hopelessly irrelevant. But evangelicals might choose to reply that they have as much right to investigate ways out of philosophy's epistemological impasse as any; and, in any case, for a movement that is rapidly gaining ground in many parts of the world among a rich variety of cultures, the European verdict that we are now post-Christian could be seen as parochial and even premature, just as were the verdicts in the 1960s and 1970s that the world was in the grip of an irreversible trend of secularization. Additionally, it is open to evangelicals to point out that the being of God has in fact played a foundational role in just about every epistemological system up to the eighteenth century, and that the rejection of this role for God was less because of the problems that arose from giving epistemology a theological basis, than because, once the Age of Reason had so successfully removed the need for God in most ordinary spheres of life, it seemed only consistent to try and do the same in the sphere of epistemology. If this latter exercise has landed us in so many difficulties, it is at least worth exploring the possibility that the reason for this is that the exercise itself was a mistake.

15. Starting with God 1: six theses

With great confidence the thinkers of the Enlightenment set out to build a system of knowledge and truth based solely on the powers of human reason. They failed; and the collapse of the Enlightenment project has led to the current collapse of confidence in reason. With the collapse of reason has come the realization that we have no basis or justification for our knowledge and belief in truth. For many this has meant the abandonment of the traditional concepts of knowledge and truth; we can know nothing, or next to nothing; and truth, at best, is no more than the individual's personal creation.

Yet such scepticism and relativism are impossible to live with. Further, despite the collapse of the foundation, the whole structure of modern knowledge that was built on the Enlightenment confidence still stands firm. Water still boils at 100°C; we can still observe, communicate, debate and discover things that we cannot but assume are objectively true. So we are forced to the conclusion that, however mistaken the Enlightenment may have been about the basis and justification for truth, their conviction that there is such a thing as truth may still be valid. What is needed is not the scrapping of the concept of truth, but the establishing of an alternative basis for it.

This, it would appear, is the only honest alternative to relativism and solipsism. For some it may be satisfactory to accept the destruction of truth, and the resulting relativism, and to continue, inconsistently, to live as though truth still exists. If we have rejected reason, they would claim, there is no need to be consistent. This might be an easier position to hold if the world around us was similarly inconsistent. But water continues consistently to boil at 100°C; things and people around us and our experience of them continue to be marked by regularities and consistencies. At the very least, it would seem that we ought to explore the possibility that there is some basis and justification for our belief that what we experience and observe in some way or other is the expression not of our subjectivity, but of what really is the case.

A basis for truth

So the search is on for something to replace reason as the basis and justification for truth. As yet, very few candidates have been put forward, and none has won much approval. The suggestion of the third section of this book is that we try returning to the practice of the pre-Enlightenment period, one that served pretty well for nearly two thousand years, and build our epistemology on God. Since there are many concepts of God, we are exploring specifically the concept of God that is held by evangelical Christians, one that emphasizes his ability to reveal and communicate truth with human beings, and to be personally involved with them on a variety of levels. Our interest is in this concept of God forming a basis not just for religious belief but for knowledge as a whole, both religious and non-religious.

In outlining an approach to a God-based epistemology that could be put forward by evangelicals, I am not wishing to suggest that the elements of it are in any way their exclusive property. Many of the points made below will be readily accepted by Christians with different theological insights, or by other theists. Nevertheless, it remains the case that evangelicalism is specially suited to develop an epistemology more or less along these lines.

Equally, I am not trying to argue that all evangelicals have necessarily seen things in the way I am going to outline. It is undeniable, for example, that at times some evangelicals appear to have ignored the fact that the source and primary locus of truth is God, and have concentrated all their attention on the Bible. But however much, in the fires of controversy, the Bible has become the centre of their attention, they would still wish to claim with Wesley and Thielicke that they are interested in the Bible only because it points beyond itself to God, and that their belief in the truth of the Bible is dependent on the prior belief that God is truth. All evangelicals would agree that, however high a view they have of the Bible, its authority and truth are only derivative; God alone is the source of truth.[1]

The accusation that evangelicals have lost sight of God by concentrating on the Bible is doubtless linked with the dichotomy that a number of their critics have tried to put forward: either propositional truth or personal truth; either truth located in the Bible or truth located in God.[2] This is a dichotomy evangelicals have steadfastly resisted. To them there seems no reason why we cannot have both. Truth can be expressed in personal and in propositional form. Personal truth can be expressed propositionally. The truth of propositions needs warrant from outside of those propositions, and, for evangelicals, this comes from God. They would see the dichotomy (either God-centred truth or propositional truth) as arising from a blinkered acceptance of Kantian dogmatism, and feel they have every right to stand by their concept of divine truth (some of which is in propositional form) and to seek to defend it.

Nevertheless, in their own thinking and in their presentation of their position to others, they would be well advised to be clear that the source and foundation of truth is nothing less than God himself. It may be (as we shall be exploring later) that they will wish to stress that personal truth and propositional truth are so closely linked that they are virtually inseparable, and doubtless they will wish to maintain a central role for the Bible in all their thinking. But, in keeping with their true heritage, they must accept that only God can be ultimate, and thus that, in this sense, the propositional truth of the Bible cannot be ultimate. Additionally, they need clearly to reaffirm the conviction of Hodge and the main evangelical tradition that the truth of God, though found in the Bible, is by no means limited to the Bible. All truth is God's truth, and must be seen as such.

There appears to be no philosophical reason why the concept of God should not play a foundational role in an epistemological system. Not only was its incorporation into such systems standard until the eighteenth century, but the Idealists and A. N. Whitehead have continued to make use of the concept into the twentieth.[3] Granted, such a step will make the resulting epistemology difficult to accept for those who deny the existence of God. But atheists are far from a majority in the world, and there are indications that their numbers are falling. So it is arguable that we need not be required to follow the programme of the last two centuries, which has sought to produce philosophies acceptable to them and their presuppositions. Further, if God can be incorporated into an epistemological system in the first place, there seems no reason to deny the possibility of his occupying an all-important position in that system once he is there.

Nor does there seem to have been any valid philosophical reason why God was rejected as the foundation for epistemology in the first place. It was more a matter of his gradually being ousted as reason was given an increasingly central role. Thinkers were confident that reason was sufficient in itself to justify knowledge and truth. So God became redundant. At the same time he was losing his role in physics, astronomy, and science in general: 'I have no need of that hypothesis.'[4] Everything could be fitted into a rational and naturalistic metanarrative or explanatory structure. Now that that structure has collapsed, and reason has been shown as inadequate for the role foisted on it, we would seem fully justified in seeking to develop a God-based epistemology.

Six theses

I shall start by putting forward six theses on the nature of an epistemology for today. Objections can, of course, be raised at a number of points, but, for the sake of the presentation of this chapter's argument, I shall defer considering them until later.

1. *There is such a thing as objective truth:* that is to say, there is some truth that is not totally subjective. We can accept that much of what we call truth may be subjective, and that all the truths we individually hold are affected by us as subject, but we cannot accept that all truth is subjective. Even the relativists claim objective truth when they say that all truth is relative. In order to live in the world, to be human, to communicate, to learn, to discuss, to develop knowledge, we have to assume the existence of at least some objective truth. To do this we do not, of course, have to assume that truth exists objectively in some sort of Platonic world of Ideas; but we do have to assume that truth is not wholly dependent on our thinking it. I do not control it totally; there is something outside of me; there is a given, something which has its roots in a reality which exists independently of my thoughts and ideas.

2. *Truth is broad.* Despite its initial vision of building up a huge body of reliable truth, the Enlightenment in fact progressively reduced the number of things we could accept as true. Since reason was the test of truth, only what could be established by reason could be accepted as truth. But reason could establish very little. The rational arguments for the existence of God, for example, were soon shown to have holes in them; no-one could produce a logically watertight conclusive argument that demonstrated once and for all that God exists. So, it was concluded, we could not claim truth for statements about God. But what applied to the existence of God also applied to the existence of other minds and of the world around us; we are just as unable to produce logically watertight conclusive arguments showing that they exist. We cannot make true statements about God, or about other people, or about trees and tables and chairs. So truth was limited to subjective beliefs within our own minds and to analytic truths like those of mathematics. And since my personal subjective truth is very much mine (and, since I have no way of telling whether you exist, I am not going to try to communicate anything to you), all we really have left is analytic truth. And even that is questionable . . .[5]

Despite this trend to reduce truth to something very narrow indeed, as human beings we do in fact find ourselves operating with a broad concept of truth. Each one of us regularly encounters and copes with many different types of truth: mathematical ('2 + 2 = 4'); logical ('If A then not non-A'); truth about the world around us ('There is a tree in the garden'); historical truth ('There used to be a tree in the garden, but we cut it down last year'); future truth ('This tree won't last for ever'); truth about values ('Every person should be free to exercise his or her human rights'); moral truth ('Destroying the planet through pollution is wrong'); relational truth ('My wife loves me'); religious truth ('The universe was created by God'); and so on.

If our epistemology, then, is going to be adequate for human experience in the real world, it will need to be broad in its interests and application, covering as fully as possible the whole range of the epistemological data. Knowledge takes many forms; there are many types of truth. Knowledge and truth exist not just in theoretical abstraction; they are an integral part of being and living. They are essentially involved in the area of human relationships, social, cultural and personal, and thus specifically in the area of communication. Elements of faith and commitment have a part to play in much if not all of our knowing. And so we could go on. Therefore an epistemology that applies just, say, in the sphere of logic and reason, but has nothing to say about human relationships, or intuition, or moral or aesthetic truth, or commitment, will not be adequate.

3. *An epistemology should do more than simply describe the data; it should supply an adequate explanation.* Besides listing differing types of knowledge and truth, it should seek to explain why we accept these as knowledge and truth, how they fit together, how we justify them, and so on. In other words, it needs to supply a full explanatory framework into which all the epistemological data can be fitted.

Given the wide range of human experience and activity that is covered by our epistemology, we clearly need a wide-ranging explanatory framework to give us adequate explanation. We experience ourselves, our thoughts, other people, other ideas, objects in the world; we make sense of our experiences. We respond in personal encounter; we engage in processes of rational thought. We come to know things; we test our beliefs; we establish truths. We are aware of others and communicate with them. We find that our experiences and thought processes generally cohere with theirs; when there are substantial differences, we find we are able to work on those differences, giving and receiving justification of why one position is to be preferred to another. In general, we find that there is a huge area in which our experiencing and thinking operate in a coherent and consistent and meaningful way, and in which our experiences and thought processes appear to tally closely with those of others. It could, of course, be that the consistency and patterns we discern and use are purely fortuitous: we (or rather I, since, if this is so, I cannot come to any conclusions about anyone else) have found that the system works, but there is no reason why it should have worked, and there is no reason why it should continue to do so. But to adopt such a position seems to require a great deal of credulity, and the willingness to settle for solipsism.

Our continued involvement in these processes presupposes that we accept them as reliable, at any rate for the most part. Though our acceptance may be more or less pragmatic (they work satisfactorily, so we use them and do not ask questions), it would seem very strange if there was no *reason* for them to work so well; and if there is a reason, then part of the human enterprise is to try to find it.

An epistemological framework, then, should supply an explanation that is broad enough to cover as wide a range as possible of epistemological phenomena. Additionally, its interest and application should include the practical as well as the metaphysical. That is to say, its interest should not be just the nature and contents of knowledge and truth, but how they function, how we use them, and so on. So it should cover the explanation of, and grounds for, things like meaning, communication, and praxis.

The project of the Enlightenment (to put forward an explanation that did not give any role to God, but made reason the sole arbiter of truth) succeeded for a time by progressively narrowing the range of epistemology, and thereby narrowing the type of material an explanatory metanarrative had to cover. But it has now ended in failure. As yet, no alternative non-theistic explanatory framework has been put forward that has gained any degree of acceptance. While it is perfectly possible that one may in due course be found, this at the very least opens up the possibility of re-introducing a theistic one. If reason cannot provide an adequate basis and justification for truth, and no other non-theistic basis is to hand, we are justified in exploring a theistic basis.

4. *An epistemological framework must be able to cope with the fact that individual truths are able to cohere into an integrated whole.* We do not retain individual truths in isolated compartments; they are built up into a body of knowledge and truth and merge into an integrated worldview.

This means the rejection of the Kantian or Wittgensteinian divided universe. We simply do not keep various types of truth in isolated compartments. We find it perfectly possible to say, for instance, 'John is grumpy because he's upset at the criminal felling of that beautiful oak tree just to get more light in the kitchen.' All sorts of truth are present in that one sentence: historical truth (someone cut the tree down); present truth ('John is grumpy'); moral truth ('criminal felling'); personal truth ('he's upset'); aesthetic truth ('beautiful'); purposive truth ('to get more light in the kitchen'). However much we may be told that we cannot mix facts and values, moral truth and scientific truth, and so on, we continually do so perfectly successfully. Our epistemology must be able to accept and account for this.

5. *In a post-foundationalist, post-Enlightenment era, we are not required to provide a logically watertight rational demonstration of the validity of an approach to epistemology.* Some would argue that such rational demonstration can never be obtained in any sphere. Others would say that it is possible in such areas as

mathematical theory, but not in the real world as we know it. It is possible, for example, to demonstrate conclusively that the internal angles of a triangle add up to two right angles. But this applies only to the idealized triangles of mathematical theory; we can never show that the angles of an actual triangle in the real world add up to two right angles, since every triangle in the real world is imperfect: its sides are not perfectly straight, and its angles not totally true. Even if they were, the sceptic would have no problem showing that it is impossible to prove rationally that, for example, the triangle we think we are observing actually is there. Total, final, rational demonstration of the mathematical-theory type is not possible in the real world.

Yet we cope very well without it. We accept the general reliability of triangles, and the existence of other people, and the reality of the world around us, even though we are unable to produce final, rational, irrefutable proof of the validity of our beliefs; and we are confident our beliefs are valid.

6. *Though conclusive logical demonstration of the validity of our epistemological framework is not called for, we ought, nevertheless, to seek to provide some justification for it.* But this justification will need to be broader than rational support alone, although it will include rational elements. It will, for example, need to be shown that the approach to epistemology is one we can live with, and one that caters satisfactorily for the whole of human personhood. Even in the more limited rational sphere, the strongest justification will be one which provides warrant in a range of ways, rather than just one.

16. Starting with God 2: his nature and image

Using the concept of God to provide the basis and justification for truth will work only if the concept adopted is broad enough to cover all the elements mentioned so far. Some concepts of God would not be adequate. If, for example, personal knowledge of individuals in relationships, or the experience of communication and the communality of knowledge, is part of the data we are trying to explain, then there must be aspects in the concept of God which provide a sufficient basis for these elements; a deistic or pantheistic God, or one incapable of communicating, would appear to be less than adequate.

The nature of God

The concept of God held by evangelicals, however, does seem to contain a range of elements that make it suitable for our purposes. In the first place, God is seen as having a wide range of characteristics. Secondly, several of the specific aspects of the nature and acts of God emphasized by evangelicals are particularly relevant to issues of epistemology. Thirdly, evangelicals are strongly placed to answer the objection that God cannot make any contribution to human epistemology because he is necessarily infinite and 'other', while epistemology is necessarily finite and tied to this world. We shall examine these three points in more detail.

First, in evangelical thinking, the range of characteristics of God is wide. He is both transcendent and immanent. He both thinks and feels. He is divine, and he is personal. He knows, he remembers, he predicts. He experiences and rejoices and is sad. He does things: he creates, he comes, he acts, he performs miracles. He loves; he forms relationships; he warms our hearts. He is holy and good; he provides standards of right and wrong. He speaks; he communicates propositionally; he reveals truth. He is the truth; he promises, he guarantees, he holds all things together. All these characteristics are found in the one God, not contradicting each other, but enriching one another. Here is a concept of God that seems broad enough to cover the range of data we were thinking of in the last chapter.

Secondly, many of the elements that evangelicals have traditionally stressed in the nature of God and in his acts have direct bearing on issues of knowledge and truth. Evangelicals are therefore able to draw on a number of their specific insights into the nature of God, and his acts, to enrich evangelicalism's contribution to a basis for epistemology.

God is *personal*, and is thus involved in personal relationships. Even before creation he contained within himself relationships in the Trinity. In creation he has chosen to make beings 'in his image' who share in personhood and are capable of relating to him and to other persons. On this understanding of the personal nature of God can be built an understanding of our own personhood, our self-awareness, and our knowledge of other persons in relationships.

God is *creator* and sustainer of all that is. Everything has its source and meaning in him. He is ultimate reality, the one who is, I AM WHO I AM; he does not need a source or explanation. But he is the source and explanation of all the created universe. His power brought it into being and holds it in being; because of him it is real and objective; it exists independently of human minds, though not independently of God. Truth, then, is to be seen as rooted in God. Additionally, God's creative and sustaining power is purposive; creation is not meaningless or capricious; it has purpose – doubtless many purposes. A chance, random universe can have no purpose, and so no meaning; but a planned and designed one will have both purpose and meaning. Since it has goals, it will operate in accordance with those goals, and thus be meaningful and consistent. Awareness of the goals, even if only partial, will lead to an understanding of the way the purposes are being worked out and of the resulting meaningfulness and consistency. As human beings, we have the ability to begin to discern and understand some of the purposes and meaning of the world, to 'think God's thoughts after him'.

In keeping with his nature, God has chosen to have a very close relationship with the created order, both maintaining it in being and shaping its structures. So both the general patterns and specific events in the universe are the product of God's providence and sovereignty. Since integrity and consistency are hallmarks of God's nature and activity, it would seem reasonable to assume that the created order will function with a high degree of coherence and consistency.

One of God's purposes in creation is *love*. This is primarily the expression of his love; but, since love at its highest is relational and reciprocal, it is also the two-way relationship of love given and received between God and his creation. This entails creating beings that are able to experience the love of God; to be aware, at least in part, of what that love is and where it comes from; and to love God, however imperfectly, in response. God has created many different types of creatures with a wide range of abilities; as human beings created 'in his image', we are aware that we have a specific ability to be loved and to love, and thus to develop a relationship of love between us and God. Besides being personal and relational, such love is volitional (involving our will) and emotional (involving our feelings); and it also includes a factual and conceptual element: in order to be able to experience the love of God (or of another person) and to love him in return, we have to accept the objective existence of God and have at least some conceptual idea of what he is like. We may not necessarily verbalize this concept, nor need we separate it clearly from our relational response to his love; but it is a part of the complexity and wholeness of the experience.

Another core element in the nature of God as seen by evangelicals is *goodness*. This is closely linked with his *faithfulness*. Because he is good, he is dependable; we can trust him to be consistent and true to his character. Love and faithfulness are also closely linked in biblical thought, particularly in the concept of steadfast or covenant love; God's faithfulness is the outworking of his love. Because he is good, God would not want persons whom he has created and loves to be seriously in error about the objects of perception and the nature of things in the world; despite the limitations in perception and understanding that must be inevitable in finite beings, he would want us to be able to live in the world and cope with its complexity. Thus it would seem reasonable that belief in the existence of a good, loving, faithful God gives us grounds for believing in the general dependability of our knowledge of the external world, and the reliability of our processes of thought.

God's love, in evangelical thinking, specifically entails the desire that we should be in a personal relationship of love with him, and this gives rise to two central concepts, that of revelation and communication, and that of salvation through the work of Christ on the cross.

The concept of God *revealing and communicating* is possible, as we have seen, because he is a personal God capable of forming personal relationships with persons he has created 'in his image'. Such relationships can be on a number of levels: spiritual, emotional, and personal. They all involve God taking the initiative and coming to us and revealing himself or something of his nature, purposes or truth to us. The revelation of himself in personal encounter is primary; but it does not preclude the revelation of truth. Indeed, it needs it, to enable us to interpret correctly the encounter experience. So he not only reveals his love and holiness and himself to us; he communicates with us in the way we communicate with each other, through words and statements. Our encounter with God thus involves various sorts of knowledge and truth: personal, experiential, moral, factual and propositional.

The revelation of truth, about himself and about the world, can take a number of forms, including 'intuitively known' moral and axiological concepts, truth arising from personal encounter, and truth in the form of propositions. Communication in a relationship is not just in one direction; besides God communicating with us, it is possible for us to communicate with him in the relationship of love, and, specifically, in prayer. Any act of communicating has two parts, that of giving and that of receiving; God undoubtedly has the ability to give communications; but our limitations and the brokenness of our relationships with him means that the receiving of communications from him is rather more problematic. The possibility of human error is always present in a fallen world. But mercy and grace constantly offer ways out of error; understanding can grow; mistakes can be corrected; counter-arguments can persuade; paradigms can shift; conversions can happen.

The truth God reveals will sometimes be such that we can grasp it adequately; for example, the truth that Jesus called his disciples to follow him, or that he calls us to live Christ-like lives. Sometimes truth will be more than we can grasp adequately; for example, that God loves us, or that those who open their lives to him have eternal life. But our inability to grasp the wholeness of a revealed truth does not take away its truth; my inability to grasp the theory of relativity or the infinite number of decimal places in *pi* does not prevent the theory being true, or the proportion measured by *pi* being an accurate fact about a circle.

For evangelicals, God's most significant act is his work of *salvation* in Jesus Christ: his incarnation, life, and supremely his death and resurrection. Quite apart from his incarnation and life being God's key act of communication, the cross and resurrection are seen as the means by which he achieved our salvation, reconciling us to him and restoring us to a full personal relationship in which we can begin to know him. Without this reconciliation, personal knowledge of God is not possible. The moral, spiritual and epistemological effects of conversion or regeneration are closely interlinked; we move from being cut off from God and spiritually dead because of our fallenness and sin, to being forgiven, spiritually alive, and able to know God and personally experience his truth. Additionally, our knowledge of God gives a new understanding of everything else; we have a new focus, a new worldview which enables us to make sense of everything else, whether it is a matter of fact, of morals, of value, or of meaning or purpose. Our restored relationship with God, who is the source of and key to all reality and truth, enables us to begin to understand and know things as they truly are.

There is a third reason why the evangelical concept of God is particularly suitable as a basis for knowledge and truth, and that is that it is able to answer the objection that God cannot make any contribution to human epistemology because he is necessarily infinite and 'other', while epistemology is necessarily finite and tied to this world. The key issue here is the evangelical conviction of the primacy of God's grace: that he takes the initiative, whether in creation, redemption, revelation, or whatever. This has radical implications, and provides a solution to a whole range of problems at the interface of the finite and the infinite, the world and God.

The Enlightenment policy of seeking to explain everything in terms of human reason necessarily rejected this concept. If we start and end with human reason, there is no place for divine intervention. But neither is there any place for God at all. The distance from the finite to the infinite is infinite, too great a gulf for reason to cross. Our finite minds are necessarily limited to the finite world; the infinite world is beyond our reach. Thus the Enlightenment inevitably led to Kant's and Nietzsche's conclusion that God, and with him eternal truth, moral absolutes, and all ultimate fixed points, were lost to us for ever. What is wholly other is wholly beyond us.

The evangelical response to this is incisive. While it is impossible for finite reason to cross an infinite gulf, it is not impossible for an infinite God, who, necessarily, has infinite capabilities. The finite cannot reach the infinite; but the infinite has taken the initiative and reached out to the finite.

This concept has many implications; we shall glance briefly at one of them, and then in a little more detail at another. The first is the issue of the timelessness of truth. The Enlightenment found it hard to bridge the gulf between the finite time-bound things we see as truths, and truths that are somehow timeless and eternal. Evangelicals, however, would see the deliberate choice of a timeless God to create a universe subject to time, and then to be involved in that universe, as providing a bridge between the timeless and the time-bound. God is in himself timeless and unchanging; human beings exist in time, with all its limitations, and are subject to change, development, process, and the like. Nevertheless, it is foundational to evangelical thinking that it is within God's capabilities to relate to his time-bound creation, and, specifically, to time-bound human creatures. Such a relationship will appear to the time-bound person as one that is deeply rooted in time, and that even develops and changes; but that does not impair the timelessness of the God we are experiencing. Similarly, though a timeless God will know every truth timelessly, he can additionally know every time-bound truth, that is, how each truth appears and functions in any context, including that of a process in time. So, for example, his timelessness does not prevent his knowing what the tomorrowness of tomorrow feels like to me, even though he also knows what it is for the thing I call 'tomorrow' to be known timelessly. Thus it is within his capabilities to express timeless truth in a form that is meaningful for time-bound creatures; such a truth will then be true in both the finite and infinite contexts. There is thus in God the possibility of integrating timeless absolute truth with the time-bound, finite and relative thing that is the nearest we are able to get to ultimate truth.

The image of God

The link between the infinite and the finite, for evangelicals, is highlighted in the concept of 'the image of God'. There is much debate over how this phrase should be understood in its biblical context. For our purposes it is sufficient to say that God has consciously built something into human persons that in some way reflects his own nature; he is not 'wholly other' from us, because he has chosen to make us in some aspects like himself. The supreme result of this is that we can relate to him, love him, and have some knowledge of him. But a further outcome is that we can relate to each other and to the world around us in a way other creatures seem unable to do; in that this form of relating is based in some way on the nature of God, we can have confidence in its validity. Thus it is possible to argue that many of the facets of our experience and our knowledge are the result of God-given abilities, arising from the 'image of God' in us.

Thus we can see the wide range of human experiences and knowledge not as something originating wholly within us, but as something planned and given by God, and so, in a sense, underwritten by him. Our capabilities to love, be glad, think, and so on, are modelled on his nature, and so he provides the basis for their validity.

We can apply this concept very broadly. Our personal experiences, for instance, can be seen as an expression of the image of God in us: loving and receiving love; knowing and relating to other persons; experiences of joy and sorrow, pleasure and hurt, awareness of good and evil; experiences of beauty, value, significance, and the like. All these are direct experiences; we do not need to think about them; we are immediately aware of them. For the most part they seem to be distinctively human experiences; we do not generally attribute them to animals, except by projection.

A further form of direct experience is our awareness of objects we encounter in the world, or of other people we meet. We do not seem to have to make an inference, such as: 'I am seeing an image of a tree, and so I infer that there is a tree there.' We see the tree, not its image; our experience is direct and immediate. Further, unless we have reason to suppose there is something wrong with our eyes, or that we are delirious, or that our neighbour enjoys setting up cardboard cut-outs of trees in our garden, we feel we are justified in being sure that what we are experiencing really is a tree. For all the doubts of the sceptical philosophers, we constantly accept direct experience as a wholly valid source of truth. Additionally, we have the ability to fit these many differing experiences together; despite their differences, we are able to integrate them, to build them into a consistent whole. Though it is very hard to demonstrate on purely rational grounds why these things should work so well, they can be seen as arising from God-given abilities implicit in 'the image of God'.

This brings us to our ability to reason. Over and above our ability to know experiences, objects and people directly, we have the ability to think, recall from memory, make deductions, abstract concepts, work through issues, come to conclusions, and all the dozens of other processes of rational thought. This ability, again, would seem to be limited largely, if not exclusively, to human beings. If computers are able to 'think', it is only because human thinkers have programmed them to copy human thought processes; without human thought there would be no 'thinking' computers. Again, though reason on its own is unable to provide adequate justification for our confidence, we for the most part feel that what we recognize as valid, rational thought processes do give us the truth; they are dependable; they work; they can be trusted.

All these capacities – the ability to relate to others in love, to experience a wide range of feelings and values and the like, to have direct awareness of objects in the world, and to follow valid processes of reasoning – are part of what it means to be human; and all of them in their different ways give us access to knowledge and truth. Again, some would choose to assume that it is purely fortuitous that as human beings we have these various abilities, and that they work so well in the situations in which we find ourselves. Evangelicals, however, would want to say that none of these elements has arisen by chance; rather, they are what God has planted in us in order to enable us to know truth. Whether or not they are specifically what the Old Testament meant by 'the image of God', they are to be seen as elements reflecting in some way the nature of God, which he has chosen to put in us to enrich our being, and to deepen our relationship with him, with others, and with the world around us.

Perhaps it needs to be emphasized that the existence of these differing elements in us do not in themselves constitute convincing evidence that there must be a God who has put them there. However much we accept that the existence of God is the best explanation for the data, no conclusive 'proof' of God's existence can be built on them. Rather, the train of thought is in the opposite direction; we start with a concept of God who is the source of everything there is, including reality and truth, and who has created human persons 'in his image', such that they can relate to him, to each other, and to things in the world. In love he has revealed himself to them, both personally and existentially and in verbal communication. Starting, then, with some such concept of God, when confronted with the need to provide an adequate basis and justification for our experience of truth, we find that God fits the bill. We feel the need to provide an adequate explanation for the fact that we do experience and discover and communicate truth, and so on, and the concept of God answers that need very well. We are not able to claim that we can provide conclusive proof that God is the correct answer, or even the only answer; an alternative answer may one day be put forward which covers the data as satisfactorily as the concept of God does. But at present, for those who are able to accept the concept of God, it is far and away the most satisfactory answer. It may be that, for some, belief in the existence of God will be made easier as a result of the above argument; but evangelicals need to be clear that their foundational conviction that such a God exists arises from something other than a conclusive rational argument.

17. Starting with God 3: observations and conclusions

In this chapter I shall pick up a number of points which arise from the use of the concept of God as a basis and justification for truth. For ease of presentation, I shall introduce each point with an observation in the form of an objection, and then comment on it. I shall then draw together some conclusions about basing our epistemology on God.

Observations

The method of producing an explanation for epistemological data by introducing a further very complex concept is unacceptable. It goes against the well-established principle, often called Ockham's razor, that the simple explanation must be the correct one.

First, it is not the intention of the suggested approach to introduce the concept of God in order to supply an explanation for meaning and truth. Rather, the suggestion is that the evangelical concept of God, which is already widely held for reasons that have nothing to do with epistemology, can be seen as (almost incidentally) supplying a satisfactory base for our confidence in knowledge, truth, and the like.

Secondly, the principle we call Ockham's razor is open to challenge.[1] It did good service through the Enlightenment period, enabling Hume and his friends to clear out large stocks of 'divinity' and 'school metaphysics' from their libraries and commit them 'to the flames'.[2] But this was because it fitted well the Enlightenment programme of reducing all explanations to the merely rational, a policy which has been shown to be inadequate. Further, as a dogmatic principle, it is impossible to show that it is correct. In fact it is not difficult to think of situations where the complex explanation is the correct one, a point illustrated by many a detective story.

Finally, even if we were to concede that Ockham's razor is a valid principle, we can point out that the presupposition of God is in this case the simplest explanation, in that no other clearly acceptable explanation is currently available.

If you use God to provide a basis for truth, what basis do you have for believing in God? And if you are able to justify this belief, how do you then justify your justification? And how do you justify that? You are locked into an infinite chain of justification; the task is impossible.

The task is impossible if by 'justification' we mean 'a proven logical case that conclusively demonstrates that the belief is true'. We have already seen that this is an impossible and unnecessary demand, based on the Enlightenment's excessive confidence in reason. Justification in real life is something much broader than logical proof. I am justified in believing that it is snowing, not because I produce a logical proof, but as the result of any number of very different factors combining to confirm that belief: I feel cold, everything looks white, flakes are landing on my outstretched hand, others are saying, 'It is snowing', and so on. Despite the occasional forays of some into evidentialism, evangelicals have always justified their belief in God on a much broader basis than that of rational argument. Foundational is the concept of God coming in grace to us; tied in with this are concepts of God speaking, the illuminatory work of the Holy Spirit, the experience of conversion and of personal encounter with God, and the awareness of his love, power and truth. Following on from the primacy of God's action is the long-term confirmation (or otherwise) that what we have taken as God coming to us really is such. This, again, is not simply a rational process, though reason will play a part in it; it is the confirmation of the reality of the encounter with God in each aspect of our personhood: emotional, spiritual, moral, relational, and so on. It is the continued outworking of the miracle of the new birth, which permeates each part of our lives.

The belief in God as the basis for knowledge and truth was rejected at the Enlightenment. It is therefore not acceptable to return to it now.

The belief was not rejected at the Enlightenment. Early Enlightenment thinkers held firmly to it; their confidence in reason rested on the conviction that reason was the light or candle that God has put in each of us so that we might know his truth.[3] Indeed, it is arguable that without the foundational belief that God is the justification for our confidence in the reliability of our reason, the Enlightenment project would not have got under way. Certainly, as soon as God was removed from the systems of the Enlightenment thinkers, the incoherence of those systems was clearly demonstrated. It was the attempt to continue the Enlightenment project without the undergirding of belief in God that led to its collapse.

The Enlightenment started with a conviction that God is the basis for everything, including human reason. It is God's purpose that we should explore his world and unlock its secrets; to this end he has gifted men and women with the ability to reason, an ability which was seen as sufficient to explain everything in the world. So far from a rejection of God, the full use of this gift was seen as an expression of piety, even of worship.[4] As the Enlightenment developed, two steps were taken away from this early 'doxological' approach.

First, there was an increasing tendency to subject God to reason. The earliest thinkers saw God as the source of reason, and so beyond its jurisdiction.[5] Revelation was seen as beyond the scope of reason's authority. As time went by, however, it was accepted that though God himself may be beyond the scope of our reason, what he did in our world was not. Therefore, just as his works in creation were subject to our reason, so his other works in the world, including revelation and miracle, were also to be subject. And since it turns out that all we can ever know about God has to be 'in the world', then, for our purposes, everything to do with him has to be subject to reason.

Secondly, it was assumed that if reason was sufficient to explain everything in the world, then reason itself did not require any explanation outside of itself; it was its own justification. These two steps tended to be assumed rather than argued; neither of them was conclusively established, and the second is now recognized as invalid.

If God is the basis for our confidence in truth, and the existence of God cannot be logically proved, then our confidence in truth is destroyed; a superstructure is only as strong as the foundation; we are no further forward.

Again, this is returning to a narrow concept of what constitutes a sufficient basis for a belief in God, based on the Enlightenment dogma that nothing can be true unless it is established beyond any possibility of doubt or refutation. Confidence or even certainty does not require logical proof. I am certain my wife loves me; those who experience God are certain that he exists. In neither case is a logical proof possible or appropriate; in both cases the content of the belief is more real than any number of mathematical formulae.

The possibility of error invalidates the concept of God as a basis for truth. A perfect God could communicate only errorless truth, yet people often have experiences they erroneously attribute to God, and we are constantly told that the Bible is full of errors.

To claim that God is the justification for our confidence in the reliability of our knowledge of the world around us is not to claim that our knowledge is infallible. I can believe that the vast majority of my experiences are of objective reality and give me true data about the things I experience, without claiming that I always interpret my experiences correctly, or that none of them is ever a mirage or dream.

As for special revelation, evangelicals continue to hold to their conviction that a God of truth will not lie, and that the Bible is the revelation of God, and so necessarily truthful. But their greater openness to the possibility of being mistaken, especially their more open approach to hermeneutics, means that they are considerably less inclined to claim definitive truth for their understanding or interpretation of revelation; we are back to Wesley's willingness to be corrected.

Once again, for those who hold to a rationalistic concept of truth in which one possibility of error necessarily destroys the whole system, such openness could be fatal. But evangelicals are not committed to this narrow concept. They are able to function without the assurance of a logically proven case. For them, there is a sufficiently broad basis for their belief in a God who is trustworthy and who reveals truth to enable them to cope with the possibility of error in our reception or understanding of truth, and with the inability to provide definitive answers to every logical problem. The situation is parallel to our knowledge of objects in the world; there is no definitive answer to the logical arguments of the sceptic who insists that since some people occasionally experience mirages, none of us can ever put any trust in any of our senses. But that in no way prevents us claiming immediate awareness and, in effect, certain knowledge, of chairs and tables and the like.

In contrast to the Kantian tradition, evangelicals have always insisted that God is capable of communicating truth about the phenomenal world, as well as theological truth; but they have equally insisted that our finiteness and, indeed, our sinfulness, mean that we shall on occasion get the message wrong. An infallible God does not guarantee infallible human understanding or knowledge. We may accept with Descartes 'the impossibility of God's ever deceiving' us,[6] but our human limitations make it inevitable that we fall short of full apprehension or perfect knowledge. But the possibility of error is offset by the grace, love and goodness of God; we may as yet see 'through a glass, darkly', but an immanent, caring God is concerned enough and gracious enough to provide for our present needs for knowledge and truth.

Why should we adopt a broad understanding of what we mean by 'truth'? Is it not better to have a clear-cut, simple concept than a complex broad one? How can you prove that the broad concept is the right one?

Anyone is, of course, able to adopt any concept of truth they choose. There are still those, for example, who hold to the view of truth held by the logical positivists, that only what can be scientifically established can count as truth; and there are those who claim that there is no such thing as truth. But, unless people are going to keep their truth totally to themselves, and never seek to put it into practice in the world, any view of truth will have to stand the tests of being shared with other people and lived out in the world. These two tests make a narrow concept of truth less viable. Our experience of the world and our interaction with other people make us realize the tremendous complexity of life. We cannot cover everything using just one single type of explanation, such as the scientific one. Issues of fact rub shoulders with issues of purpose, moral concepts, value judgments, and the like. People do claim truth as much for 'The cat ought not to be on the mat' as for 'The cat is on the mat', even though the two types of truth seem to be very different. A concept of truth that is sufficient to cover the data of real life needs to be a broad one.

Again, the 'proof' for this is not in the form of a logically watertight case; but that type of proof is not available for any concept of truth. Logical positivism declined because it was seen to be based on an initial presupposition that was quite unprovable. 'Only scientific truth exists' is as much an article of faith as is 'The concept of truth is as valid in ethics as in science'. Instead of demanding conclusive proof, we need to test our concept of truth against our experience of living in the world. How does it fit with the experiences we and the people around us actually have, the way we function and communicate, and so on?

Granted that there are different types of truth, we must carefully distinguish between them and keep them apart. Moral truth, for example, should be kept apart from scientific truth; above all, theological truth should be kept on its own and not mixed up with other sorts of truth; truth in God is necessarily totally different from human truth.

Of course there is value in separating out different types of truth for the purpose of analysis. But the fact is that in real life we regularly use different types of truth together, and find that everything works satisfactorily. If we say, 'It's a beautiful morning', we are making both a value judgment ('It is beautiful') and a factual statement ('It is morning'), and we have no problem in doing so. In the same way, evangelicals want to insist that theological truth, though different in some ways from other sorts of truth, can happily fit in with them. If God reveals truth to us, he is not limited to revealing theological truth; he can tell us historical, moral or factual truth. Indeed, we could argue that, for God, all the truths we call historical, moral or factual are theological, in the sense that they are his acts, or events in his world, or expressions of his goodness, or aspects of his truth.

It is hard to see how it would be possible to establish that truth in God is necessarily totally different from human truth. This is an assumption that many have made, along with the assumption that everything else in God, from his love to his existence, is totally other than our love, our existence, and so on. Evangelicals can counter this assumption with their belief that an infinite God would have infinite capabilities; thus he undoubtedly knows truths that are far beyond us in ways that we cannot begin to imagine; but he is also capable of knowing that the cat is on the mat in a way that is parallel to our knowledge of it. God's involvement in the world, in creation, in providence, in the incarnation, and so on, demonstrates that he is not wholly other in every respect; and the concept of the image of God in human creatures provides a further bridge between him and us.

Conclusions

For the evangelical Christian, God is the source and ground of everything. If something is real, it is because he creates and sustains it. If something is good, it is because it expresses his character. If something is true, it is because it is one with his creative action and purpose in the world.

Truth can be known because he is truth, and he has chosen to make truth knowable to human creatures. There is a parallel with his goodness: he could have created us amoral beings; but he chose to create us with an ability to be aware of goodness and evil, and so to do good or evil. In the same way he chose to create us with an awareness of truth; so we can know truth and live truth. He did not have to create us this way; most of his creatures do not have the ability to know either goodness or truth in the way that we do. But he did so, and thus gave us the opportunity to find, know, follow and do the truth.

God's interest is more in our living the truth than in our simply knowing it. Truth is much more than cerebral or factual. It is moral, practical and relational. At its best it is Jesus Christ, who is the way, the truth and the life. These are not three isolated concepts; rather they are three words conveying one concept; when our lives are one with him, we have found the way to live truth.

We are back, then to Hodge's assertion: 'The ultimate ground of faith and knowledge is confidence in God.'[7] This applies not just to 'theological' truth, but to all truth. Given the existence of God, the purposes of God, the nature of God, the involvement of God in the world, and the love of God for the human persons he has made in his image, then we have a firm basis for knowledge and truth. We also have a basis for accepting the dependability of our reason. If, with the early Enlightenment thinkers, we root our confidence in reason in God, it becomes a firm enough basis on which to build a consistent picture of the world. Reason is dependable because it is God-given; the world is consistent because God has made it that way. When reason refused to accept its derivative nature and set itself up as an absolute, it did not take long for its inadequacy to be revealed. Reason that does not claim to be ultimate can continue to be relied upon and used in dialogue with our experience of the world, of other persons, of God, and of all the other elements that go to make up human personhood, in a continuing process of discovery and development. In such a process, no one element will claim ultimate authority; direct awareness of objects in the world, or our personal encounter with God, will not have to give way to the demands of reason; but, equally, reason will not have to be dispensed with when we are dealing with direct experience or encounter with God. The various elements are able to work together to establish the truth, in the confidence that each of them is an essential God-given part of human personhood, and that all have essential roles to play. This is a concept we shall be exploring further in the next chapter.

Evangelicals are thus in a position to accept with integrity the mass of knowledge that is the heritage of the Enlightenment period. They may legitimately believe that water boils at 100°C, that other people exist, that the surface of Mars is permanently frozen, and so on. In contrast to those who go on believing these things despite believing at the same time that the basis or justification for them has been demolished, they are able to fit these truths within an overall worldview which provides an adequate basis and justification for them. They agree with the postmodernists that reason has failed as an ultimate justification for truth, but they are able to retain both reason and truth as a result of their foundational concept of God. Here is an adequate framework, a total explanation, which not only is sufficient to make sense of all the data in a way that the confidence in reason on its own never could, but also, because of its broad scope, is able to supply something that in itself is rich and wide-ranging, and contains the potential for continuing discovery and development in the future.

18. The wholeness of truth

Fragmentation

I have referred a number of times to the resistance by evangelicals to the almost universal trend to fragment truth. This trend was caused partly by the overwhelming growth in the amount of truth there was to be known. Up to the seventeenth century it was possible for one individual to be well informed and capable of making positive contributions in all areas of human knowledge, from physics to theology, political theory to geography. But increasing knowledge meant that no one person was able to keep up with everything; specialization was inevitable. So knowledge, the established and agreed body of truth about the world, became divided; the scientists pursued their science, the historians their history, the theologians their theology, and so on. As they grew apart, it became more difficult and less important to relate the different areas together. Indeed, keeping them apart, and thus concentrating on limited areas of truth, was found to be very fruitful, and there was little motivation to seek to integrate them all.

Additionally, as we have seen, the fragmenting process was accentuated by philosophical considerations. Seventeenth-century thinkers had a vision of all knowledge and truth following the same basic pattern; the ideal for them was mathematics, where truth could be known clearly and precisely; it could be established logically, and in such a way that any reasonable person would have to accept it. But it did not take long for the vision of all truth conforming to the mathematical model to be abandoned. In physics, for example, it worked well enough, at any rate for three centuries. But it never worked well in history, ethics or theology; attempts to make these disciplines conform to the mathematical model were soon accepted as failures. So historians and the like either had to abandon any claim to be producing truth in their particular discipline, or they had to claim that the truth they were producing was every bit as true as the mathematicians' truth, but that it was a different type of truth, operating in a different way, according to a different logic.

The conclusion was therefore drawn that different areas of knowledge contain differing types of truth; moral truth is different from historical truth or factual truth. They operate in different ways, according to different rules. Long before Wittgenstein proposed his 'language games', it was widely recognized that theologians cannot make theological pronouncements about matters of scientific fact, or that we cannot move from 'is' to 'ought'. Different types of truth need to be kept apart.

Besides this fragmenting of knowledge and of truth itself, there was a fragmenting of the knowing subject. Despite specialization, individuals found that they still had to continue to operate in a wide range of areas of truth. The scientist still had to make moral decisions, to relate to others on a personal basis, and so on. In the laboratory, love could be analysed in chemical formulae; but that would not do for love back home in the family. So, in a sense, there had to be two people: the scientist in the laboratory, and the family member back home, just as David Hume found he had to switch off from his philosophy in order to live in the world of people.[1] Thus theories of human personhood were developed, splitting it up into various 'faculties', such as our emotions, our intellect, and our soul. Human reason was split into 'ordinary' reason and 'higher' reason. The human person, the knowing subject, became as fragmented as truth itself.

Evangelicals have resisted both these trends. Because God plays such a key role in their system, they were able to retain him as the integrating factor when others were finding that coping without him was leading to fragmentation. Evangelicals thus refused to follow the Kantian option, parting company with the rest of Protestantism, who were only too relieved to solve the pressing problem of apparent contradictions between the discoveries of science and the content of religion by divorcing the two areas of truth.

Integration

Thus, after the primacy place given to God, the second core emphasis in an evangelical approach to epistemology is the integration of truth and of the knowing person. All truth is one, because all truth is God's truth, and God is one. This is not to deny the varied nature of the differing types of truth. Evangelicals need to retain a very wide concept of truth, covering many different types, as we saw in chapter 15. Truth is not to be narrowed down to comply with some reductionist theory. Rather, our understanding of it must be broad and rich enough to cover all the different forms in which we encounter it.

So truth is varied, rich, and complex; evangelicals can accept that it operates in different ways in different spheres. In maths, for example, it is very clear-cut; we can readily distinguish between truth and falsehood. The statement '2 + 2 = 4' is clearly true; '2 + 2 = 5' is clearly false. But in, say, ethics, we often have to operate with less clear-cut edges. Most people would accept that 'Breaking the law is wrong' is true, but they could want to insist that it is only generally true; we can all think of examples when it would be right to break the law. So the edges here between the truth and falsehood are rather more fuzzy. But it would be a major mistake to conclude that, since we have to operate without clear-cut mathematical-type truth in ethics, then we have to abandon the concept of truth in ethics altogether. The fact is, we do use concepts of truth in ethics. It makes perfect sense to say, 'I know it is generally true that we ought to keep the law of the land, but it is also true that sometimes we are justified in breaking it.' It may be harder to analyse the way truth functions in ethics than in maths; but there can be no question but that the concept of truth applies as much in the one as in the other, even though it operates differently.

However, none of this should be allowed to obscure the insight that truth is one. However tempting it may be, abandoning an integrated concept of truth because of the difficulties involved in working it out not only goes against our general experience (where, as we have seen, we find no difficulty in making statements that contain several types of truth sitting happily next to each other in one meaningful sentence); it also fragments our universe, and, very probably, fragments us as well.

A distinction needs to be made at this point between subjective and objective truth. Evangelicals are clearly not claiming that all subjective truth is one; that would be quite untenable. But they do wish to claim that objective truth, whatever its form, is one; objective moral truth and objective scientific truth and objective historical truth can all be built into one total view of the world. Again, they need to concede that purely objective truth is rarely, if ever, found; we each bring something of our subjective selves to every experience and act of believing or knowing. But allowing that objective truths are accompanied by subjective elements does not destroy their objectivity. Even in ethics, one of the greatest strongholds of subjective relativism, it is impossible to get by without an at least minimal objective core. The relativist's statement, 'What I call good you are entitled to choose to call evil', is meaningful only if there is some agreed (and so non-subjective) content to the words 'good' and 'evil'. Some would argue that it is impossible to separate subjective from objective elements; once we have allowed that a statement can be partly subjective and partly objectively true, we have lost the objective truth because we can never tell which is the subjective part and which is the objective. But in practice this is not a great problem. One person says, 'It is great to have that tree chopped down'; another says, 'Cutting down that tree was a criminal act.' We can accept the contrast in subjective reaction; but there is an irreducible objective content, namely that a tree has been cut down.

All objective truth, then, is one. The objective core of our experience of things around us, of our encounter with other people and with God, of the truths of mathematics, of moral principles, of scientific fact, and so on, can all be built into one integrated view of the world. This can happen because, for the evangelical, the world is one; it was planned and made as an integrated whole by a God who is faithful and consistent and works in the world according to his own coherent and consistent purpose. Admittedly, the overall picture is so rich and complex that it is far beyond us to grasp it all at once; only God is capable of that. But, because it is one, the relatively small sections of it that we can grasp must in themselves be one. The limits of our knowledge may result in apparent inconsistencies, or areas where we cannot conceive how differing truths fit together. But even then we operate on the principle that the different truths can ultimately be integrated; we do not have to settle for incompatibilities or a fragmented universe.

This, of course, is how we in fact approach the data of knowledge and truth in ordinary life. Whatever our philosophical or theological convictions, confronted with any new truth, we immediately seek to integrate it with the whole body of truth we already possess. It may take time to do so, and there may well have to be adjustments, either to the new truth, or to our formerly held beliefs; but we seem inevitably to seek to make truth an integrated whole. Philosophy may call for fragmentation; life demands integration.

Truth is to be seen as multi-dimensional. The pressure has been on us to isolate single types of truth, that are thus one-dimensional. We say, for instance, that the biologist's task is to explore the possibilities of genetic engineering in a purely scientific way without any reference to, say, the moral implications, or to the personal feelings of whoever is produced as a result of the engineering. But an integrated approach to truth could not allow this. Though we can choose to look at just one isolated dimension of a truth, if we are going to see the real thing we shall need to see it multi-dimensionally. 'The cat is on the mat', taken one-dimensionally, conveys the truth that a specific animal is on a particular bit of floor-covering. But if anyone in real life ever says 'The cat is on the mat', it is likely that the truth he or she is seeking to convey is much richer than that. Perhaps someone has heard a screech of brakes outside; could it be that the cat has been run over? Where is the cat? 'The cat is on the mat', in that context, conveys reassurance, comfort, even a rebuke for paranoia. On top of its immediate content, the statement 'The cat is on the mat' carries all sorts of connotations, of cosiness and domesticity, perhaps, or possibly a moral implication: 'That mat is worth a lot of money; you should never allow the cat on it.'

Even individual truths, then, are multi-dimensional. And no one truth is to be taken in isolation; any statement draws much of its meaning, and so its truth, from its context: the situation in which it is spoken, from the person who speaks it, the hearer, the motive, the feelings expressed as the words are uttered, and so on. If the mat is worth a lot of money, and the words 'The cat is on the mat' were spoken in an accusing tone, part of its truth claim could be: 'It is your fault she's there.' An appropriate denial of the statement 'The cat is on the mat' would then be: 'But *I* didn't let her in.' Those who insist on strict logic and one-dimensional truth would have difficulty with this; but in real life we cope with the richness and complexity of claims to truth with very little difficulty.

This brings us to the nature of ourselves as knowing subjects. We have seen that the trend to fragment truth also fragments the person who holds the truth. One part of me believes a scientific truth, another part a theological truth, another a moral truth, and so on. Such an approach raises all sorts of difficulties over how we analyse these different aspects and fit them to their specific fields of interest, and over how we relate the different parts of the person together. But, as we have seen, the strongest argument against this approach is that we are each aware that we simply do not function that way. In real life we do mix factual, moral and theological truth together, and we respond to the result as a whole integrated person, not as several different departments.

It has been part of the distinctiveness of evangelicalism that it has insisted on this integration of the person. Doubtless on occasion this has led to a rather simplistic view of what it is for an integrated person to believe a truth; but there is no reason why evangelicals should not accept both the rich complexity and the unity of the believing subject. This complexity needs to cover the experiential, the relational, the volitional, the moral, the rational, and maybe other aspects as well.[2]

Personhood

The *experiential* aspect of human personhood is the most obvious means by which we find truth. We see a cat; we feel its soft fur, we hear it purring; our direct experience convinces us that there truly is a cat there. Granted, there is an outside possibility that we are dreaming or hallucinating or that in the poor light we are being deceived by a cardboard cut-out. But we all have useful ways of telling the difference between a dream or cardboard and living reality or cat. Even if we should on the very rare occasion get it wrong, we soon check it out with the whole of our experience and, if we find it does not fit, put it right. Despite the philosophers, this possibility of error does not as a rule lessen our confidence in truth; it can even increase it: 'I was once caught out by a very good cardboard cut-out of a cat, so now I always look twice to make sure the cat is real.'

Direct experience, then, is a very powerful source of truth. Seeing is believing. Traditionally, direct experience has been necessarily channelled through one or more of the so-called five senses: sight, hearing, taste, smell, and touch. But, again, this seems to be an unnecessarily restrictive list. Why only five? By which of the five senses, for example, do we have the experience of joy? Joy is a valid experience which we all have directly; could it be that we experience it by a sixth sense? Could it be that there are other senses, seventh, eighth, and so on, giving us a wide range of different ways of having direct experiences? Better, perhaps we ought not to regard our response to direct encounter with any specific object or situation in the world as channelled through just one 'sense', all neatly tied up and segregated, such as apprehending a cat through sight, a gas leak through smell, and good news through my joy faculty. Rather, we should say that *we* as persons, whole persons, experience cats, gas leaks and good news. True, sight, smell or excitement may be the most significant element involved in that experience, but it is, after all, *my* experience, not that of my eyes, nose, or inner being.

As the Enlightenment developed, it tended to play down direct experience as a source of truth: our experiences may be fallacious; only reason can be relied on to give us truth. But the fact is that we do continually accept as truth what we directly experience: 'I saw it with my own eyes'; 'If you don't believe there is a wall there, try walking through it.' Indeed, we can claim that our direct experience always is the truth. If error does creep in, it is not at the direct experience stage, but at the next stage, when our reason begins to get to work on what we have experienced. We see a white shape moving in the garden at night; the experience is totally truthful: there is a white shape moving in the darkness. Error creeps in if we conclude, 'It is a ghost', instead of 'There's a towel hanging on the line'. So, in contrast to the Enlightenment view, then, we can say that direct experience is an extremely reliable source of truth; it is reason that, in this case, is leading us astray.

For evangelicals, included in the range of direct experience will be direct experience of God. Just as we experience objects, emotions, and other people, we experience God himself. Those who do not believe in God, and those whose God is necessarily wholly beyond human experience, are not able to accept the possibility of such an experience. But it fits well in the evangelical framework; God, though infinite and transcendent, is personal and capable of revealing and expressing his love, reality, goodness, and so on, to human persons he has made. This experience is, like our experience of cats or other people, a direct one. When our reason gets to work on it and we try to understand it, we may have problems and even make mistakes; after all, God is considerably more complex than cats. But that does not call into question the truth of the direct experience: we truly experience God, even if we cannot grasp or express all the implications of that truth.

There is no reason, then, why we should not take our experience of God, checked out and verified with other sources of truth, including God's revelation in the Scriptures, as a wholly reliable source of truth. If God is, as evangelicals believe, personal, loving, and eager to develop relationships with human persons made in his image, such direct experience seems fully acceptable.

This brings us to a second element of human personhood which needs to be fitted into the integrated whole: the *relational*. This is more than an inert, passive relation. Ben Nevis is higher than Snowdon, but it would not make any difference to Ben Nevis if Snowdon were 500 metres higher, or even ceased to exist. Though much of our relating is on such a passive level, a distinctive element of human personhood is that we are capable of relating to objects, situations and people in a much more active way. I can choose to ignore something or somebody, or I can choose to relate to them. On a country walk I can pass by tree after tree; but then one catches my eye. I stop, and look at it, and admire it. Something happens beyond the basic direct experience. There is a response; the tree is doing something to me, changing me in some way, giving me joy, or annoyance, or whatever. Even richer is the experience of relating to other people. Here we use the word 'know' in a much deeper way than in mathematics or even than in 'I know Snowdon very well'. If I know someone, I imply that there is a relationship between us that is more than passive acquaintance. I have gone beyond directly experiencing the person and have in some way responded to her; she has affected me, annoyed me, delighted me, enlightened me. If I know her well, I should probably say that not only has she affected me but I have affected her. The relationship is two-way; both of us are changed and enriched by it.

The model for the knowledge of truth that still permeates our culture is that of the deliberately detached and unaffected observer gathering data. Clearly this is applicable in certain circumstances, but we need to insist that it is not the whole story. If we are truly human, one aspect of our knowing the truth will be that it affects us; our relationship to it is personal; it changes us. We do not remain detached; we open ourselves up to the truth; we are involved; we let it affect us. The deepest human relationship is, of course, love. However alien the concept may be to our culture, we are almost back to Plato's approach, which saw philosophy as 'love of wisdom', and knowledge as love of beauty or goodness rather than mere awareness of facts. Love is, after all, the richest of human relationships; perhaps it is time evangelicals went against our current culture and set themselves to work out an alternative philosophy and epistemology in which love plays a key role.[3]

We have looked at two aspects of human personhood, the experiential and the relational. These two are clearly very close. In no way do we wish to separate them out into two distinct 'faculties'; rather, they are to be seen as the one integrated person experiencing and responding.

Similarly, our third aspect, which we have called *volitional* – the aspect of us that covers choice and our wills and the process of commitment – is to be seen as closely integrated with these two. Some have tried to suggest that our wills are in effect the source of truth; we choose to believe something as true, and commit ourselves to it, and that then is truth. This could work only if the 'volitional' part of us were a separate faculty, working in isolation. But it is not. We are not free to create our own truth in this way, conjuring it up, as it were, from nowhere. In real life we do involve our wills in the act of knowing truth, but we use them alongside the rest of our personhood. In particular, rather than setting our wills to work with a blank sheet before them, we integrate our volitional activity with the data of our relating and direct experience. We do not create truth; we do not choose with every option open; we do not commit ourselves to some totally blind leap in the dark.[4] Rather, we choose to respond to the data of experience.

Commitment plays a significant role in the building up of any worldview. None of us can wait until we have satisfactorily established our worldview to start living. We have to choose to accept our foundational beliefs provisionally and go ahead with living by them, testing them as we do so, and either confirming them or, if necessary, modifying them or in due course abandoning them. There will thus be an initial commitment to them, which is often unconscious; though in the case, say, of a religious conversion, it may be made deliberately and consciously. Such a commitment will rightly involve a degree of tenacity. We shall not abandon the worldview the first time some difficulty turns up; scientific theories are not abandoned on the strength of one contrary instance. But not even the strongest commitment should be allowed to get right out of step with, say, the data of experience or the voice of reason; a commitment which refuses to listen to any of the other parts of human personhood is very dangerous. Again, this element of our personhood needs to be closely integrated with all the other aspects.

The fourth aspect of human personhood we listed was the *moral*. The inability to find any way of linking the way things are with the way things ought to be has been a major feature of the post-Kantian world. Once God was removed as the basis for morality (and for everything else), no adequate alternative basis could be found. Attempts were made to define good in terms of (for instance) the greatest happiness of the greatest number, or the preservation of the human race, or, more recently, the preservation of the ecology of planet Earth. But it is always possible to ask, 'Is human happiness, or the preservation of the human race or of Earth's ecology, necessarily good?' The concept of goodness seems to stand behind and judge even these principles, so it cannot itself be defined in terms of them.

We have referred a number of times to the disastrous way our culture separates matters of fact and matters of goodness and rightness. The resistance of evangelicals to this has always been firm, as has been their insistence that morality in the human person is not to be divorced from the other aspects of our personhood. The element of choice and commitment we have just been looking at has strong moral overtones. We have freedom of choice, and have to be committed to some principles of action or worldview. But the choice and commitment are not amoral; there is a standard inbuilt into the universe and into us as creatures made in the image of God, and that is the standard of the nature of God himself. In the last analysis, the way our human personhood has functioned will be assessed by putting it alongside the way God himself, or God incarnate in Christ, functioned. If we say that we, as integrated persons, choose to respond to the data of experience, we need to add that in so doing we cannot avoid exercising moral responsibility for our choices. Some, perhaps, would prefer not to, and many would wish to shed responsibility for wrong choices; but moral accountability, in the evangelical worldview, is an integral part of human personhood.

The final aspect in our list was the one that has received the most attention, the *rational*. Leaving it to the end of our discussion does not mean that it is unimportant; evangelicals would want to say that it is as impossible for us as persons to operate without reason as it is to operate without morality or experience. There is no scale of relative importance in the aspects of our personhood; they all depend on each other and complement each other, and go to make up a single integrated whole. It is the rational person who makes moral choices; the moral person who has experiences; the relational person who reasons, and so on. Reason plays a vital part in interpreting the data of experience and checking them against the rest of what we hold to be true, and either incorporating them into the overall system, or deciding what adaptations or corrections need to be made. Our relational response to experiences, to other people and to God may at times be spontaneous, but it is not irrational. Our choices and commitments need to be monitored by God-given reason; evangelicals have always been suspicious of irrational faith.

19. Conversion and certainty

Evangelicalism has a significant contribution to make to the contemporary search for a new epistemology in that it offers a way of seeing truth as one, and the knowing subject as an integrated whole. We have listed some of the aspects of the human person that go to make up this whole, and which are together involved in the process of knowing and responding to the truth. There is, however, a further dimension which is central to the evangelical approach. If God is the source of and key to everything, and we are made in the image of God, then our knowing and living the truth will be seriously inadequate unless God has his rightful place in it. And this rightful place, again, will not be achieved merely by our giving him an intellectual acknow-ledgment and allowing him some theoretical place in our worldview, but by a holistic acceptance and experience of all that is implicit in the evangelical concept of God: personal, moral, experiential, and so on.

Conversion and its consequences

This brings us back to the concept of conversion or the new birth, one which has always been a central theme for evangelicals. Though they have from time to time been prepared to make certain concessions over this concept (for example, allowing that it does not have to be a dramatic 'Damascus road' experience, but may be a longer process), they have stuck to the belief that the new birth is both essential (without it a person is not a true Christian) and something that radically affects every part of life. A favourite text would be 2 Corinthians 5:17: 'If anyone is in Christ, he is a new creation; the old has gone, the new has come!' This radical change covers passing from spiritual death to life, reconciliation to God, forgiveness, and much else.

Conversion also has significant epistemological implications. Evangelicals have frequently used biblical texts such as: 'I was blind but now I see!' (Jn. 9:25); 'You will know the truth, and the truth will set you free' (Jn. 8:32); and 'The man without the Spirit [understood as the unregenerate person] does not accept the things that come from the Spirit of God . . . The spiritual man makes judgments about all things' (1 Cor. 2:14–15). Such passages are interpreted as saying that before conversion we are in ignorance and error; at conversion the life of God is poured into us, and so for the first time the truth of God is open before us. That is not to say that we apprehend it all at once; it has to be explored and learned and experienced. Wesley drew a close parallel between human birth and the new birth:

> Before a child is born into the world he has eyes, but sees not; he has ears, but does not hear. He has a very imperfect use of any other sense. He has no knowledge of any of the things of the world, or any natural understanding. To that manner of existence which he then has, we do not even give the name of life. It is then only when a man is born, that we say he begins to live. For as soon as he is born, he begins to see the light, and the various objects with which he is encompassed. His ears are then opened, and he hears the sounds which successively strike upon them . . . How exactly doth the parallel hold in all these instances! While a man is in a mere natural state, before he is born of God, he has, in a spiritual sense, eyes and sees not; a thick impenetrable veil lies upon them: he has ears, but hears not; he is utterly deaf to what he is most of all concerned to hear. His other spiritual senses are all locked up: he is in the same condition as if he had them not. Hence he has no knowledge of God; no intercourse with him; he is not at all acquainted with him. He has no true knowledge of the things of God, either of spiritual or eternal things; therefore, though he is a living man, he is a dead Christian. But as soon as he is born of God, there is a total change in all these particulars. The 'eyes of his understanding are opened;' (such is the language of the great Apostle;) and, He who of old 'commanded light to shine out of darkness shining on his heart, he sees the light of the glory of God,' his glorious love, 'in the face of Jesus Christ.' His ears being opened, he is now capable of hearing the inward voice of God, saying, 'Be of good cheer; thy sins are forgiven thee;' 'Go and sin no more.' This is the purport of what God speaks to his heart; although perhaps not in these

very words. He is now ready to hear whatsoever 'He that teaches man knowledge' is pleased, from time to time, to reveal to him.[1]

For Wesley the results of the new birth in the area of our understanding are very closely integrated with those in other areas. He goes on to list further ways in which the regenerate person feels 'the mighty working of the Spirit of God': a 'peace which passeth all understanding', joy, the love of God, an exercising of spiritual senses, through whose use 'he is daily increasing in the knowledge of God, of Jesus Christ who he hath sent, and of all the things pertaining to his inward kingdom'.[2] This emphasis on the strongly experiential nature of what the Spirit teaches the regenerate person was central in Wesley's thinking; his own evangelical conversion contained the twin elements of understanding and heart-warming, and he clearly expected all who were converted to experience the same. 'Now if God should ever open the eyes of your understanding, must not the love of God be the immediate consequence?'[3]

It might appear from Wesley's language that evangelicalism entails a radical split between the truth that is accessible to non-Christians and that which is accessible to Christians. We have seen that evangelicals reject the Kantian division between ordinary truth and theological truth which would put an unbridgeable gulf between them. But are they rejecting this radical division only to create another which is equally radical, placing the gulf not between ordinary truth and theological truth, but between truth known by Christians and truth known to others? Are they claiming that the regenerate have access to a new type of knowledge, unavailable to the unregenerate, and quite different from any other knowledge?

Certainly some of the descriptions of the radical change brought about by conversion could be used to argue that this is the evangelical position. But that would, I feel, be unfair to the main thrust of evangelicalism, and, if held, would greatly damage its contribution to the current debate on truth. The claim here is not (or should not be) one of a new type of knowledge, a *gnōsis* open only to the regenerate. Rather, it is that when God works in us through the Holy Spirit, each part of us, including our minds, is deeply affected. We still have the same mind, and the same body, but God has begun a process of change, renewing our minds and our lives. Wesley claimed a new peace and joy and love for the Christian, as well as a new understanding. He was not claiming that these were wholly other than the peace and joy and love experienced before conversion, but rather that these things take on a new dimension because they are now empowered by the Holy Spirit and expressing the new life that God has given. There is, then, a new dimension to knowledge, understanding, peace, joy, and love; but it is not to be seen as something wholly other; it is the same mind and the same body living in the same world, but with the added dimension of the personal experience of God's grace and presence through the Holy Spirit.

In practice, evangelicals readily allow that experiences of God's love and even existential encounters with Christ are not in fact limited to Christians.[4] Saul of Tarsus, for example, was presumably unregenerate when he had his encounter with Christ on the Damascus road. With the possible exception of some Calvinists, evangelicals would want to say that it would have been quite open to Saul to reject Christ at that point, and so never to be regenerated. No special *gnōsis*, then, available only to the regenerate, is required to encounter God, to hear his voice, and to know his reality and power. What is required is that God should take the initiative and come to us and reveal some aspect of himself to us. Some would no doubt claim that in their case he has never done this, though a surprising number of people who are not professing Christians do claim supernatural experiences of one sort or another. But the point remains that experiences of God are not limited to the regenerate; all may have them.

Conversion often includes a change from rejecting specific truths about God, incorporated in Christian doctrine, to accepting and believing them. But this is not necessarily so: an unconverted person may already accept theological doctrines and know them to be true; many an evangelical sermon has used James 2:19 to point out that people may believe facts about God and matters theological but not be regenerate: 'You believe that there is one God. Good! Even the demons believe that – and shudder.' Doubtless, believing theological truths is to be preferred to not believing them, though, in the last analysis, evangelicals are convinced that mere head knowledge of theological truth that is not personally appropriated is not worth having.[5]

The key to the epistemological significance of conversion is something deeper, then, than an experience of God or believing a doctrine, though both of these elements will be present. It is an all-embracing change, a Copernican revolution, in which God becomes, for the individual, the centre or the key which gives reality, meaning and life to everything else. Again, this is not just an intellectual thing; it is a matter of the will, heart and body, as well as of the mind. It is the recognition and appropriation of the fact that if God is going to have any part in our lives, he must be the centre and source of and key to everything. Such an act of recognition and appropriation, according to evangelicals, itself needs the power of the Holy Spirit; it is not a matter of the individual adopting a new God-centred view of the world and way of living. God himself gets to work on our minds and our lives to bring about this radical change.

The change, like conversion itself, can be seen as both instantaneous and gradual. There is a moment of radical reorientation; and there is a long process of working out the implications of this reorientation. Because the moment of reorientation is something supernatural, the light of God breaking through, the power of God changing our thinking and feeling and all our being, it is often a dramatic experience, parallel, say, to Saul's on the Damascus road. This is not always the case; many evangelicals describe their moment of change in terms similar to C. S. Lewis's: 'The choice appeared to be momentous but it was also strangely unemotional.'[6] But there will always be a profound reorientation, a *metanoia*, a change of worldview.[7] We move from one in which God has played little or no real part to one in which he is central, not just in the sense that he has the key role in our system of beliefs and truths, but in the sense that he directs us morally, indwells us personally, instructs and empowers and changes us through the Holy Spirit, and so on. God thus becomes the key to our understanding of the world (and so of truth), and the key to living the truth.

But the full process of the renewing of our minds and the conforming of our lives to the truth is not something that is accomplished all at once. Some elements of conversion, according to evangelicals, are more or less instantaneous: forgiveness, and a new status before God, for example. But the changing of our minds and of our lives so that they conform to the truth is a longer, slower process. It may well start some time before the moment of regeneration; it will certainly go on afterwards as God continues to work in us and change us. It takes more than a lifetime to complete the task of renewing our minds; even at best 'we know in part'; full knowledge will not be attained until heaven. The conforming of our lives to the truth of God also takes time; for most of us, a lot of time.

The regenerate Christian, then, for whom God is, or is increasingly becoming, the centre of everything, would appear to have a key to understanding and living in the world that the non-Christian lacks. But this does not mean either that the non-Christian is unable to find truth, or that there are no limits on the Christian's ability to grasp the fullness of truth. Few evangelicals would follow the more extreme Calvinist teaching that in our unregenerate state our minds are totally blinded, and we are incapable of any good action. Rather, they would agree with the more optimistic view that is found in some passages in Calvin: that the image of God, though seriously affected by sin, still remains in us and enables us to know and live the truth within limits.[8] At conversion, these limits are significantly but not completely removed; we still know only 'in part', and our ability to live the truth continues to be conditioned by our humanness, even though the illumination and indwelling of the Holy Spirit are available to counter the effects of our fallenness and sinfulness.

Because of the image of God and his common grace, then, evangelicals have generally been ready to accept that those who are not regenerate can and do have knowledge of the full range of truth.[9] This can include knowledge of theological (that is to say doctrinal) truth, and even experiential knowledge of God, should God choose to reveal himself to them. Their knowledge will be in a sense incomplete, in that they will have knowledge of specific truths, but lack the awareness of the total framework or metanarrative into which all the specific truths fit, and which gives them their meaning. In this sense, truth as known by those who do not know God is attenuated, a rather shadowy thing, both because it is divorced from the God who is the source of reality, truth and meaning for all things, but also because it is almost certain to lack the full integration and application to every area of life that is the richness of the evangelical experience of truth.

Certainty and its scope

Evangelicals have traditionally made claims to certainty: both doctrinal certainty (that we can know for sure that specific propositional statements, especially those in the Bible, are true) and personal certainty (or assurance of one's own experience of God and personal salvation). Thus J. I. Packer sums up the evangelical doctrine of Scripture: 'Its text is word for word God-given; its message is an organic unity, the infallible Word of an infallible God, a web of revealed truths centred upon Christ.'[10] Hodge claimed that 'assurance is not only attainable, but a privilege and a duty';[11] and many evangelical hymns, from the Wesleys onward, have spoken of the confidence, peace, and assurance of the believer.[12] But mainstream evangelicalism, for all its insistence on an infallible God, has never claimed infallibility for human beings, whether for personal experience or even for interpretation of Scripture. Packer writes:

> The infallibility and inerrancy of biblical teaching does not, however, guarantee the infallibility and inerrancy of any interpretation, or interpreter, of that teaching; nor does the recognition of its qualities as the Word of God in any way prejudge the issue as to what Scripture does, in fact, assert. This can be determined only by careful Bible study. We must allow Scripture itself to define for us the scope and limits of its teaching. Too often the infallibility which belongs to the Word of God has been claimed for interpretations of Scripture which are, to say the least, uncertain and which make Scripture pronounce on subjects about which it does not itself claim to teach anything. The Bible is not an inspired 'Enquire Within Upon Everything'; it does not profess to give information about all branches of human knowledge . . . It claims in the broadest sense to teach all things necessary to salvation, but it nowhere claims to give instruction in (for instance) any of the natural sciences, or

in Greek and Hebrew grammar, and it would be an improper use of Scripture to treat it as making pronouncements on these matters.[13]

Even the acceptance of an infallible Bible, then, does not allow us to claim infallibility for our specific understanding of what the Bible says. Similarly, Hodge allows that 'there may indeed be assurance, where there is no true faith at all'.[14] Personal assurance does not guarantee the truth of which we are assured. We saw in chapter 13 that contemporary evangelicalism is even more ready to allow the possibility of being mistaken, though still retaining a very high level of confidence in the Bible and the evangelical worldview.

A clear distinction needs to be made between the rational certainty of a logically proven belief, and the personal certainty of something which is not logically proven but which we are convinced is true. Evangelical certainty cannot be the former; indeed, we have seen that not even science is able to claim this sort of certainty for its statements. Those still strongly influenced by Enlightenment thought may argue that the second type of certainty can never be valid: if there is any element of uncertainty, then certainty is impossible. But this is unrealistic. We are in fact certain of many things, any one of which a sceptical philosopher would be able to cast doubt on: 'I am certain I am reading this book' ('But you may be dreaming'); 'I am certain I can't walk through that wall' ('But the fact you've tried many times before and always got a bruised nose proves nothing'); and so on. In real life it is even possible to say, for example, 'I am certain my wife loves me; I accept that it is conceivable that she is just putting on an act, but I am sure she isn't'; the admission of the possibility of error does not destroy the element of certainty.

This is, of course, because real-life certainty, like evangelical certainty, is something much bigger than rational proof. We are back to a holistic approach, a combination of personal, experiential, volitional, moral and rational elements, each bearing the other out, and leading to a conviction or assurance or certainty. In acceptance of the truths of Scripture, or personal knowledge of God, or assurance of salvation, evangelicals would stress the element of the divine initiative, the Spirit of God working in us. But this does not operate in a vacuum; other elements will also be involved. We believe that 'God loves us', for example, because the Bible teaches it and the Spirit confirms the truth of the Bible to us, and because we personally experience the love of God. But we also hold that belief because we are committed in our wills to a worldview that is built on the concept of a God who loves the creatures he has made; and, further, both the holding of this worldview and this specific belief are rational in the sense that we have tested them by rational criteria, and will continue to do so. So far at least, they have passed the test.

Certainty, like truth, is broader and richer than Enlightenment thinking has allowed. The collapse of the Enlightenment view of both of these concepts does not, therefore, entail the loss of either. Evangelicalism, with its combination of the rational with the personal, and its foundational belief in a God who loves and communicates and is to be trusted, offers a viable alternative to relativism and subjectivity in both of these areas.

20. God's truth

We have been exploring the viability of basing an epistemology upon the concept of God held by evangelicals. We have found that this gives us a rich and integrated concept of truth that fits the whole range of our experience. In this chapter we shall further explore the nature of truth as it is in God and, in particular (since evangelicals stress so strongly the centrality of the Bible), as he communicates it to us in the Scriptures.

Truth in God

Clearly, truth in God is going to be very rich and broad, and something that is fully integrated with all other aspects of his being. Despite the tendency of philosophers and dogmaticians to separate out the attributes of God, we need to view them as integrated aspects of the one God, not in any way as independent elements. So truth in God is one with his holiness, his love, his power, his eternity, his saving acts, and so on. His truth will be holy, loving, powerful, eternal, saving; his holiness, love, power, eternity, salvation, will be true. We must resist thinking of his truth in isolation; it must always be holy truth, saving truth, powerful truth, and so on. Carl Henry was right to stress that truth is rooted in the Logos of God, but we should be wrong to view the Logos as a merely 'intellectual attribute' of God, isolated pure reason or merely cerebral word. The prologue to John's Gospel lists creativity, life, light, glory, fullness and grace as integral to the Logos, along with truth. This in no way belittles truth as it is in the Logos; again, it greatly enriches it.

One aspect of truth in God especially worth noting is its active nature. The Enlightenment tended to picture truth as something inert and passive, something we discover and put into textbooks. The existentialists and postmodernists see it as something we create. In God, truth is very far from passive, and is certainly not something we create. In that it is an expression of the nature of God himself, it is living and active – even, in a sense, creative. The word of God creates; if he declares a truth, it is. His truth is saving truth; just as the righteousness of God makes righteous, and the holiness of God makes holy, so the truth of God makes true. When it gets to work on our lives or on the world it changes them; it sets free, it shapes, it makes true. It is possible, of course, for us to resist the truth of God, preventing it, for a time, from changing us. But this does not make it inactive; it continues to be active, but now its activity is more in terms of judgment and conviction, and ultimately of condemnation and destruction of what is false.

We need also to keep in mind that truth in God is inextricably linked with love. If the truth of God is active and living, it is so because it is God's love in action. His love cannot leave us in darkness; it reaches out to us in illuminating and liberating truth. Love desires our wholeness – that we should be 'true' people, freed from falsehood and corruption. Love speaks too of a relationship that is 'true', a restored right relationship with God. A link between truth and love is an unfamiliar one in our culture, but, as we saw in chapter 2, it would not have been strange to Plato, who saw love as the appropriate response in us when confronted with truth.

The concept of truth in God as something rich and integrated allows us, as we have seen, to avoid the trap that insists that God-given truth is either personal or factual but cannot be both. In particular it allows us to accept that revelation is both God revealing himself and revealing truth about himself. We can accept that the primary datum of revelation is God himself, but we do not have to assert that personal revelation precludes God communicating truth to us in other ways, and, in particular, verbally in the Scriptures. To do so would limit God's abilities in a wholly unacceptable way, and deny two central convictions of evangelicalism: that God has in fact come to us, and has communicated verbally with us in the Bible.

Indeed, the fact that we are rational beings as well as beings who experience, relate, choose, love, and so on, would cause us to expect that a God who chose to make us able to communicate rationally and verbally and receive communication from others would communicate verbally with us through our reason as well as in other ways. Further, there seem no grounds for holding that a strong stress on God coming to us personally should in any way detract from a very high view of the reliability of God's revelation in

Scripture. Indeed, the two can be seen as complementing each other. On the human level a close relationship would normally be developed and enriched by verbal communication, and verbal communication is more meaningful and more likely to be trusted and accepted where there is a close relationship.

It is therefore quite unreasonable to dismiss *a priori* the possibility of God's communicating truth to us in the Scriptures, just as it would be unreasonable to rule out the possibility of his revealing himself to us personally, morally, or in the exercise of our wills. But since the claim to God-given truth, with its implication of the infallibility or inerrancy of the Scriptures, has caused considerable controversy, we need at this stage to pick up some of our earlier discussion in order to clarify what it would entail in the light of the concept of truth we have been developing.

Truth in the Scriptures

Perhaps we should start with some negatives. The claim to God-given truth in the Scriptures does not, first, have to require adopting some form of mechanical dictation theory of inspiration. Both the divine and the human authorship of the biblical documents can be fully accepted. It is surely a very limited view of God's abilities that claims he could not use the words of sinful and fallible individuals to communicate truth. A God of infinite wisdom and power must be able to communicate a perfect message even through imperfect channels. The fallibility of the writers does not have to entail that their statements are in any way false; even weather forecasters are capable of making true statements. Further, the fact that, say, the person who produced the 'With deepest sympathy' card I sent to a friend the other day has not an ounce of sympathy in his or her whole body does not in any way negate the truth of the message that I expressed through it.

Nor need a concept of God-given Scriptures necessitate a naïve, 'literalistic' hermeneutic. Since no statement can be made without the clothing of its cultural context, any more than it can be made without the clothing of a specific language, the scriptural writings need to be understood in their cultural context, and reinterpreted into ours, just as much as they need to be translated from Hebrew or Greek into English. The statement 'The sun rose' does not have to be taken as implying for us a geocentric view of the universe, even though the writer of Genesis 32:31 presumably held such a view. As it happens, our culture has no difficulty understanding the truth of 'The sun rose' even though, scientifically speaking, we know it to be false. But other differences between aspects of biblical cultures and our culture may appear more serious, and we need the help of scholars trained in sound hermeneutical principles to avoid misunderstanding. One point worth bearing in mind is that the almost universal tendency to assume that if two cultures clash in some aspect, it must be my culture that is right, may often need to be firmly resisted.

That brings us to a third point. A belief that the Scriptures are God-given truth should not involve a rejection of scholarship, whether that scholarship is conducted by those who share this presupposition or by those who are unhappy with it, or even by those who reject the Christian message altogether. A policy of openness to criticism from any quarter is not a sign of lack of confidence in basic presuppositions; quite the reverse. Where serious issues are raised, we must engage with them.

Fourthly, we do not have to produce a logically watertight case for this belief in order to be justified in holding it. As we have seen, the Enlightenment demand was for logical proof. When, say, the arguments for the existence of God were shown to be less than watertight, there were those who concluded that belief in God had been shown to be unjustified. That is by no means the case; we all have many beliefs that are perfectly justified, even though they would never be accepted by a sceptical philosopher as logically proved. We may choose to say we have sufficient evidence to justify our belief in God, or we may choose to call it 'properly basic', or we may found it on existential experience; each of these is a valid and sufficient basis for holding a belief in God. Similarly, our belief that the Scriptures are the verbal communication of God may be held on what we accept as sufficient evidence, or as properly basic, or as a result of hearing God speaking in the Scriptures. Either belief, in God or in the inspiration of the Scriptures, thus to some extent becomes vulnerable to counter-evidence. But that is true of all our beliefs. We may accept that our belief in God, in the Bible, in other minds, or in the existence of the external world is open to question from the sceptics, and that there is a logical possibility that it may one day be disproved, yet still justifiably remain fully committed to it.

Nor do we need to claim, fifthly, that we have excluded all textual errors and arrived at a correct understanding of every verse in order to hold that the Scriptures are God-given truth. When I recently attended a performance of *Cymbeline*, I had no difficulty in accepting that what I heard was the work of Shakespeare, even though there are textual uncertainties in the play, and the performance was to some extent the work of the producer and actors who very probably did not interpret Shakespeare's message exactly as he would have done. The possibility of textual corruption, misinterpretation or indeed mistranslation in the Scriptures is always there; but the influence of these factors is on the whole small and, thanks to the work of scholars, continually decreasing. The margin of uncertainty they introduce is not large enough to warrant rejecting the Bible as God-given truth.

Finally, it goes without saying that in claiming the Scriptures are God-given truth, we are in no way seeking to limit the truth of God to what is written in the Bible. Nor do we need to reject the concept on the grounds that the truth of God is too great to put into words. Of course the truth of God in its fullness is far greater than words, even the words of Jesus or the Bible; but that does not prevent the words of Jesus or of the Bible being true. The incarnation may have entailed kenosis (self-emptying), but the incarnate Son of God was fully divine. What God has communicated to us in the Bible is only a small part of the great total of divine truth, but it is still divine truth.

Positively, in clarification of the concept of the truth of the Scriptures, we can observe that the overall richness and variety of all God's dealings with us are repeated in his speaking to us in the Scriptures. Contemporary philosophy has emphasized the variety of types of spoken or written disclosure, and it need not surprise us to find that God has chosen to use a range of methods of communicating his truth verbally to us in the Scriptures.

There appears, for example, to be variation in the means by which God used the biblical writers to record his message. There are some passages where there seems to be something very near to dictation, as in the letters to the seven churches in Revelation 2 and 3 or in passages prefixed by 'This is what the LORD says'. Then there are the records by the evangelists of the sayings of Jesus, where the evangelists produce verbatim what he said. It may be that sometimes, rather than a verbatim record, the prophets were expressing God's message in their own words, or the evangelists were summarizing Christ's teaching. In this case we might say that God's Spirit helped to direct their summarizing or remembering so that what they wrote was what God wanted to be written; it would be safe to presume that these writers (or speakers) were consciously open to the Spirit's direction as they spoke or wrote. A parallel conscious openness to God's Spirit would have been present in Paul and others as they wrote their letters. There may be some passages in Scripture (for instance some of the Old Testament narratives which draw on material from outside the Jewish tradition) where the original authors were not consciously dependent on God; in this case we might suppose either that he overruled what they wrote in some way, or directed by his Spirit those who later edited and incorporated these passages into the Scripture writings. The distinction might be parallel to a committee chairperson either carefully supervising a secretary who is writing the minutes of a meeting to ensure that they are correct, or allowing the secretary to compile the minutes and then endorsing them by signing them as a correct record.

Further, there is a rich range of literary styles; the writers were very varied, and from a variety of cultural and historical settings. Some parts of the Scriptures were written by individuals; others appear to be more of a team effort, compiled and supplemented by a number of people, sometimes over a long period of time, each person being a key link in the chain of transmission and development.

Then there is the wide range of literature types: narrative, poetry, worship, command, story, prophecy, and so on. The variety is great and brings both richness and complexity to the truth of what God is saying in the Scriptures. Our understanding of it will be impaired if we fail to take account of this richness and complexity – if we were to treat poetry as a straightforward historical account, for example. But of itself the variety in the ways God has communicated to us in the Scriptures enables the truth it conveys to be far richer and broader than if it had all been monochrome.

In the Scriptures God speaks truth to us. Whatever he speaks is truth, and the truth of any specific passage of Scripture will be appropriate to the means by which he is speaking. Narrative, factual and historical passages will be narratively and factually and historically true (in a way appropriate to concepts of narrative and fact and history held by the biblical writers); poetic passages will be poetically true; promises and prophecies will be true in the way that is appropriate for them; and, though the concept is rather foreign to our culture, the Bible is able to speak about even commands and worship being true.

Additionally, all the truth of the Scriptures will be holy truth, loving truth, saving truth, and so on. It will never be isolated from the wholeness of God. Some passages may highlight this or that specific aspect – a worship passage emphasizing holiness, or a gospel story highlighting grace – but it will never be bare truth on its own, for God's truth can never be separated from God.

Given the richness and complexity of truth, including God-given truth, it is hardly surprising that evangelicals have had some difficulty defining exactly what they mean when they claim that the Bible is God-given truth. All evangelicals wish to say that the whole of the Bible, rightly received and interpreted, is a true and trustworthy communication from God. At the same time, no evangelical wishes to claim, say, that because Genesis 32:31 tells us the sun rose we are committed to geocentrism, or that every word of the advice of Job's friends is God's true message to us today. A number of formulae have been put forward, using terms such as 'infallible', 'without error', 'trustworthy', and the like;[1] but, not surprisingly, any formula needs considerable unpacking in the light of the Scriptures themselves, and of our developing understanding of them. Nevertheless, despite the intricacies of the debate, evangelicals have rightly insisted on maintaining a very high view of the truthfulness of the Scriptures. They would seem justified, given the kind of qualifications we have outlined above, in continuing to use descriptions like 'completely true and trustworthy', 'infallible' or 'inerrant' to state their firm commitment to the truth of the Scriptures.

Scriptural truth and other truth

Since God's truth is one, we can expect the written truth we find in the Bible to be one with other forms of truth. With Hodge we can claim that ultimately, though not necessarily immediately, the 'two great sources of knowledge', the Scriptures and what we learn through reason and experience, will be 'consistent in all their valid teachings',[2] provided, of course, that we are rightly interpreting and applying both the words of the Bible and the data of experience.

In particular, we can stress the basic unity between the truth of the biblical writings and existential or kerygmatic truth. My wife's love for me is something I experience personally and existentially; but she also from time to time leaves little notes about the place, saying 'I love you.' Thielicke was wrong when he asserted that holding the propositional truth of the Bible would destroy our existential experience of its truth; my wife's notes in no way detract from, but rather enhance, our personal relationship. In fact, I do not find it necessary to draw a clear line between the ways in which she communicates the truth of her love to me; the truth is one, however it is expressed. Further, evangelicals have always held that, since it is very possible for us to misinterpret our personal experience of God, or even to claim that a specific experience is of God when it is not, the truth of God in the Scriptures has an essential normative role; no true experience of God will run counter to biblical teaching.

Nor am I at all sure that Thielicke is right in suggesting that trust in the Scriptures is necessarily dependent on and subsequent to our personal experience of God coming to us. However much we stress that the basic datum of revelation is God himself, and not words spoken by God, *in the experience of the individual* it seems quite possible that acceptance of the truth of Scripture may precede the personal existential experience of God. We may believe the Scriptures because we have met with God, or our acceptance of the truth of the Bible may lead us to seek and find him. Again, we may be wise not to draw too strong a line between the two; after all, Thielicke's preaching of the message depended at least to some extent on the presupposition that the biblical writings from which he preached were trustworthy.[3]

Additionally, within the Bible itself, truth will basically be one. For all the attacks on, say, the historicity of the Scripture narratives, it is still possible to hold that all parts of the Bible are God-given truth; we do not need to take refuge in the concept that the Bible is theologically true though historically false. Indeed, it is unfair to the Scriptures themselves to separate off some passages or concepts as theological and others as non-theological ('mere narrative'). There is no 'mere narrative' in the Bible; it is all the record of God's dealings with his people, his story, and so fundamentally theological.

Rejection of the call to differentiate strongly between types of truth in the Scriptures may help us over the issue raised, for example, by Thielicke's quotation from C. H. Spurgeon: 'When the Spirit of God departs, then even the truth itself becomes an iceberg.' Whether Spurgeon intended it or not, the quotation seems to imply that there are two clear-cut possibilities: Scriptures enlightened and applied by the Spirit, and totally Spirit-less Scriptures. This is open to challenge. To return to *Cymbeline*; granted that Shakespeare was not present in person at the performance at Stratford-upon-Avon last month, that by no means entails that it was a totally Shakespeare-less experience; Shakespeare (one could almost say the spirit of Shakespeare) dominated the whole thing. To extract the Spirit of God totally from the Scriptures would not leave us with the bare, cold words; it would leave us with nothing, just as, according to Thiselton, removing the cultural clothing of the Scriptures would leave us with nothing. It is not a case of '*either* Scriptures in which we have a dynamic personal experience of God *or* totally Godless words strung together'. Rather, there is a whole range of levels at which we encounter God and his truth as we read the Scriptures, from the richest existential or evangelical experience to one in which we are left cold as ice by what we read. But none of them is totally Godless or Spirit-less, and, though we may choose to reject what we read, none of them is devoid of truth. Just as it remained true that the Earth was spherical when everyone believed it was flat, so the truth of God's revelation remains intact, even if it is rejected. We can, of course, say that it is true in an objective and absolute sense; but our stress on the active or loving truth of God allows us to say that it is true in a further, dynamic sense, in that God continues actively to express his love and speak his truth even when we are not listening. The Logos is the light that 'shines in the darkness' even though 'the darkness has not understood it' (Jn. 1:5). God's truth in the Bible is far from inert and passive.

Receiving the truth

The truth of God that reaches out to us remains intact even if we refuse it; but if we do receive it, what difference does our understanding of ourselves as integrated persons make?

Given the Enlightenment stress on reason, we perhaps ought to start with a negative. We are not to receive the truth of God with our reason alone; nor are we to allow our reason to overrule all other aspects of our personhood. However innocently it was introduced, the Enlightenment concept that all divine truth must be compatible with our reason inevitably led to the conclusion that if something appears to be unreasonable, then it cannot be divine truth, and on to the rejection of just about everything that involved supernatural intervention. This development took the heart from Christianity, for it effectively made our reason the ultimate, instead of accepting God as the ultimate.

But that is the point at which we have to start. Almost by definition, a Christian is one who accepts that God is God, that Jesus is Lord, that our basic condition is creaturehood, and that our innate rebellion against God is to be replaced by acceptance of his lordship and by submission to him. This acceptance of God's lordship is necessarily a holistic thing, involving every aspect of us; it cannot be something that involves just one part of us (say, our religious part) and ignores the rest; nor can it be something that submits most of us but allows ultimate freedom to one aspect, such as our reason. What is more, it is (or should be) a total, unreserved thing, responding to Christ's call to total discipleship and reflecting Paul's concept of himself as a slave of Christ.[4]

Such an attitude of openness and commitment to God is, admittedly, a risky thing. We have no logically provable guarantee that when we jump he will catch us. But it is not a leap in the dark; it is a response to his prior coming to us, whether in our experience or in the Scriptures (or very probably both). His truth, love and power reach out to us, and give us excellent grounds for our response. Such love can be trusted. Our hearts respond to the life and teaching of Jesus. The internal and external evidence that the Bible is God-given truth is strong.

This is something richer than a merely rational acceptance of the presuppositions that there is a God and that he has come to us in Christ and spoken to us in the Bible. It will include that, but it will be an act of the will as well as of the reason, and an expression of love, and the submission of our personhood and life and each part of our being. It will be accompanied by the continuing work of God's grace, indwelling us by his Spirit, warming our hearts and renewing our minds.

As integrated persons, then, we are to receive the truth of God in all aspects of our being. We shall resist the tendency to dichotomize, receiving something with our heart, for instance, but not our will, or accepting a truth intellectually but not letting it affect our living.[5] In particular, we shall accept the Scriptures holistically, receiving their teaching, allowing them to correct us, letting them direct our living, and experiencing their power to set our hearts on fire (2 Tim. 3:15–16, Lk. 24:32). There will doubtless be passages of Scripture we find hard to accept, perhaps because they run counter to what seems to us morally right, rationally coherent, or personally acceptable. Rather than allowing our moral sense, reason or will to dictate our response to the specific problems, we shall need to set the issue in the larger context of our acceptance of the truth of God. If, for example, the problem occurs in an Old Testament passage, we might focus on Christ as both the truth and the key to all the Scriptures, specifically seeking 'the mind of Christ' on the issue through the illumination of the Spirit, checking out his teaching about the Old Testament, seeing how he would have understood it, acknowledging his lordship over it, listening for what he wants to say through it, and so on. This may well provide a clear solution to the specific problem; but even if it does not, it sets the issue in its proper context. Very few would be so bold as to claim that they have solved all the problems connected with, say, the Trinity, the incarnation, eschatology, or the truth of the Bible. Most of us have to 'walk by faith' over such issues, seeing them in proper perspective as we set them in the context of our experience of God, his revelation in Jesus and the Scriptures, and the work of the Spirit in our lives and in the world.

21. Truth

The collapse of the Enlightenment concept of truth does not have to lead to relativism. There is an alternative. It involves reinstating key elements of the pre-Enlightenment concept of truth, enriched by the insights of evangelicalism. It means we reject a narrow concept of truth, and adopt something that is broad. This allows for the complexity and richness of the world in which we find ourselves; there is much more to truth than bare scientific facts. It also allows for the complexity and richness of the knowing subject: we are persons, not just thinking machines.

God the basis of truth

This alternative entails reintroducing God as the source and basis for all that exists, and, specifically, as the source and basis for truth. This God, understood in evangelical terms as personal, creator, loving, good, faithful, communicating, saving, unlimited in ability, and choosing to take the initiative and be involved in the world, is big enough to hold all else in being and direct it according to his purposes. This means that the universe expresses and reflects his mind; it is consistent and reliable; so truth about it can be known. Additionally, God has given to some of his creatures the ability to know truth, both about the world and about himself.

Those who start from atheistic, pantheistic or deistic presuppositions will choose to reject this approach. If they are willing to justify this rejection or to defend their own views, they will not be able to do so on the basis of their own presuppositions. Nor will those who accept this approach be able to defend their position or attack others on the basis of their presuppositions. Rather, each side will have to seek to show that the overall explanation, worldview or way of life arising out of their presuppositions is comprehensive and sufficient for all the data, and does a better job than the worldviews based on rival presuppositions. This is a huge task, and one that could never be completed. But it has to be attempted, and, as in almost all other areas of life, action can be taken long before complete logical demonstration has been achieved. In real life it is not at all uncommon for people to reach the point where they feel they have good grounds to make a paradigm shift from, say, atheistic presuppositions to theistic ones (or *vice versa*). This may sometimes be the result of a single factor: an atheist has a religious experience, and comes to believe in God, or a theist finds that a prayer for healing is not answered, and decides that God does not exist. More likely, it will be the result of a combination of factors, covering different aspects of what it means to be human: the rational, the moral and the volitional intertwined with the experiential, and often as the culmination of a process.

In that everyone has to hold, consciously or otherwise, a basic set of presuppositions, those who hold to a theistic and evangelical view are as entitled to their starting-point as others are to theirs. Indeed, if they can show that their resulting worldview is more comprehensive and satisfactory for the whole of life than that of others, they may justifiably claim that their position is stronger than that of their rivals. Equally, of course, they have to be open to the possibility that serious weaknesses will be found in their position, and that these will require them to revise or abandon it.

The collapse of the narrow, rationalistic, Enlightenment concept of truth has opened up the possibility of restoring the broader and richer concept that had been dominant for nearly two thousand years, and developing it further with evangelical insights. Truth is not to be limited to what can be logically established, like a geometric theorem; it reaches, as Plato held, well beyond the merely intellectual; it is intimately bound up with reality and with goodness, and with God. Any individual truth may be multi-dimensional, with emotional, moral or religious, as well as factual, connotations. Truth is for doing and living, not simply for believing; it has a teleological element, a purpose, a rightness. Above all, truth is personal, not in the weak sense of being merely subjective, but as something that requires the richness of a human (or divine) person to relate to it. The ultimate definition of truth is found in the words of God incarnate: 'I am the way and the truth and the life' (Jn. 14:6).

Locating truth ultimately in God, or allowing God to play a significant role in establishing and justifying truth, cuts against the dominant trend in the Enlightenment and in the Renaissance before it. This was essentially humanistic; the source of and justification for truth are to be found in us as human beings; we do not need to look outside of ourselves to some external authority or source. In particular, our reason, something over which we have full control, is sufficient on its own to establish and justify truth.

This was in effect a denial of creaturehood. Though it took centuries for God to be completely erased from the scene, it was a claim to self-sufficiency; 'man come of age' no longer needed God. In contrast, Protestant and evangelical thinking continued to see us as created, contingent and dependent beings. The essential role of God as source and upholder and lord over all was deduced from biblical statements such as the following: 'All things were created by him and for him. He is before all things and in him all things hold together' (Col. 1:16b–17); 'In him we live and move and have our being' (Acts 17:28); 'From him and through him and to him are all things' (Rom. 11:36); and 'Apart from me you can do nothing' (Jn. 15:5b). Dooyeweerd and Thielicke specifically attacked the concept of the autonomous self, with its implicit denial of creaturehood and contingency; but all evangelicals would see it as a mark of the human race's rebellion against God, and of our rejection of his lordship and authority.

Our creaturehood and truth

The acceptance of creaturehood and contingency means that we are open to the possibility that truth and its justification are not 'all our own work'; and that, however significant a role we may play, ultimately both truth and its justification are given; they come from an authority which is other than ourselves, and to which we choose to submit. This was something specifically highlighted by Forsyth; but it is a concept common to all evangelicals. All truth is in some sense given; whenever we encounter something in the world around us, we are encountering the active and dynamic handiwork of God. Theological truth is also given. As we have seen, there has been much debate over whether the authoritative givenness of theological truth is communicated through the Bible or through the personal experience of the work of the Holy Spirit in our lives. The straightforward answer to that question is to refuse to accept a dichotomy and allow that God communicates his truth and himself in a whole range of ways: personally, experientially, verbally, and so on. This is not to be seen as a range of isolated options, as though God at one time chooses to communicate through the Bible without any involvement of the Holy Spirit, and then at another time reveals himself to an individual in an experience that is quite unrelated to the biblical revelation. Rather, biblical revelation, the work of the Holy Spirit, personal encounter, the stirring of our emotions, even physical experiences, are all to be seen as interweaving aspects of the revealing of the one God. Whatever their particular emphasis may be, all evangelicals must accept that the only ultimate authority and source of truth is God himself.

Not only is truth given; we are designed to receive it. Part of our creaturehood is that we have been given the capacity to know, accept and benefit from truth. Again, the issue here is not a merely factual one. We are made in the image of God not simply in order to enable us to amass more and more information. If all truth is God-given, it will reflect the richness of God. It will be beautiful, good, ethical and practical as well as factual. It will be multi-dimensional, a simple truth containing within itself interweaving factual, moral, personal and practical implications. So our God-given ability to receive truth is broad, so broad that it affects every part of us. God has made us so that we can respond to a given truth in a whole range of ways: with joy, with understanding, with excitement, with fear, with love, with action, and so on. News of a terrorist bomb in London is not just filed away in our minds as a piece of information; it makes us angry, or fills us with sympathy for the victims, or warns us to be on the lookout when we are next in London. We discover that a friend of ours has a criminal record, or was abused as a child, or is the heir to a fortune; in subtle ways we find that this affects the relationship between us. Bad news depresses us; good news excites us. Exploring the details of the world around us leads us to worship the God who planned and made them; learning of the mess we have made of this world makes us determined to do something about it.

Admittedly, our current culture is so geared to producing information that for much of the time we are simply unable to respond holistically to every item of truth as it is presented to us. We read books or newspapers, watch news bulletins, and so on, and one truth after another is flung at us. The terrorist bomb is followed by a breakthrough in medical research, plans for a new sports centre, a protest over the construction of a new road, the antics of politicians, the cricket score, the weather forecast, and so on. It is too much to cope with at once; we cannot let it affect us personally. We accept the information, but refuse to let it do anything to us, or to take action regarding it. Our responses become stunted. We take refuge in being detached observers; truth becomes mere facts to be filed away.

Perhaps this is inevitable, and, in the case of much of the information that comes our way, it does not matter a great deal. But this kind of response should not be seen as the paradigm. It is not the real response; it is only a pale shadow of what receiving truth should be, an emergency measure adopted when we are presented with more truth than we can cope with. The paradigm is the holistic response, allowing truth to affect each part of us as appropriate:

our feelings, our worship, our mind, our body, our living, our choosing, our doing.

As human persons, then, we have God-given abilities to receive and respond to truth. We also have God-given abilities to communicate truth. There is much more to these than the mere passing on of factual information, as though we were no different from a fax machine or a television screen. When we state something as the truth, we are putting something of ourselves into the statement; there is a moral, volitional and personal element to it. The biblical concept of truth has strong elements of faithfulness, integrity and reliability about it, all of them with personal connotations; when I tell you that something is true, I am committing myself personally to it, entrusting something of myself to you. Communicating truth, at its best, is an act of the whole person.

The Enlightenment insistence on our autonomy as knowing subjects not only led to the rejection of the concepts of truth as given from outside of us and ourselves as designed by God to receive it; it also led to a stress on the role we have in shaping truth and the neglect of the concept of truth shaping us. But the role of truth in affecting, changing and shaping our lives is a substantial one, whether we are operating at the level of 'There is a wall there and you cannot walk through walls' or 'You will know the truth, and the truth will set you free' (Jn. 8:32). If truth does affect us holistically, and if we live it as well as believe it, then our whole lives are being shaped by the truth — whether the truths of the world around us, or of other people and situations, or of God.

But that is not to deny that we also have a role in shaping what comes to us as truth. With Thielicke, we can accept that 'the slate has a hand in what is written on it'. Though it comes to us as given, the response it evokes is not automatic; it is, at least to some extent, within our control. We can choose not to be affected by it, or to be annoyed rather than pleased by it, to misinterpret it, or to disbelieve it. Quite apart from our freedom of choice, our reaction to a given truth will be affected by the total pattern of presuppositions, beliefs, experiences and attitudes that go to make up the complex whole of our human personhood. For example, our emotional response to the news of a terrorist bomb may depend on whether we are for or against the particular terrorist group. Data from a space probe to Mars have to be interpreted in the light of our already existing understanding of the composition of the solar system. We interpret a specific religious experience or Bible passage in the context of our overall understanding of God, the Bible and the Christian gospel. Again, we bring ourselves to the task of receiving the truth. Because each of us is a unique and very complex person, with God-given freedom and creativity, no two individuals will respond identically to any given truth.

This does not mean, however, that we are back to subjectivism and relativism. That would apply only if our power to shape the truth were total. It is not. The truth has considerable power to shape us; but, as we have seen with walking through walls, there are definite limits to our powers to shape it. Our relationship with truth is a two-way one; it shapes us and we shape it; but in most cases the largest part of the shaping is done to us and not by us. Allowing that we have any power at all to shape the truth means, of course, that we have to let go of claims to the kind of absolutely undoubtable certainty that was the goal of the early Enlightenment; we can never produce a total logical proof that we have got a truth absolutely right. But, as we have seen, such a goal was unrealistic, and we do not in fact need it in order to have sufficient personal confidence in what we believe to be the truth to enable us to live.

To return to the theme of creaturehood: our Creator, in putting his image in us, has included elements of freedom and creativity. This means that we are more than passive receivers of the truth; we share in a dynamic relationship with it over which we have elements of control. But because, in his love, God does not want us to be totally in error, he has set limits to the degree of control we are able to exercise. We may freely choose to believe this and respond negatively to that; we have the ability to create concepts, theories and even metanarratives. But we do not have the ability to create the world; that has already been done. In the last analysis it is not the truth that we are controlling at all; rather, it is our relationship with it. That much God allows us; but he does not allow us to re-create the whole.

Additionally, though the gift of freedom is a real one, and, in fallen humanity, one that is often used to pervert or reject the truth, concepts of the immanence and grace of God, and of revelation and the illumination of the Holy Spirit, mean that God himself is actively engaged in revealing the truth to us. Jesus opened blind eyes and healed deaf ears; the Holy Spirit, 'the Spirit of truth', is given to guide us into all truth (Jn. 16:13). There is light shining in the darkness, and we each are free to come into the light so that it may be clear that we live by the truth (Jn. 3:21).

The understanding of truth as something broad, and the holistic nature of our relationship with the truth, means that we can satisfactorily incorporate into our concept of truth the range of emphasis covered by evangelical and other thinkers. We do not have to make a choice between truth as propositional and truth as personal; it is both. It is historical, and it is existential. It is factual, and it is relational. It is particular, and it is eternal. It is doctrine, and it is life. These are no longer to be seen as irreconcilable elements, conflicting with each other; rather, they are complementary, enriching each other. They are all united in God himself, who is personal and able to communicate in verbal propositions and doctrines, and in personal encounters. Though eternal and infinite, he has chosen to be involved in history, in the factual and the particular, in existence and in life.

Thus we are able to welcome the distinctive insights of, say, Forsyth, or the fundamentalists, or Thielicke, without being pushed into accepting the implicit 'either/or' that, perhaps as the result of controversy, appears in their works. Forsyth rightly stressed 'the effectual primacy of the given', and that what was given was God himself, come to us in Christ, and challenging us in our wills. But we do not have to accept the dichotomies 'either words about Christ or Christ himself', 'not truth but action', 'the will and not the intellect'. The validity of Forsyth's distinctive insights can be accepted, while retaining a key role for words about Christ and for truth and the intellect.

Similarly, the fundamentalists rightly affirmed the oneness and objectivity of truth, and stressed the supernaturally revealed cognitive truth of the Scriptures. But this does not have to lead to a rejection of scholarship or of developments in interpretation, or to a denial of the validity of some forms of personal experience of God. There is no inconsistency in having a very high view of the truthfulness of the Scriptures coupled with an openness that is willing, like Wesley, to allow the possibility of personal error in our understanding of them.

In contrast to the fundamentalists, Thielicke stressed the dynamic nature of truth, and the centrality of the active work of the Holy Spirit. He is a God who comes to us; we have not just a revelation in a book, but the Revealer himself, bringing us to being in the truth. But Thielicke's consequent rejection of verbal inspiration as a concept which necessarily involves 'mechanical' dictation and 'slavish obedience' does not follow at all; it is perfectly possible to combine a concept of a dynamic God who comes to us with a concept of a God who inspires writers to record just such dynamic acts in the Scriptures. It is at this point that Thielicke parts company with the almost universal evangelical emphasis on the unity of truth, and follows the Kantian dichotomy between transcendent truth (our encounter with truth in God) and historical or other forms of this-worldly truth. But with concepts of truth and revelation that are as broad and as rich as the God who is their source, we do not have to let these dichotomies push us to an 'either/or'. Truth is big enough for 'both/and'.

Good news

We close our survey of evangelicals and truth with a final look at the word 'evangelical'. Etymologically, it means those who announce good news; the cognate term 'evangelist' is particularly associated with those who preach with a view to a life-changing response. Evangelicals earned their name because they claimed and demonstrated that they were proclaimers of life-changing good news.

The good news is, of course, the gospel of Jesus Christ, and supremely of what he has done for us on the cross. But in drawing on the evangelical concept of truth to provide an alternative to relativism and chaos in our postmodern age, we can extend the concept of life-changing good news to the whole of truth. Truth, we could say, is evangelical. It is, or should be, good news that is life-changing.

That is not to say that every item of truth is good news; often quite the reverse seems to be the case in our current society. But we are back with Plato and his belief that there is an intimate connection between the true and the good. Without minimizing the badness of bad news at all, we would all accept that true bad news is in at least some sense better than false good news. If there has been a terrorist bomb and people have been killed, it is, generally speaking, good that the truth should be told. Unless there are overriding security reasons for hushing it up, it is bad if we are told that nothing has happened, even if we are closely related to one of those who have been killed. Most of us would prefer to live in an open society than in one where truth is manipulated by those in power.

Truth as a whole is good. Discovering and knowing the truth, even when it hurts, is in the long run preferable to living with lies. In a further sense, if we accept the foundational concept of God as the source and basis of all truth, and believe that God himself is wholly good, then in this way, too, truth is good. The world he has made, and the abilities he has given us to discover truths about that world and about himself, are all themselves good. Truth is friendly because God is friendly; it is not to be feared, but to be welcomed.

Central to welcoming it is the willingness to let it change us and shape our lives. The concept of submitting to the truth is almost as alien to our contemporary culture as the concept of truth being good. But, to pursue the parallel with the evangelical gospel, it is only when we reach the point where we admit that alone and unaided we cannot make sense of the world around us, of life, or even of ourselves, that we become willing to listen to the truth that comes to us from outside with answers that we could never have thought of. Those answers are much broader, richer and in many ways more demanding than the secure and ordered little structures of our own making. Mystery and wonder are also concepts that we have long since lost; but maybe they still have a place as we accept the greatness of truth, and admit to our own smallness.

But truth, for all its greatness, is not given to emphasize our smallness. It is given to transform our smallness, to enrich our poverty, to enable us to benefit from the whole of reality. It brings us into closeness with others; we share truth. There is a heritage of truth, an ocean of truth for the good of all. It enables us to live in harmony with the world around us; and it puts us in touch with the purposes and the heart of God.

Truth is good news. It may be a long way off, and removed even further by the detours into narrow Enlightenment rationalism and despairing postmodern relativism; but there is still a promise of truth prevailing and setting us free.

Glossary

Age of Reason The period, especially in the eighteenth century, when reason was seen as the basis for and criterion of all knowledge and truth; the Enlightenment.

a priori Prior to experience. An *a priori* truth is one that we know intuitively, independently of experience.

autonomy Freedom from external authority. The ability to establish truth, morals, *etc.*, without reference to God.

axiological Concerning values.

axiom A belief or principle on which other beliefs are built, but which cannot itself be finally established as true; a presupposition.

contingent That may or may not be the case; a *contingent* being is one that may not have existed.

deism The rationalist religious/philosophical approach which rejects the possibility of the intervention of God in the world through revelation, incarnation, miracle, and the like.

deduction The process of reasoning that limits its conclusions to what is wholly contained within its premises; contrast *induction*. From the statement 'This animal has four legs and barks' we can deduce 'It has legs' and 'It makes a noise', but not 'It is a dog'; that would be *induction*. Given the truth of the premises, deduced conclusions are always true.

determinism The denial of personal freedom; all events and actions are fixed by external forces, or by God.

dichotomy Radical division; 'either/or', with no possibility of 'both/and'.

empiricism The view that all true knowledge is derived from experience, usually through the five senses. Traditionally, empiricists have not accepted the validity of religious experience.

Enlightenment The philosophical movement, focused in the eighteenth century, but in effect covering the whole modern period, which made reason the criterion for knowledge and truth.

epistemology The branch of philosophy that covers the nature of truth and our knowledge of it.

evidentialism An approach to Christianity which stresses the importance of establishing the truth of its claims rationally, by means of adequate evidence.

existentialism A philosophical approach, or way of reacting to 'Being' (usually expressed in literary forms rather than as a systematized philosophy), which stresses the existence of the person, subjectivity, the absurdity of the world and our alienation from it, dread, freedom, choice, and personal authenticity.

fideism An approach that holds that religious beliefs should be adopted totally by faith, without the use of reason.

forms A Greek concept for the realities which lie behind objects and make them what they are. Plato believed that the forms exist independently of the objects and of our minds.

foundationalism A philosophical approach that believes it is possible to have a conclusively established belief or set of beliefs which acts as a foundation on which we can build our system of knowledge.

fundamentalism An element within twentieth-century evangelicalism characterized by commitment to traditional Christian doctrines (the 'fundamentals') and the inerrancy of Scripture, and by a rejection of contemporary critical scholarship.

hermeneutics The area of theology or philosophy that deals with interpretation, especially the understanding and interpretation of the Scriptures in their original setting, and their application in our contemporary setting.

idealism A term used with a wide range of meaning; in particular it holds that ultimate reality is non-material, and so mental or spiritual.

illumination The work of the Holy Spirit enlightening and enabling us to know truth.

immanence Involvement (of God) in the world.

induction The process of reasoning (contrast *deduction*) that draws a conclusion or general principle from a range of instances or items of information about a specific topic, and then uses that conclusion or principle as a general truth. The process is not an infallible one; however many corroborative instances we may assemble of water boiling at 100°C at sea level, we can never claim with logical certainty that all water boils at 100°C at sea level.

inerrancy The quality of being wholly without error. In the debate over the truth of the Bible, a claim of *inerrancy* is generally used to stress that the Scriptures are free from all falsehood.

infallibility The quality of being completely trustworthy. In the debate over the truth of the Bible, *infallibility* tends to be used to indicate that the Scriptures, when interpreted by the Holy Spirit, will not lead us astray.

intuition A truth we know immediately, without a process of reason.

language games A concept, particularly used by Wittgenstein and his followers, that recognizes that we use words and language in a wide variety of ways according to the type of discourse, and that this affects both meaning and truth. 'My heart's in the Highlands' may be scientifically false but poetically true.

latitudinarianism A 'broad-minded' movement, particularly in the Church of England in the seventeenth century, which stressed the role of reason over against that of revelation in establishing religious truth.

liberalism An approach to Christian theology that rejects biblical authority and many of the traditionally held Christian doctrines.

logical positivism A philosophical approach which claimed that only what was logically necessary or (at least potentially) verifiable by empirical or scientific experience could be meaningful.

metanarrative A comprehensive explanation or system that makes sense of everything.

modernism The western worldview of the modern period, from the seventeenth to twentieth centuries, particularly characterized by its confidence in reason.

naturalism An approach that rejects the supernatural and seeks to explain everything in this-worldly or scientific terms.

noetic structure The pattern according to which the mind operates.

objectivity The quality of being external to and independent of the personal observer; the converse of *subjectivity*. A table could be said to exist *objectively* if it continues to exist even when no-one is observing it or thinking about it. A table's subjective existence would cease as soon as the observer or thinker (the subject) stops contemplating it.

ontological argument A type of argument for the existence of God which claims that there is something about the very concept of God that entails his existence. For example: God, by definition, has all positive qualities; existence is a positive quality; therefore God exists.

ontology The study of being; the essence of a thing.

pantheism A religion or philosophy that denies that God is other than the universe. For the pantheist, the world, nature or some basic essence of the universe is God.

paradigm shift The abandoning of a set of beliefs, system of explanation, or worldview, in order to adopt a significantly different one.

pietism A movement, starting in Germany in the seventeenth century, which stressed the personal, spiritual and devotional aspects of Christianity.

postmodernism An approach to philosophy and culture which rejects modernism, especially the confidence in reason that was central to the Enlightenment. Besides being anti-rational, it rejects belief in structures and worldviews that supply overall explanations (metanarratives), and fully embraces relativism.

presupposition A (foundational) belief or principle on which other beliefs are built, but which cannot itself be finally established as true.

propositional truth Truth expressed in a statement or sentence; a proposition is a form of words that makes a claim to truth; for example, 'The cat is on the mat.'

ratiocination Process of reasoning.

rationalism The view that knowledge and truth are established by reason alone. In its narrow sense, the term would exclude any experience as a source of truth; in a looser sense, it would allow anything that appears acceptable to reason.

relativism The belief that truth (or morals, *etc.*) is not fixed, objective, or universal, but relative to each person, situation, culture, and the like.

Renaissance The period following the Middle Ages which stressed the abilities and potentials of human persons, and began to break away from ecclesiastical authoritarianism.

scholasticism The approach to philosophy and theology by medieval and some early Protestant thinkers characterized by respect for authority, careful attention to detail, and logical argument. The term has generally been used disparagingly, though there is now an increasing willingness to recognize the validity of their approach.

solipsism Scepticism pushed to the extreme of holding that no knowledge or truth is possible, except that the sceptic exists.

subjectivity The quality of being dependent on an observing/thinking mind (the subject) for reality, existence, or validity; the converse of *objectivity*. Subjective truth is truth dependent for its validity on the person believing it; it has no independent or objective validity.

theism Belief in one God, particularly one, such as the Judeo-Christian God, who relates to and is involved in the universe he has created.

theocentricity The centrality of God, especially in a system of beliefs.

transcendence The quality of being beyond the world. A transcendent God is one who exists beyond and independently of the created universe.

volition An act of the will.

Notes

1. Truth and evangelicals

1. F. Nietzsche, *Die fröhliche Wissenschaft* 125, , trans. W. Kaufmann, in W. Kaufmann (ed.), *Existentialism from Dostoevsky to Sartre* (New York: New American Library, 1975), pp. 126–127.
2. *Ibid.*
3. D. W. Bebbington, *Evangelicalism in Modern Britain: A History from the 1730s to the 1980s* (London: Unwin Hyman, 1989), p. 1.
4. *Ibid.*, pp. 105–109.
5. W. G. McLoughlin, *The American Evangelicals 1800–1900* (New York: Harper Torch Books, 1968), p. 1.
6. These statistics are from P. Johnstone, *Operation World* (Carlisle: OM Publishing, 1993), p. 25. Accurate statistics are elusive; estimates vary according to criteria used, *e.g.* membership, community, inclusion of pentecostals, 'Catholic evangelicals', *etc.* See also D. Barrett, 'Status of Global Mission 1995' in *World Evangelization*, January 1995.
7. Bebbington, *Evangelicalism in Modern Britain*, pp. 2–17.
8. 'Nothing in the Christian system is of greater consequence than the doctrine of Atonement . . . Undoubtedly, as long as the world stands, there will be a thousand objections to this scriptural doctrine. For still the preaching of *Christ crucified* will be foolishness to the wise men of the

world. However, let *us* hold the precious truth fast in our heart as well as in our understanding.' Wesley saw the atonement as propitiatory and substitutionary, citing the anger and mercy of God, and Is. 53:5 and 2 Cor. 5:21. J. Telford (ed.), *The Letters of the Rev. John Wesley* (8 vols.; London: Epworth, 1931), letter to Mary Bishop, 7 February 1778; vol. 6, pp. 297–299.

9. Bebbington, *Evangelicalism in Modern Britain*, p. 11.
10. Preface to J. Wesley, *Sermons on Several Occasions* (3 vols.; London: Wesleyan Conference Office, 1874), vol. 1, p. 5.
11. The Lausanne Covenant 2, in J. D. Douglas (ed.), *Let the Earth Hear His Voice: International Congress on World Evangelization, Lausanne* (Minneapolis: World Wide Publications, 1975), p. 3.

2. Plato to postmodernism 1

1. I am not claiming that the questions as I have put them were necessarily issues the various thinkers consciously faced. But they are relevant to their thinking, and give us some help in analysing their approaches.
2. Cited as 'attrib.' in the *Bloomsbury Dictionary of Quotations* (London: Bloomsbury Publishing, 1987), p. 374.
3. 'This, then, which imparts truth to the things that are known and the power of knowing to the knower, you may affirm to be the Form of the good. It is the cause of knowledge and truth, and you may conceive it as being known, but while knowledge and truth are both beautiful, you will be right in thinking it other and fairer than these. And as in the other world it is right to think light and sight sunlike, but not right to think them the sun, so here it is right to think both knowledge and truth like the good, but not right to think either of them the good. The state or nature of the good must be honoured still more highly.' Plato, *The Republic* 6.508–509, trans. A. D. Lindsay (London: J. M. Dent and Sons, 1923), p. 231.
4. See R. Campbell, *Truth and Historicity* (Oxford: Clarendon, 1992), p. 56, for a fuller list, with references.
5. 'Philosophy' is derived from Greek *phileō* (to love) and *sophia* (wisdom).
6. Plato, *Republic*, 5.475 – 6.48.
7. The exact relationship to God of the forms, and so of truth, was a matter of long debate. Some, like the Jewish thinker Philo, who was alive at the same time as Jesus Christ, suggested that the forms were not eternal but were created by God before he created anything else, and that they thus exist as a kind of blueprint for the world as we know it. However, Plotinus (204–270), the most influential Neoplatonist, maintained the eternity of the forms by making them an integral part of God which did

not need to be created. Christian thinkers tended to follow his lead, partly because they did not like the idea of an additional level of being between God and the rest of creation, and partly because the forms seemed to fit well with biblical concepts of the divine wisdom and the divine Logos; since these were equated with Christ, who was uncreated, they too had to be uncreated.

8. 'Eternal truth and true love and beloved eternity: you are my God . . . I said, "Surely truth cannot be nothing, when it is not diffused through space, either finite or infinite?" And you cried from far away: "Now, I am who I am" (Exod. 3.14). I heard in the way one hears within the heart, and all doubt left me.' Augustine, *Confessions* VII.x (16), trans. Henry Chadwick (Oxford: Oxford University Press, 1991), pp. 123–124.

9. Augustine, *De libero arbitrio*, 2.XV.153–156.

10. The concept of divine illumination had its main roots in the Christian teaching of divine grace taking the initiative in revelation; but there are clear parallels with Plato's use of the sun as the source of illumination. In his famous allegory of the cave, he calls the sun 'in a manner the author of all those things which he and his fellow-prisoners used to see'. Plato, *Republic*, 7.516.

11. Augustine, *De libero arbitrio*, 2.X.113.

12. In the *Confessions* Augustine claims that he found all the truths of John 1:1–5 in the works of the pagan Neoplatonists; what he did not find were the truths of verses 11–12. *Confessions*, VII.9 (13).

13. Augustine, *In Iohannis Evangelium tractatus*, 29.6. This principle, repeated several times by Augustine, was based on the Latin of Isaiah 7:9, *nisi credideritis non intelligetis*, 'Unless you believe you will not understand', and was taken up by Anselm in his *credo ut intelligam*, 'I believe in order to understand.'

14. Anselm's interest in establishing the doctrines of Christianity by the use of reason unaided by revelation was largely apologetic.

15. Hebrew thinkers were able to speak of 'doing' the truth as well as 'believing' it; John 3.21, strictly translated, is 'He who does the truth comes to the light.'

16. 'If doing the truth and doing good have the same opposite term, namely, doing evil, then they are not different in their signification. But everyone maintains that whoever does what he is supposed to do does what is good and what is right, or correct. So it follows that to do what is right, or correct, is to do the truth. For it is evident that to do the truth is to do what is good, and to do what is good is to do what is right. Therefore, nothing is clearer than that the truth of an action is its rightness.' Anselm, *De veritate* 5, trans. J. Hopkins and H. Richardson (Cambridge: Cambridge University Press, 1965).

17. '[God's] being is not only in conformity with his intellect, but is his very act of knowing; and his act of knowing is the measure and cause of all other being and all other intellect; and he himself is his own being and his own act of knowing. Hence it follows not only that truth is in God but also that he is the supreme and original truth.' Aquinas, *Summa Theologiae*, 1a. 16, 5. (Blackfriars translation; London: Eyre and Spottiswoode, 1964–6).

18. 'There is a double canon for the theological truths we profess. Some surpass the ingenuity of the human reason, for instance the Trinity. But others can be attained by the human reason, for instance the existence and unity of God, also similar truths demonstrated in the light of philosophical reason.' Aquinas, *Contra Gentes* 1.3.2, in T. Gilby (ed. and trans.), *St Thomas Aquinas: Philosophical Texts* (London: Oxford University Press, 1951), p. 29.

19. Aquinas, *Summa Theologiae*, 1a, 16, 1 and 2.

3. Plato to postmodernism 2

1. Bacon's confidence in the powers of the new learning was unbounded; he specifically stated that 'Knowledge itself is power'. *Religious Meditations,* 'Of Heresies'.

2. Scepticism claims that we cannot have knowledge, or that we cannot have knowledge in specific areas, *e.g.* of the world around us or of the future. Those who start with a concept of knowledge that requires unquestionable certainty are very open to scepticism, since just about anything can be doubted.

3. R. Descartes, *Discourse on the Method of rightly directing one's Reason and of seeking Truth in the Sciences*, part 4, in E. Anscombe and P. T. Geach (eds. and trans.), *Descartes: Philosophical Writings* (London: Nelson, 1970), p. 32.

4. J. Locke, *An Essay concerning Human Understanding,* 4.19.14.

5. 'He that takes away reason to make way for revelation, puts out the light of both; and does much-what the same as if he would persuade a man to put out his eyes, the better to receive the remote light of an invisible star by a telescope.' *Ibid.*, 4.19.4.

6. *Ibid.*, 4.4.3.

7. 'Besides all that endless variety of ideas or objects of knowledge, there is likewise something which knows or perceives them, and exercises divers operations, as willing, imagining, remembering, about them. This perceiving, active being is what I call *mind, spirit, soul,* or *myself.* By which words I do not denote any one of my ideas, but a thing entirely distinct from them, wherein, they exist, or, which is the same thing,

whereby they are perceived – for the existence of an idea consists in being perceived.' G. Berkeley, *A Treatise Concerning the Principles of Human Knowledge*, 1.1.2.

8. 'My intention . . . is only to make the reader sensible of the truth of my hypothesis, *that all our reasonings concerning causes and effects, are derived from nothing but custom; and that belief is more properly an act of the sensitive, than of the cognitive part of our natures.'* D. Hume, *A Treatise of Human Nature*, 1.4.1.

9. Bertrand Russell, *History of Western Philosophy* (London: George Allen and Unwin, 1961), pp. 645–646.

10. Kant, *Critique of Pure Reason*, A41–42/B59, in N. Kemp Smith (ed. and trans.), *Immanuel Kant's Critique of Pure Reason* (Basingstoke: Macmillan Education Ltd, 1933), p. 82. The word 'intuition' (*Anschauung*) might better be translated 'way of seeing things' or 'viewpoint'.

11. *Ibid.*, B16.

12. The word Kant used for ordinary reason (reason in the ordinary or phenomenal world, covering scientific reason, logic and the like) was *Verstand*; the other, higher, reason he called *Vernunft*.

13. F. Nietzsche, *Die fröhliche Wissenschaft* 125, trans. W. Kaufmann, in W. Kaufmann (ed.), *Existentialism from Dostoevsky to Sartre* (New York: New American Library, 1975), pp. 125–127.

14. S. Kierkegaard, *Concluding Unscientific Postscript*, trans. D. F. Swenson and W. Lowrie (Princeton: Princeton University Press, 1941), 2.2.2; chapter heading and p. 182.

15. Jean-François Lyotard, in *The Postmodern Condition: A Report on Knowledge* (Manchester: Manchester University Press, 1984), *passim*, uses the Wittgensteinian concept of language games. Michel Foucault, in *Power/Knowledge: Selected Interviews and Other Writings 1972–1977* (New York: Pantheon, 1980), uses ideas reminiscent of Nietzsche in his view that what we claim to be truth is in fact a means of gaining control.

16. Lyotard, *The Postmodern Condition*, p. xxiv.

17. For further discussion of relativism, see Peter Hicks, 'Mission, Meaning and Truth', in A. Billington, T. Lane and M. Turner (eds), *Mission and Meaning* (Carlisle: Paternoster, 1995), pp. 306–318.

18. The challenge of the collapse of the traditional western concept of truth has been met with a wide range of responses from contemporary philosophers, most of whom refuse to accept the conclusions of postmodernism. Many have chosen to go back to specific aspects of Enlightenment thought, and sought, for example, to redevelop elements of the philosophy of George Berkeley or logical positivism. Rather fewer have explored pre-Enlightenment concepts.

4. The Reformation legacy

1. 'Human reason, with all its wisdom, can bring it no further than to instruct people how to live honestly and decently in the world, how to keep house, build &c., things learned from philosophy and heathenish books. But how they should learn to know God and his dear Son, Christ Jesus, and to be saved, this the Holy Ghost alone teaches through God's word; for philosophy understands nought of divine matters. I don't say that men may not teach and learn philosophy; I approve thereof, so that it be within reason and moderation. Let philosophy remain within her bounds, as God has appointed, and let us make use of her as of a character in a comedy; but to mix her up with divinity may not be endured.' Luther, *Table Talk* 48, trans. W. Hazlitt (London: Geo. Bell, 1895), p. 23.

2. 'Before faith and the knowledge of God, reason is mere darkness; but in the hands of those who believe, 'tis an excellent instrument. All faculties and gifts are pernicious, exercised by the impious; but most salutary when possessed by godly persons.' *Ibid.*, 76, p. 34.

3. Luther saw reason as bypassing revelation and putting the focus on human activity rather than on divine grace, arrogantly building a tower of Babel to reach heaven rather than humbly receiving salvation by faith. See B. A. Gerrish, *Grace and Reason* (Oxford: Clarendon, 1962), especially pp. 10–27 and 100–113.

4. Duns Scotus (?1266–1308) took a somewhat more Augustinian/Neoplatonist position than Aquinas, arguing, for example, for the need of divine illumination to know 'sure and pure truth'.

5. The vision was William Tyndale's, who is reported to have said to a priest: 'If God spare my life, ere many years pass, I will cause a boy that driveth the plough shall know more of the Scriptures than thou dost.' He published his English New Testament in 1525.

6. The Anabaptists and their congregational successors tended to stress the local congregation as the means through which the Holy Spirit interprets the Scriptures.

7. E. Cameron, *The European Reformation* (Oxford: Clarendon, 1991), pp. 139–144.

8. A. E. McGrath, *The Intellectual Origins of the European Reformation* (Oxford: Blackwell, 1987). p. 173.

9. For the Reformers, there was a double need of God's grace: in revelation, since without the Bible we have no access to the truth of God; and also in illumination, since without the work of the Holy Spirit we cannot receive the Word. See note 12 below, and the further quotations in chapter 19 note 8.

10. J. Calvin, *Institutes of the Christian Religion* 1.7.5, ed. J. T. McNeil, trans. F. L. Battles (Philadelphia: Westminster, 1960), p. 80.

11. These two quotations are taken from W. R. Godfrey, 'Biblical Authority in the Sixteenth and Seventeenth Centuries: A Question of Transition', in D. A. Carson and J. D. Woodbridge (eds.), *Scripture and Truth* (Leicester: IVP, 1983), pp. 225–243, 227. Godfrey claims that Luther and Calvin can be seen as allies for contemporary evangelicals who argue for inerrancy.

12. 'Without the illumination of the Holy Spirit, the Word can do nothing . . . And it will not be enough for the mind to be illumined by the Spirit of God unless the heart is also strengthened and supported by his power. In this matter the Schoolmen go completely astray, who in considering faith identify it with a bare and simple assent arising out of knowledge, and leave out confidence and assurance of heart . . . Therefore as we cannot come to Christ unless we be drawn by the Spirit of God, so when we are drawn we are lifted up in mind and heart above our understanding . . . The Word of God is like the sun, shining upon all those to whom it is proclaimed, but with no effect among the blind. Now, all of us are blind by nature in this respect. Accordingly, it cannot penetrate into our minds unless the Spirit, as the inner teacher, through his illumination makes entry for it . . . It now remains to pour into the heart itself what the mind has absorbed. For the Word of God is not received by faith if it flits about in the top of the brain, but when it takes root in the depth of the heart that it may be an invincible defense to withstand and drive off all the strategems of temptation. But if it is true that the mind's real understanding is illumination by the Spirit of God, then in such confirmation of the heart his power is much more clearly manifested.' Calvin, *Institutes* 3.2.33–36, pp. 580–583.

13. 'This truth and instruction is contained in the written books and in the unwritten traditions, which, after they had been received by the apostles from the mouth of Christ Himself or from the apostles, the Holy Spirit dictating, have come down to us, transmitted as it were from hand to hand; and following the example of the orthodox fathers, it receives and venerates with equal devotion and reverence all the books both of the Old and of the New Testament (since one God is the author of both) and also said traditions, both those pertaining to faith and those pertaining to morals, as dictated either orally by Christ or by the Holy Spirit and preserved by a continuous succession in the Catholic Church.' *The Council of Trent*, The First Decree, in M. Chemnitz, *Examination of the Council of Trent* (St Louis: Concordia, 1971), part 1, p. 37.

5. Edwards and Wesley

1. G. Whitefield, *A Short Account of God's Dealings* 2, in *George Whitefield's Journals* (Edinburgh: Banner of Truth, 1960), p. 58.

2. 'Being in secret prayer, I felt suddenly my heart melting within me, like wax before the fire, with love to God my Saviour; and also felt, not only love and peace, but a longing to be dissolved and be with Christ, and there was a cry in my inmost soul which I was totally unacquainted with before, "Abba, Father! Abba, Father!" I could not help calling God my Father; I *knew* that I was His child and that He loved me and heard me. My soul being filled and satiated, cried, "It is enough; I am satisfied. Give me strength, and I will follow Thee through fire and water!" I could say I was happy indeed! There was in me a well of water springing up to eternal life; and the love of God was shed abroad in my heart by the Holy Ghost.' Quoted in H. J. Hughes, *Life of Howell Harris* (London: James Nisbet and Co., 1892), pp. 12–13.

3. 'God from all eternity did, by the most wise and holy counsel of his own will, freely and unchangeably ordain whatsoever comes to pass . . . God, the great Creator of all things, doth uphold, direct, dispose and govern all creatures, actions and things, from the greatest even to the least, by his most wise and holy providence.' The Westminster Confession of Faith (1647), 3.1; 5.1.

4. There were many affinities between the Puritans and Locke, and they welcomed his philosophy as supportive of their own, rejecting his sceptical conclusions in favour of his more positive passages.

5. J. Edwards, *Personal Narrative*, in O. E. Winslow (ed.), *Jonathan Edwards: Basic Writings* (New York: New American Library, 1966), p. 93.

6. Edwards, *A Faithful Narrative of the Surprising Work of God*, in *The Works of Jonathan Edwards* (1834 edn; rpr. Edinburgh: Banner of Truth, 1974; 2 vols.; referred to hereafter as *Works*), vol. 1, p. 348.

7. Edwards, *A Treatise Concerning Religious Affections*, 1.2.1, in *Works*, vol. 1, pp. 237–238.

8. Edwards, *Notes on Natural Science*, quoted in H. G. Townsend (ed.), *The Philosophy of Jonathan Edwards*, p. 17, cited in E. Flower and M. G. Murphy, *A History of Philosophy in America* (2 vols.; New York: G. P. Putnam's Sons, 1977), vol. 1, p. 144.

9. *Ibid.*

10. Edwards, *Remarks in Mental Philosophy – The Mind*, 10, in *Works*, vol. 1, p. ccxxv. Section 15 of this treatise reads:

    TRUTH. After all that has been said and done, the only adequate definition of Truth is, The Agreement of our ideas with existence. To explain what this existence is, is another thing. In abstract ideas, it is nothing but the ideas themselves; so their truth is their consistency with themselves. In things that are supposed to be without us, it is the determination and fixed mode of God's exciting ideas in us. So that Truth, in these things, is an agreement of our ideas with that series in God. It is existence; and that is all that we can say. It is impossible that we should explain a perfectly abstract and mere idea of existence; only we always find this, by running of it up, that God and Real Existence are the same.

Coroll. Hence we learn how properly it may be said, that God is, and that there is none else; and how proper are these names of the Deity, JEHOVAH, and I AM THAT I AM.

11. Edwards' concept of the ideas of God was a dynamic one. It is God's will, as much as his mind, that holds things in being (*ibid.*, section 13, p. ccxix). He can speak of the existence of things as God's action: 'The existence of these things is in God's supposing of them . . . The supposition of God, which we speak of, is nothing else but God's acting, in the course and series of his exciting ideas, as if they (the things supposed) were in actual idea.' *Ibid.*, section 40, p. ccxviii. Edwards' answer to the problem of causation was an immanent and active God.

12. Cambridge Platonism was a seventeenth-century movement which shared the century's confidence in reason ('Reason . . . is the very Voice of God', Benjamin Whichcote, *Aphorism* 76) but reacted against the prevailing empiricism seen in Bacon and later in Locke, by seeking to return to Platonism, or (more accurately) Neoplatonism. Advocating 'latitude' or tolerance, they were opposed to Calvinism and its dogmatism, and to irrational 'enthusiasm'.

13. The leading, and perhaps most mystical, of the Cambridge Platonists, Henry More (1614–87), claimed both an innate sense of the divine, 'that exceeding hail and entire sense of God which nature herself had planted deeply in me', and a 'conversion' experience in which he turned from a thirst for intellectual knowledge to true illumination of the soul by the light of God which was at the same time both rational and experiential. See Basil Willey, *The Seventeenth Century Background* (London: Routledge and Kegan Paul, 1979), pp. 123–154.

14. Wesley shared much of the confidence in reason that was the hallmark of his age, and was always eager to seek to demonstrate to his opponents that his position could be supported by rational arguments. Nevertheless, he readily accepted reason's limits: 'In spite of all my logic *I cannot so prove* any one point in the whole compass of Philosophy or Divinity as not to leave room for strong objections, and probably such as I could not answer.' Letter to Samuel Furley, 21 May 1762, in J. Telford (ed.), *The Letters of John Wesley* (8 vols.; London: Epworth, 1931), vol. 4, p. 181.

Conviction was the work of the Spirit, not of the reason. See also *An Earnest Appeal to Men of Reason and Religion* 28, in G. R. Cragg (ed.), *The Works of John Wesley* (Oxford: Clarendon, 1975), vol. 11, p. 55: 'We join with you then in desiring a religion founded on reason, and every way agreeable thereto.' But he makes it clear that the reason he bases his religion on is 'eternal reason', rooted in knowledge of God.

15. Wesley, *Journal*, 21 March 1770.

16. Wesley, sermon 'On Faith' 1.1–9, in *Sermons on Several Occasions* (3 vols.; London: Wesleyan Conference Office, 1874–76, hereafter referred to as *Sermons*), vol. 3, pp. 219–227. Compare the sermon 'The Marks of the New Birth' 1.2–3, in *Sermons*, vol. 1, pp. 235–247, where mere 'assent to all the propositions contained in our creed, or in the Old and New Testament', including 'Jesus is the Christ' 'is no more than dead faith'.

17. Wesley, sermon 'On Faith' 1.10.

18. Wesley, sermon on the 'Catholic Spirit' 1.12–13, in *Sermons*, vol. 1, pp. 548–561.

19. Wesley, sermon on 'The Great Privilege of those that are born of God' 1.1, in *Sermons*, vol. 1, pp. 248–259. 'When he is born of God, born of the Spirit, how is the manner of his existence changed! His whole soul is now sensible of God . . . "The eyes of his understanding" are now "open," and he "seeth Him that is invisible".' *Ibid.* 1.8–9.

20. Wesley, sermon on 'The Witness of the Spirit: Discourse II' 4.8, in *Sermons*, vol. 1, pp. 136–148. Wesley argued strongly for 'experimental religion', on the grounds that it was biblical, but rejected unbiblical 'religious' experience as readily as non-appropriated biblical doctrine. 'It is objected, first, "Experience is not sufficient to prove a doctrine which is not founded on Scripture." This is undoubtedly true; and it is an important truth.' *Ibid.*, 4.1.

21. Section 5 of the Preface to *Sermons*, vol. 1, p. 4.

22. *Ibid.*

23. *Ibid.*, section 9.

24. Wesley, sermon on 'Christian Perfection' 1.4, in *Sermons*, vol. 2, pp. 1–18.

25. *Ibid.*, 1.1.

26. Edwards, *A Treatise Concerning Religious Affections* 1.2.1, in *Works*, vol. 1, p. 237.

27. Wesley, sermon on 'Original Sin' 2.3, in *Sermons*, vol. 2, pp. 51–61.

28. Edwards, sermon on 'A Divine and Supernatural Light immediately imparted to the Soul by the Spirit of God, shown to be both a Scriptural and Rational Doctrine', in *Works*, vol. 2, p. 17.

6. Charles Hodge

1. For an eye-witness account, see Peter Cartwright, *Autobiography*, in W. G. McLoughlin, *The American Evangelicals 1800–1900* (New York: Harper Torch Books, 1968), pp. 47–49.

2. See E. R. Sandeen, *The Roots of Fundamentalism* (Chicago: University of Chicago Press, 1970), pp. 116–117; J. Barr, *Fundamentalism* (London: SCM, 1977), pp. 274, 276.

3. Hodge developed lasting friendships with Johann Neander (Professor of Church History at Berlin), Ernst Hengstenberg (Professor of Theology at Berlin), and especially with Friedrich Tholuck (Professor of Theology at Halle). Friedrich Schleiermacher (1768–1834), accepting the Kantian unknowability of God, developed an understanding of Christianity in terms of feeling.

4. For a fuller treatment of Hodge's epistemology see Peter Hicks, *The Philosophy of Charles Hodge; a Nineteenth Century Evangelical Approach to Reason, Knowledge and Truth* (Lewiston, New York: Edwin Mellen, 1997).

5. Reid was Professor of Philosophy at King's College, Aberdeen, and knew Hume personally and debated with him. His *An Inquiry into the Human Mind on the Principles of Common Sense* was published seventeen years before Kant's *Critique of Pure Reason*, and was very widely read throughout Britain, America and Europe.

6. American thinkers tended to call the Scottish common-sense philosophy 'the English philosophy', Scotland being seen as part of England. Despite 1776, the consciousness of English (or Scots) roots of American society ran very deep, and it was natural for Americans to look on the Scottish philosophy as their own.

7. C. Hodge, *Systematic Theology* (3 vols.; London: Nelson; New York: Charles Scribner, 1871–73), vol. 1, p. 52.

8. *Ibid.*, vol. 1, pp. 608, 616.

9. *Ibid.*, vol. 1, p. 56.

10. R. Descartes, *Fifth Meditation*, in E. Anscombe and P. T. Geach (eds. and trans.), *Descartes: Philosophical Writings* (London: Nelson, 1970), p. 108.

11. R. Descartes, *Fourth Meditation*, in *ibid.*, p. 92.

12. *Cf.* A. A. Hodge, *Outlines of Theology* (London: Nelson, 1863), p. 49. A. A. Hodge (Charles's son) described his *Outlines* as little more than abridgments of his father's lectures (*ibid.*, p. ix).

13. C. Hodge, *Princeton Review* 23 (1851), p. 343.

14. 'As has often been stated before, the Scriptures do not make the sharp distinction between the understanding, the feelings, and the will, which is common in our day. A large class of our inward acts and states are so

complex as to be the acts of the whole soul, and not exclusively of any one of its faculties.' Hodge, *Systematic Theology*, vol. 3, p. 91.

15. Samuel Taylor Coleridge (1772–1834), the poet, was very influential in advocating the views of the post-Kantians in Britain and America.

16. C. Hodge, *Princeton Review* 22 (1850), p. 661; *Princeton Sermons* (London: Nelson, 1879), p. 214.

17. Hodge, *Systematic Theology*, vol. 1, p. 56.

18. *Ibid.*, vol. 3, p. 699.

19. *Ibid.*, vol. 1, pp. 194, 200; vol. 2, pp. 666, 683; vol. 3, p. 70; *Princeton Sermons*, pp. 205–207.

20. There is considerable evidence that Hodge in his early period was much more open to a moderate Kantian position than later in life. I have argued in *The Philosophy of Charles Hodge* (see note 4) that the turning-point was the publication of *The Limits of Religious Thought Examined* by H. L. Mansel (1858). The moderate Kantians wanted to accept Kant's conclusions and yet retain some objective content to religious belief. After 1858 Hodge was convinced this could not be done; either Kant or objective truth had to go.

7. Warfield, Machen and fundamentalism

1. G. M. Marsden, *Understanding Fundamentalism and Evangelicalism* (Grand Rapids: Eerdmans, 1991), pp. 38–39.

2. D. J. Tidball, *Who are the Evangelicals?* (London: Marshall Pickering, 1994), pp. 17–18. Though broadly correct, many fundamentalists and some evangelicals would not be happy with some elements of this analysis.

3. The Princetonians, though rightly looked on as forerunners of fundamentalism, were in fact different from many of their successors in several significant points. Fundamentalism was closely allied to revivalism; the 'either/or' mentality of the revivalists (one is either saved or lost, spiritual or worldly, in the truth or in error) helped to bolster fundamentalism's dogmatism and militancy. The Princetonians were increasingly suspicious of revivalism, questioning not only its excesses, but its basic approach. The Princetonians were Presbyterians, committed to Calvinistic confessionalism and scholasticism; the fundamentalists tended to be Baptists, with considerably less weight of theological tradition behind them. Nor could the Princetonians accept the fundamentalists' wholesale rejection of evolution or their exclusive commitment to premillennialism.

4. Mark Noll contrasts Warfield's rationalism with the position of Hodge, 'who often downplayed rational argumentation', citing Warfield: 'We

believe in Christ because it is rational to believe in Him . . . The action of the Holy Spirit in giving faith is not apart from evidence, but along with evidence.' This set Warfield against not just the liberals, but also evangelicals who stressed the direct activity of the Holy Spirit, and even against Dutch Reformed evangelicals, such as Abraham Kuyper, who did not share Warfield's strong rationalism. M. A. Noll (ed.), *The Princeton Theology 1812–1921* (Grand Rapids: Baker, 1983), p. 242.

5. B. B. Warfield, *Biblical and Theological Studies* (Philadelphia: Presbyterian and Reformed, 1968), pp. 5, 21.

6. Warfield was not alone in calling theology a science. His opponents also used the term (but not with objective implications) in phrases such as 'the science of faith', or 'the science of religion'.

7. Warfield, 'The Idea of Systematic Theology', in Noll (ed.), *Princeton Theology*, p. 244.

8. *Ibid.*, p. 245.

9. *Ibid.*, pp. 244–245.

10. Warfield, 'Theology a Science', in J. E. Meeter (ed.), *Selected Shorter Writings of Benjamin B. Warfield* (2 vols.; Phillipsburg: Presbyterian and Reformed, 1970), vol. 2, p. 210.

11. Warfield, 'The Idea of Systematic Theology', in Noll (ed.), *Princeton Theology*, p. 260.

12. *Ibid.*, pp. 260–261.

13. Warfield, 'Authority, Intellect, Heart', *The Presbyterian Messenger* (1896), pp. 7–8, in Meeter (ed.), *Selected Shorter Writings*, vol. 2, p. 668.

14. *Ibid.*, p. 671.

15. *Ibid.*, p. 669.

16. Warfield, *Biblical and Theological Studies*, p. 455.

17. *The Fundamentals* (12 vols.; Chicago: Testimony Publishing Co., 1910–1915), vol. 1, pp. 21, 27.

18. Quoted in B. B. Warfield, *Revelation and Inspiration* (New York: Oxford University Press, 1927), p. 70.

19. *Ibid.*, p. 39.

20. Warfield, 'The Divine and Human in the Bible', *The Presbyterian Journal* (3 May 1894), in Meeter (ed.), *Selected Shorter Writings*, vol. 2, p. 546.

21. *Ibid.*, p. 543.

22. N. B. Stonehouse, *J. Gresham Machen: A Biographical Memoir* (Edinburgh: Banner of Truth, 1987), p. 337.

23. J. G. Machen, *What is Faith?* (Grand Rapids: Eerdmans, 1925), p. 32.

24. J. G. Machen, *Christian Faith in the Modern World* (London: Hodder and Stoughton, 1936), p. 62.

25. Machen, *What is Faith?*, p. 249.

26. So Marsden, *Understanding Fundamentalism and Evangelicalism*, p. 192.

Marsden accepts that 'Machen does not seem to have referred to Scottish Common Sense philosophy directly', but still feels that, like so many of his contemporaries, he was unconsciously influenced by it.

27. *Ibid.*, p. 190.
28. Machen, *What is Faith?*, p. 27.
29. *Ibid.*, pp. 27–28.
30. Machen, *What is Faith?*, p. 242.
31. Machen, *Christian Faith in the Modern World*, pp. 62–64.
32. Machen, *Christianity and Liberalism* (Grand Rapids: Eerdmans, 1923), p. 58.
33. Machen, *Christian Faith in the Modern World*, p. 212.
34. Machen, *Christianity and Liberalism*, pp. 78, 72, 122; *Christian Faith in the Modern World*, pp. 83–86.
35. Machen, *Christianity and Liberalism*, pp. 44, 71; *Christian Faith in the Modern World*, pp. 89–91.
36. Machen, *Christianity and Liberalism*, p. 55.
37. Machen, *Christian Faith in the Modern World*, p. 92.
38. Machen, *Christianity and Liberalism*, p. 73.
39. *Ibid.*, p. 73; *Christian Faith in the Modern World*, pp. 55–56.
40. *Ibid.*, p. 66.
41. *Ibid.*, p. 72.
42. The scholarly and reasonable tone of *The Fundamentals* was not always maintained; an article by Philip Mauro, Counsellor-at-law, New York City, on 'Modern Philosophy', is a splendid example of how not to expound Colossians 2:8; *The Fundamentals*, vol. 2, pp. 85–105. In contrast to Mauro's wholesale rejection of philosophy, E. Y. Mullins, President of Louisville Southern Baptist Seminary, allowed that it had a role to play provided it accepted the validity of religious experience; 'The Testimony of Christian Experience', *The Fundamentals*, vol. 3, pp. 76–85.
43. C. R. Erdman, 'The Coming of Christ', *The Fundamentals*, vol. 11, p. 98.
44. Notably the British contributors, *e.g.* W. H. Griffith Thomas (vol. 8, p. 6) and James Orr (vol. 9, p. 33). About a quarter of the essays in *The Fundamentals* were by British writers. Their contributions tended to be on the moderate side, and fundamentalism never became the divisive issue in the United Kingdom that it did in America. *The Times* was able to comment in 1929 that Britain had been saved 'from a fundamentalist controversy such as that which has devastated large sections of the church in America' (cited in Marsden, *Fundamentalism and American Culture*; Oxford: Oxford University Press, 1980, p. 222).
45. J. Orr, 'Science and the Christian Faith', *The Fundamentals*, vol. 4, p. 103.
46. In a speech to 'an Infidel Club in Chicago'. Cited in Marsden, *Fundamentalism and American Culture*, p. 217.

47. A. W. Pitzer, 'The Wisdom of this World', *The Fundamentals*, vol. 9, p. 23.
48. Thomas Whitelaw, 'Christianity, No Fable', *The Fundamentals*, vol. 3, pp. 86–97.
49. James M. Gray, 'The Inspiration of the Bible – Definition, Extent and Proof', *The Fundamentals*, vol. 3, p. 41.
50. Though not, for example, for *The Fundamentals* contributer James Orr: see his *Revelation and Inspiration* (London: Duckworth, 1909), pp. 212–217.
51. The Chicago Statement on Biblical Inerrancy, in Norman Geisler (ed.), *Inerrancy* (Grand Rapids: Zondervan, 1979), pp. 496, 500–501.
52. *Ibid.*, pp. 501–502.

8. Forsyth and Denney

1. P. T. Forsyth, *Positive Preaching and the Modern Mind* (London: Hodder and Stoughton, 1909), pp. 282–283.
2. P. T. Forsyth, *The Person and Place of Jesus Christ* (London: Independent Press, 1909), p. 84.
3. Forsyth, *Positive Preaching*, pp. 249–250.
4. P. T. Forsyth, *The Cruciality of the Cross* (London: Independent Press, 2nd edn 1948), p. 23.
5. P. T. Forsyth, *The Principle of Authority* (London: Independent Press, 2nd edn 1952), p. 6.
6. Forsyth, *Faith, Metaphysic, and Incarnation*, p. 697, cited in A. P. F. Sell, 'P. T. Forsyth as Unsystematic Systematician', in T. Hart (ed.), *Justice the True and Only Mercy: Essays on the Life and Theology of Peter Taylor Forsyth* (Edinburgh: T. and T. Clark, 1995), p. 132.
7. Forsyth, *Revelation and the Person of Christ*, p. 111, in S. J. Mikolaski (ed.), *The Creative Theology of P. T. Forsyth: Selections from his Works* (Grand Rapids: Eerdmans, 1969), p. 49.
8. Forsyth, *Principle of Authority*, pp. 82, 108.
9. Forsyth, *Positive Preaching*, pp. 210–212; *Principle of Authority*, p. 124.
10. *Ibid.*, p. 372.
11. Forsyth, *Revelation and the Person of Christ*, in Mikolaski (ed.), *Creative Theology*, p. 52.
12. Forsyth, *The Church and the Sacraments* (London: Independent Press, 2nd edn 1947), p. 101.
13. *Ibid.*, p. 305.
14. Forsyth, *Revelation and the Person of Christ*, p. 109, in Mikolaski (ed.), *Creative Theology*, pp. 47–48; *Principle of Authority*, p. 53.
15. 'The essence of Christianity is not in the bare fact, but in the fact and its

interpretation. It is not in a mere historic Jesus, evidentially irresistable, but in a Christ evangelically irresistable, a Christ who is the mediator of the grace of God.' Forsyth, *Person and Place of Jesus Christ*, p. 168.

16. *Ibid.*, p. 179.

17. Forsyth, *Positive Preaching*, p. 38.

18. Forsyth, *Person and Place of Jesus Christ*, pp. 180–181.

19. Forsyth, *Principle of Authority*, p. 174.

20. *Ibid.*, p. 365.

21. P. T. Forsyth, *Faith, Freedom and the Future* (London: Independent Press, 1955), pp. 115–116.

22. *Ibid.*, p. 120.

23. Forsyth, *The Place of Spiritual Experience in the Making of Theology*, in Mikolaski (ed.), *Creative Theology*, p. 28.

24. Forsyth, *Principle of Authority*, p. 146.

25. *Ibid.*

26. *Ibid.*, p. 162.

27. *Ibid.*, pp. 168–169.

28. Forsyth, *The Grace of the Gospel as the Moral Authority in the Church*, cited in Sell, 'P. T. Forsyth as Unsystematic Systematician', in Hart (ed.), *Justice the True and Only Mercy*, p. 127.

29. Forsyth, *Principle of Authority*, p. 146.

30. *Ibid.*, p. 147.

31. *Ibid.*, p. 174.

32. Quoted in J. R. Taylor, *God Loves Like That! The Theology of James Denney* (London: SCM, 1962), pp. 26, 40.

33. *Ibid.*, pp. 40–41.

34. J. Denney, *Letters of Principal James Denney to W. Robertson Nicoll 1893–1917* (London: Hodder and Stoughton, 1920), p. xvi.

35. 'We have enough and to spare of the kind of man who splits the world into two unrelated sections called historical and spiritual, but mostly they do not quite realise what they are doing.' *Ibid.*, pp. 100–101.

36. J. Denney, *Studies in Theology* (London: Hodder and Stoughton, 1904), pp. 2–4.

37. *Ibid.* p. 4.

38. *Ibid.*, pp. 12, 14, 16–17.

39. Denney, *Letters*, p. xxxii.

40. J. Denney, *Jesus and the Gospel* (London: Hodder and Stoughton, 1909), p. 161.

41. Denney, *Studies in Theology*, p. 15.

42. J. Denney, *The Christian Doctrine of Reconciliation* (London: Hodder and Stoughton, 1917), p. 9.

43. Denney, *Jesus and the Gospel*, p. 108.

44. Denney, *Studies in Theology*, p. 11.
45. *Ibid.*, p. 13.
46. Denney, *Christian Doctrine of Reconciliation*, p. 109.
47. Denney, *Jesus and the Gospel*, p. 376.
48. Denney, *Christian Doctrine of Reconciliation*, p. 199.
49. Denney, *Studies in Theology*, p. 17; *Christian Doctrine of Reconciliation*, p. 7.
50. Denney, *Studies in Theology*, pp. 202–203.
51. *Ibid.*, p. 209.
52. Denney, *The Atonement and the Modern Mind*, p. 9, cited in Taylor, *God Loves Like That!*, p. 139.
53. David Wright, 'Soundings in the Doctrine of Scripture in British Evangelicalism in the First Half of the Twentieth Century', *Tyndale Bulletin* 31 (1980), pp. 87–106.
54. T. C. Hammond, *In Understanding be Men* (London: Inter-Varsity Fellowship, 5th edn 1954), pp. 17, 30–36.

9. Carl Henry

1. C. F. H. Henry, *God, Revelation and Authority* (6 vols.; Waco: Word, 1976–1983), vol. 1, p. 17, title of introductory chapter. The large majority of my references to Henry's work are to his *magnum opus* or to his most recent work, *Toward a Recovery of Christian Belief* (Wheaton: Crossway, 1990).
2. Henry, *Recovery of Christian Belief*, p. 49.
3. The 'Christian philosopher is under no intellectual compulsion . . . to accept rival premises, however fashionable, as the starting point for advancing his or her theistic worldview'. *Ibid.*, p. 65.
4. Henry, *God, Revelation and Authority*, vol. 1, p. 228.
5. Henry, *Recovery of Christian Belief*, p. 49.
6. Henry, *God, Revelation and Authority*, vol. 5, pp. 21, 11.
7. *Ibid.*, vol. 2, p. 17.
8. Henry, *Recovery of Christian Belief*, p. 29.
9. Henry, *God, Revelation and Authority*, vol. 6, pp. 11–34.
10. Henry, *Recovery of Christian Belief*, p. 27.
11. Henry, *God, Revelation and Authority*, vol. 6, p. 79.
12. *Ibid.*, vol. 5, p. 334.
13. Henry, *Recovery of Christian Belief*, p. 50.
14. 'Truth is truth because God thinks and wills it; in other words, truth depends on the sovereignty of God. God sovereignly upholds the truth; he establishes and preserves whatever is true. As creative, the Word of God is the ground of all existence; as revelatory, it is the ground of all human knowledge.' Henry, *God, Revelation and Authority*, vol. 5, p. 334.

15. Henry, *Recovery of Christian Belief*, p. 70.
16. *Ibid.*, p. 54.
17. Henry, *God, Revelation and Authority*, vol. 3, p. 248.
18. Henry discusses a wide range of interpretations of the 'image of God' in *God, Revelation and Authority*, vol. 2, pp. 124–142.
19. *Ibid.*, pp. 125–126.
20. Henry, *Recovery of Christian Belief*, p. 57.
21. Henry, *God, Revelation and Authority*, vol. 4, p. 129, thesis twelve.
22. Henry, *Recovery of Christian Belief*, pp. 78, 103.
23. *Ibid.*, pp. 48, 50, 56, 58, 71–74.
24. *Ibid.*, p. 74.
25. Even if the evidentialists' case for the historical fact of the resurrection is indubitably established, this still does not prove, says Henry, that 'the transcendent Deity had raised Jesus from death never to die again, and raised him moreover as the firstfruits of an end-time general resurrection'. For these things revelation and Scripture are essential. *Ibid.*, p. 82.
26. Henry, *God, Revelation and Authority*, vol. 2, p. 123.
27. *Ibid.*, vol. 1, p. 183.
28. *Ibid.*
29. Henry, *Recovery of Christian Belief*, pp. 43, 74–78.
30. *Ibid.*, p. 45.
31. 'Christianity has no less right to affirm its ultimate explanatory principles than do other world- and life-views. One who is persuaded on other grounds needs neither empirical nor existential nor speculative arguments to state his case . . . As revelationally grounded and intelligible faith, Christianity sets out from the ontological priority of the living God and the epistemological priority of divine revelation. From these basic postulates it derives and expounds all the core doctrines of the Christian religion.' *Ibid.*, p. 59.
32. *Ibid.*, p. 50.
33. Henry, *God, Revelation and Authority*, vol. 1, p. 74.
34. *Ibid.*, vol. 1, p. 77.
35. *Ibid.*, vol. 2, p. 132.
36. C. F. H. Henry, *Remaking the Modern Mind* (Grand Rapids: Eerdmans, 2nd edn 1948), p. 237; *God, Revelation and Authority*, vol. 1, p. 232.
37. 'There can be no decisive choice between alternatives if we disavow any external referent by which to judge truth claims. The crucial question is not whether a scholar must begin with faith; the critical question, rather, is whether such faith is nonrational belief.' Henry, *Recovery of Christian Belief*, p. 53.
38. Henry, *God, Revelation and Authority*, vol. 1, p. 238.
39. 'Logical inconsistency sacrifices plausibility; a logically inconsistent system

cannot be valid or true. Logical consistency may not decisively establish the truth of intellectual claims, but it is nonetheless a potent negative test.' Henry, *Recovery of Christian Belief*, p. 53.

40. *Ibid.*, p. 88; *God, Revelation and Authority*, vol. 1, p. 237.

41. *Ibid.*, vol. 1, pp. 233–234.

42. Henry, *Recovery of Christian Belief*, pp. 81, 67.

43. Henry, *God, Revelation and Authority*, vol. 1, p. 250.

44. Henry, *Recovery of Christian Belief*, p. 69.

45. Henry, *God, Revelation and Authority*, vol. 1, p. 91.

46. Henry, *Recovery of Christian Belief*, p. 40.

47. *Ibid.*, pp. 70, 54, 59.

48. *Ibid.* p. 59.

49. Henry, *God, Revelation and Authority*, vol. 2, p. 8.

50. *Ibid.*, vol. 2, p. 11.

51. *Ibid.*, vol. 4, pp. 201–202.

52. 'Verbal inerrancy implies that God's truth inheres in the very words of Scripture, that is in the propositions or sentences of the Bible, and not merely in the concepts and thoughts of the writers. We are not free to formulate the doctrine of inspiration as if verbal expression lay wholly outside its scope in some sections of Scripture so that in some places only concepts and not words are involved. Thoughts can be properly expressed only by certain pertinent words. What God reveals is truth, and the inspired writers' exposition of the content of that revelation is true; inerrant inspiration is what assures the absence of logical contradictions and verbal misrepresentations.' *Ibid.*, vol. 4, pp. 205–206.

53. 'I believe that divine revelation is rational, that the inspired biblical canon is a consistent and coherent whole, that genuine faith seeks understanding, that the Holy Spirit uses truth as a means of persuasion, that logical consistency is a test of truth, and that saving trust in Christ necessarily involves certain propositions about him.' 'The Concerns and Considerations of Carl F. H. Henry', *Christianity Today* (13 March 1981), p. 21, cited in B. E. Patterson, *Carl F. H. Henry* (Waco: Word, 1983), p. 164.

54. 'While evidentialists seek to erect a case for the infinite on the basis of the finite and profess to derive God as a conclusion from nature, rational presuppositionalists derive the cosmos instead from God.' Henry, *Recovery of Christian Belief*, p. 112.

55. Henry is as eager as any to claim that such investigations all confirm our acceptance of biblical inspiration. See *God, Revelation and Authority*, vol. 4, pp. 129–161.

56. 'The Christian knows, moreover, that it is only by divine grace that he believingly participates in the epistemic and ontic realities affirmed by the Biblical heritage.' Henry, *Recovery of Christian Belief*, p. 51.

10. Helmut Thielicke

1. H. Thielicke, *Between Heaven and Earth*, trans. J. W. Doberstein (London: James Clarke, 1967), pp. xv, xvi.
2. Thielicke, *Between Heaven and Earth*, pp. 16–17.
3. *Ibid.*, p. 17.
4. H. Thielicke, *Modern Faith and Thought*, trans. G. W. Bromiley (Grand Rapids: Eerdmans, 1990), p. 53.
5. 'In Descartes religious understanding is based on thought and not on a real encounter with God.' *Ibid.*, p. 75.
6. *Ibid.*, p. 34.
7. *Ibid.*, p. 52.
8. *Ibid.*, pp. 47–48.
9. *Ibid.*, pp. 275–276.
10. H. Thielicke, *The Evangelical Faith*, trans. G. W. Bromiley (3 vols.; Grand Rapids: Eerdmans, 1982) vol. 1, p. 117.
11. Thielicke, *Modern Faith and Thought*, p. 281.
12. *Ibid.*
13. 'The self is itself a relation, whether to God who has posited it to others, or to the outside world in general. If I were to define a human being I should have to speak about a relation.' *Ibid.*, p. 283.
14. *Ibid.*, p. 287.
15. 'The basic epistemological problem of theology is that God is not one object among others, that he thus escapes objectification, and lies outside the radius of human reason, which is limited by the horizon of experience . . . Even though he makes knowledge possible, he himself is not knowable as the basis of knowledge. He upholds the world nexus but is not himself to be found in it.' Thielicke, *The Evangelical Faith*, vol. 3, p. 6.
16. *Ibid.*, vol. 2, pp. 55–56.
17. Thielicke, *Modern Faith and Thought*, p. 275.
18. Thielicke, *The Evangelical Faith*, vol. 2, p. 8.
19. *Ibid.*, vol. 1, pp. 207–208.
20. *Ibid.*, vol. 1, p. 207; vol. 2, p. 14.
21. *Ibid.*
22. *Ibid.*, vol. 1, p. 212.
23. *Ibid.*, vol. 1, p. 159.
24. *Ibid.*, vol. 1, p. 160.
25. *Ibid.*, vol. 1, p. 154.
26. *Ibid.*, vol. 3, p. xxii.
27. Thielicke, *Modern Faith and Thought*, p. 7.
28. Thielicke, *Between Heaven and Earth*, p. 4.

29. Thielicke, *The Evangelical Faith*, vol. 3, pp. 195–198.
30. *Ibid.*, vol. 3, p. 194.
31. Thielicke, *Modern Faith and Thought*, p. 285.
32. Thielicke, *Between Heaven and Earth*, p. 7.
33. Thielicke, *The Evangelical Faith*, vol. 3, p. 107.
34. *Ibid.*, vol. 1, p. 193–194.
35. *Ibid.*, vol. 1, p. 194.
36. *Ibid.*, vol. 1, p. 211.
37. *Ibid.*
38. *Ibid.*, vol. 2, pp. 38–39.
39. *Ibid.*, vol. 3, pp. 107–108.
40. 'Much more important than the difference between the original witness of the evangelists and apostles and that of later witnesses, we contend, is the difference between the incarnate Word and the human word that bears witness to it, no matter whether it be that of prophets, evangelists and apostles, or the Word of God that is proclaimed today and tomorrow.' *Ibid.*, vol. 3, p. 107.
41. Thielicke, *Modern Faith and Thought*, p. 285.
42. Thielicke, *The Evangelical Faith*, vol. 1, p. 157.
43. *Ibid.*, vol. 2, p. 38.
44. *Ibid.*, vol. 2, p. 51.
45. *Ibid.*, vol. 1, p. 211.
46. *Ibid.*, vol. 1, pp. 202–205.
47. 'Our concern is with a particular style of truth. This is a truth that we cannot control, that has not entered the heart of man, that the natural man cannot perceive. It is a truth which leads me to being in truth and which thus transforms me. This transforming character of truth is what is brought to light by the active Word that mediates it. This Word is plainly the instrument of the miracle of the Spirit, bringing new birth and the new creation of the spiritual man. This hermeneutics of the Holy Spirit means that the truth intended cannot possibly fall under the general categories which are the epistemological conditions for the usual definition of truth.' *Ibid.*, vol. 1, p. 202.
48. Thielicke, *Between Heaven and Earth*, p. 34.

11. Reformed epistemology

1. C. F. H. Henry, *God, Revelation and Authority* (6 vols.; Waco: Word, 1976–1983), vol. 1, p. 238.
2. N. L. Geisler, *Philosophy of Religion* (Grand Rapids, Zondervan, 1974), pp. 190–226; phrases from p. 224.

3. Geisler presents a fuller form of his argument in *Christian Apologetics* (Grand Rapids: Baker, 1976), pp. 237–258. He summarizes it as follows (pp. 238–239):

    1. Some things undeniably exist (e.g. I cannot deny my own existence).

    2. My nonexistence is possible.

    3. Whatever has the possibility not to exist is currently caused to exist by another.

    4. There cannot be an infinite regress of current causes of existence.

    5. Therefore, a first uncaused cause of my current existence exists.

    6. This uncaused cause must be infinite, unchanging, all-powerful, all-knowing, and all-perfect.

    7. This infinitely perfect Being is appropriately called 'God'.

    8. Therefore, God exists.

    9. This God who exists is identical to the God described in the Christian Scriptures.

    10. Therefore, the God described in the Bible exists.

4. H. Dooyeweerd, *In the Twilight of Western Thought* (Nutley: Craig, 1975), pp. 1–2.

5. H. Dooyeweerd, *A New Critique of Theoretical Thought*, trans. D. H. Freeman and W. S. Young (4 vols.; Philadelphia: Presbyterian and Reformed, 1969), vol. 1, p. 61.

6. *Ibid.*, vol. 1, p. 8.

7. C. Van Til, *The Case for Calvinism* (Philadelphia: Presbyterian and Reformed, 1964), p. 137.

8. C. Van Til, *Christian-Theistic Evidences* (Philadelphia: Westminster Theological Seminary, 1961), p. 55.

9. C. Van Til, *In Defense of the Faith 2: A Survey of Christian Epistemology* (Philadelphia: Westminster Theological Seminary, n.d.), p. 131.

10. Van Til, *Christian-Theistic Evidences*, p. 54.

11. *Ibid.*, p. 53.

12. Schaeffer studied under Van Til at Westminster Theological Seminary.

13. F. A. Schaeffer, *The God Who is There* (London: Hodder and Stoughton, 1968), p. 179.

14. F. A. Schaeffer, *He is There and He is Not Silent* (London: Hodder and Stoughton, 1972), pp. 27–28.

15. Schaeffer, *The God Who is There*, p. 178.

16. *Ibid.*, p. 121.

17. Schaeffer, *He is There and He is Not Silent*, pp. 33–44.

18. *Ibid.*, p. 73.

19. Schaeffer was as critical of evangelicals who said 'Don't ask questions, just believe' as he was of Barth and his followers. F. A. Schaeffer, *The Church*

at the End of the Twentieth Century (London: Norfolk Press, 1970), pp. 124–125.

20. Schaeffer, *The God Who is There*, p. 156.

21. *Ibid.*

22. After his first three apologetic books, *Escape from Reason* (London: Inter-Varsity Fellowship, 1968), *The God Who is There* and *He is There and He is not Silent*, Schaeffer published books on ecology, sociology, ecclesiology, art, psychology, genetics and ethics.

23. A. Plantinga, *Warrant: The Current Debate* (New York: Oxford University Press, 1993); *Warrant and Proper Function* (New York: Oxford University Press, 1993). Plantinga's analysis of warrant is in terms of the proper functioning of our cognitive faculties in the producing and holding of beliefs in a suitable environment according to a design plan. The quotation is by Richard Foley and is cited on the cover of *Warrant: The Current Debate*.

24. N. Wolterstorff, 'Introduction', in A. Plantinga and N. Wolterstorff, *Faith and Rationality* (Notre Dame: University of Notre Dame Press, 1983), p. 7.

25. Plantinga, 'Reason and Belief in God', in Plantinga and Wolterstorff, *Faith and Rationality*, pp. 47–48.

26. *Ibid.*, pp. 17–18.

27. *Ibid.*, pp. 67–68.

28. *Ibid.*, p. 66.

29. *Ibid.*, pp. 78–82.

30. *Ibid.*, p. 83.

31. For a critique of Reformed epistemology from a pro-Wittgenstein perspective, see D. Z. Phillips, *Faith after Foundationalism* (London: Routledge, 1988), pp. 14–114; for one from the rational Catholic tradition, see L. Zagzebski (ed.), *Rational Faith: Catholic Responses to Reformed Epistemology* (Notre Dame: University of Notre Dame Press, 1993).

12. The quiet revolution

1. J. Calvin, *Institutes of the Christian Religion* 2.2.21, trans. H. Beveridge (Grand Rapids: Eerdmans, 1989), p. 241.

2. James Barr, for example, in *Fundamentalism* (London: SCM, 1977), claims that Hodge's confidence in reason was 'unbounded' (p. 272). He cites a passage from Hodge's *Systematic Theology* (3 vols.; London: Nelson; New York: Charles Scribner, 1871–73), vol. 1, p. 53, in support of this claim; but his case is considerably weakened by Hodge's explicit statement in the

middle of the passage cited (which Barr chooses to omit) that 'the demonstration of the Spirit' is needed before we can believe 'the things of the Spirit'.

3. Hodge, *Systematic Theology*, vol. 2, p. 660.

4. B. Ramm, *Protestant Biblical Interpretation: A Textbook of Hermeneutics* (Grand Rapids: Baker, 3rd edn 1973) p. 289.

5. *Ibid.*, p. 157.

6. *Ibid.*, p. 160.

7. B. Ramm, *After Fundamentalism: The Future of Evangelical Theology* (San Francisco: Harper and Row, 1983), pp. 44–45.

8. *Ibid.*, p. 45.

9. *Ibid.*, p. 27.

10. Ramm's analysis is open to challenge. Sandeen and Barr criticized fundamentalism for being pre-Kantian; fundamentalism's rationalism has most often been seen as the result of the Enlightenment's reliance on reason, mediated through American 'Scottish common-sense' philosophy.

11. 'This book has a very narrow compass . . . The leading themes are as follows: (1) The Enlightenment was a shattering experience for orthodox theology from which it has never fully recovered. (2) Neither religious liberalism nor orthodoxy had the right strategy for interacting with the Enlightenment with reference to the continuing task of Christian theology. (3) Of all the efforts of theologians to come to terms with the Enlightenment, Karl Barth's theology has been the most thorough. (4) He thereby offers to evangelical theology a paradigm of how best to come to terms with the Enlightenment.' Ramm, *After Fundamentalism*, p. vii.

12. *Ibid.*, p. 9.

13. *Ibid.*, p. 28.

14. *Ibid.*, p. 114.

15. *Ibid.*, p. 118.

16. *Ibid.*, p. 116.

17. *Ibid.*, p. 12.

18. *Ibid.*, p. 119.

19. E. D. Radmacher and R. D. Preus (eds.), *Hermeneutics, Inerrancy, and the Bible* (Grand Rapids: Zondervan, 1984), pp. 881–887.

20. A. C. Thiselton, *The Two Horizons* (Exeter: Paternoster, 1980), p. xx.

21. *Ibid.*

22. *Ibid.*, p. 11.

23. *Ibid.*

24. *Ibid.*, p. 16.

25. *Ibid.*, p. 20.

26. A. C. Thiselton, *New Horizons in Hermeneutics* (London: HarperCollins, 1992), pp. 281–282.

27. The 'speech-act' theory developed in the context of the decline of logical positivism, which had limited meaning within very narrow bounds. It was the realization that, in actual use, words and phrases have a rich range of meaning, even when their factual content appears to be nil (*e.g.* 'Stop!' or 'Possibly'), and that non-verbal factors can radically affect that meaning (*e.g.* an ironic tone of voice), that led Wittgenstein and others, particularly J. L. Austin, to begin to investigate speech-acts. See Thiselton, *New Horizons*, pp. 16–19.

28. *Ibid.*

29. Originated by Elizabeth Anscombe and used by J. R. Searle. Thiselton, *New Horizons*, p. 294.

30. *Ibid.*, pp. 294–295.

31. *Ibid.*

32. *Ibid.*, pp. 298–300.

33. *Ibid.*, p. 281.

34. *Ibid.*, pp. 283–284.

35. My colleague, Dr Steve Motyer, points out that in practice the application of speech-act theory in evangelical scholarship has led largely to an emphasis on the performative effect of the text on its first readers.

36. F. P. Cotterell and M. Turner, *Linguistics and Biblical Interpretation* (London: SPCK, 1989), p. 67.

37. *Ibid.*, p. 68.

38. *Ibid.*, p. 72.

39. *Ibid.*, p. 69.

40. *Ibid.*, p. 70.

41. Thiselton, *The Two Horizons*, pp. 85–92.

42. *Ibid.*, pp. 92, 91.

43. In a personal conversation, Turner accepted that as Christians we can and do have spiritual assurance (*e.g.* of the love of God or the holiness of God) that may well be the result of the work of the Holy Spirit; but he is unwilling to allow a claim for certainty for even this, since there are cases where people have claimed such spiritual assurance and have ultimately been proved wrong. Such cases may be very much in the minority, but he feels they prevent our making unequivocal claims to truth.

13. The contemporary scene

1. For example M. A. Noll, *The Scandal of the Evangelical Mind* (Grand Rapids: Eerdmans; Leicester: IVP, 1994); O. Guinness, *Fit Bodies, Fat Minds* (Grand Rapids: Baker, 1994); D. F. Wells, *No Place for Truth* (Grand Rapids: Eerdmans, 1993).

2. P. Johnstone, *Operation World* (Carlisle: OM Publishing, 5th edn 1993), p. 26.

3. S. M. Burgess and G. B. McGree (eds.), *Dictionary of Pentecostal and Charismatic Movements* (Grand Rapids: Zondervan, 1988), pp. 812–813.

4. One of the earliest scholarly studies of non-western pentecostalism was organized by the World Council of Churches and published as C. Lalive d'Epinay, *Haven of the Masses; A Study of the Pentecostal Movement in Chile* (London: Lutterworth, 1969). Pertinent comments in his description of a typical pentecostal church are: 'In the Pentecostalist message, the declaration of divine omnipotence is not an abstract theological postulate, but a truth experienced by faith' (p. 47); 'The experience of conversion is always marked by a feeling of change, both physically and in one's sensations' (p. 48); 'Gradually the atmosphere warms, the Spirit is manifested . . . those who are inspired sing and dance and the excitement mounts; sometimes a few collapse on the floor and show symptoms of ecstasy; others are seized by fits of laughter or of trembling or weeping' (p. 52); 'the accesses of emotion which accompany worship . . . permit people to participate in a direct and personal way in religious manifestations and in the congregation. They are forms of participation, they are the languages of those who have no language, the means of expressing their experience of encountering something greater than themselves' (pp. 53–54); 'A social catharsis accompanies the individual's catharsis' (p. 48); 'Pentecostalism teaches how to believe and live, not how to think' (p. 55); 'Chilean Pentecostalism . . . has effected a metamorphosis of Western Christianity, by its own spontaneous acculturation' (p. 63).

5. In Britain, Sheffield Academic Press has published a number of studies on the theology of the pentecostal movement.

6. This is not to gainsay the principle of openness outlined in the next section. The Enlightenment was a peculiarly western thing, and I would suggest we have no right to engage in intellectual imperialism and subject the rest of the world to it, particularly when we are now beginning to feel that, for all its benefits, in its key features it was mistaken. If pentecostalism in the non-western world is going to be of an open texture, then it must be open to the culture in which it finds itself. In fact, as we saw in the case of Chile, it has an encouraging record of enculturalization.

7. For an account of the founding and development of Fuller Seminary see George Marsden, *Reforming Fundamentalism: Fuller Seminary and the New Evangelicalism* (Grand Rapids: Eerdmans, 1987).

8. Noll sums up his book as a call to a 'search for a Christian perspective on life – on our families, our economies, our leisure activities, our sports, our attitudes to the body and to health care, our reactions to novels and

paintings . . . to take seriously the sovereignty of God over the world he created, the lordship of Christ over the world he died to redeem, and the power of the Holy Spirit over the world he sustains each and every moment.' Noll, *Scandal of the Evangelical Mind*, p. 253.

9. Evangelicals are very well represented in the field of biblical studies. A leading example in Britain is I. Howard Marshall, Professor of New Testament Exegesis at Aberdeen University. In the 1991 Laing Lecture he wrote: 'There is an important difference between evangelicalism and fundamentalism in that the evangelical is not tied, as the fundamentalist professedly is, to an unquestioning view of Scripture, but is open to new understanding of Scripture. Where they are united, however, and this is of crucial importance, is in firmly affirming the *truth* of Scripture.' I. H. Marshall, 'Are Evangelicals Fundamentalists?' *Vox Evangelica* (1992), p. 22.

10. D. L. Wolfe, *Epistemology: The Justification of Belief* (Downers Grove and Leicester: IVP, 1982), p. 65.

11. *Ibid.*, p. 77.

12. The Evangelical Alliance Relief Fund; £20 million annually is given through this fund by British evangelicals for a range of projects to eradicate poverty.

13. *Third Way* was founded to 'present Biblical perspectives' on a very wide range of social, political, cultural, artistic and ethical issues.

14. Significantly, though these organizations are evangelical in foundation and ethos, for the most part they are willing to work with those of other persuasions, a further sign of evangelical openness.

15. For a summary of possible reasons see D. J. Tidball, *Who are the Evangelicals?* (London: Marshall Pickering, 1994), pp. 186–188.

16. See, for example, J. Pollock, *John Wesley 1703–1791* (London: Hodder and Stoughton, 1989), pp. 230–236.

17. Tidball, *Who are the Evangelicals?*, p. 181.

18. For example J. Barr, *Fundamentalism* (London: SCM, 1977), p. 312.

15. Starting with God 1: six theses

1. Evangelicals have not been alone in their tendency to limit truth to propositional truth. The same tendency has been widespread among philosophers in the modern period, and it has been strongly represented in the twentieth century by logical positivism and linguistic philosophy.

2. '*There is no such thing as revealed truth . . . What is offered to man's apprehension in any specific Revelation is not truth concerning God but the living God Himself.*' W. Temple, *Nature, Man and God* (London: Macmillan, 1935), pp. 317, 322 (his italics). Jesus 'has imparted no information about

God at all . . . He does not *communicate anything*, but *calls men to himself.*'
R. Bultmann, *Theology of the New Testament* (2 vols.; London: SCM,
1955), vol. 2, p. 41 (trans. Kendrick Grobel; his italics).

3. The Idealists' and Whitehead's concepts of God varied considerably and
were quite different from that of evangelicals. Nevertheless, the concepts
played an important role in their systems. 'The positive relation of every
appearance as an adjective to Reality, and the presence of Reality among
its appearances in different degrees and with diverse values – this double
truth we have found to be the centre of philosophy . . . The Reality
comes into knowledge, and, the more we know of anything, the more
in one way is Reality present within us . . . Reality is spiritual.' F. H.
Bradley (1846–1924), *Appearance and Reality* (London: George Allen
and Unwin, 1897), pp. 551–552. 'God is the infinite ground of all
mentality, the unity of vision seeking physical multiplicity.' A. N.
Whitehead (1861–1947), *Process and Reality* (London: Macmillan, 1929),
p. 244.

4. Attributed, probably incorrectly, to P.-S. Laplace (1749–1827), French
mathematician and astronomer.

5. Perhaps the final attempt to give expression to the Enlightenment vision
of all truth contained within the bounds of reason was logical positivism.
This in effect stated that meaning, and so truth, were limited to analytic
statements such as 'A triangle has three sides', or to statements that could
be verified according to the then accepted methods of science. All other
forms of truth were to be rejected as purely subjective. But it was soon
pointed out that there were many difficulties in the way of the
verification concept; the kind of verification required simply was not
possible; and in the end we are left with the unacceptable notion that
analytic statements are the only ones that can be true.

17. Starting with God 3:
observations and conclusions

1. William of Ockham (*c.* 1285–1349): 'Plurality should not be posited
unnecessarily.' *Scriptum in Librum Primum Sententiarum, Opera Theologica*
1.74, cited in A. J. Ayer and J. O'Grady (eds.), *A Dictionary of Philosophical
Quotations* (Oxford: Blackwell, 1992), p. 459. Also attributed to Ockham
are the sayings: 'It is vain to do through more what can be done through
fewer', and 'Entities are not to be multiplied more than necessary'; the
latter is a summary of his view rather than a direct quotation.

2. D. Hume, *An Inquiry Concerning Human Understanding*, 12.3.132.

3. 'Reason is natural revelation, whereby the eternal Father of light, and Fountain of all knowledge, communicates to mankind that portion of truth which he has laid within the reach of their natural faculties.' J. Locke, *An Essay Concerning Human Understanding*, 4.19.4.

4. 'Philosophy and human learning . . . are an effectual inducement to the exaltation of the glory of God.' F. Bacon, *The Advancement of Learning* (London: Heron Books, n.d.), p. 41. For a discussion tracing a strong connection between Bacon and American nineteenth-century 'doxological science', see T. D. Bozeman, *Protestants in an Age of Science: The Baconian Ideal and Antebellum American Religious Thought* (Chapel Hill: University of North Carolina Press, 1977).

5. 'The prerogative of God extendeth as well to the reason as to the will of man; so that as we are to obey His law, though we find a reluctation in our will, so we are to believe his word, though we find a reluctation in our reason.' Bacon, *The Advancement of Learning*, p. 209.

6. R. Descartes, *Fourth Meditation*, in E. Anscombe and P. T. Geach (eds. and trans.), *Descartes: Philosophical Writings* (London: Nelson, 1970), p. 92.

7. C. Hodge, *Systematic Theology* (3 vols.; London: Nelson, New York: Charles Scribner, 1871–73), vol. 1, p. 52.

18. The wholeness of truth

1. In the conclusion of Book 1 of *A Treatise of Human Nature*, Hume struggled with the incompatibility between his sceptical philosophy and real life. 'I am first affrighted and confounded with that forlorn solitude in which I am placed in my philosophy, and fancy myself some strange uncouth monster, who not being able to mingle and unite in society, has been expelled all human commerce, and left utterly abandoned and disconsolate . . . Here then I find myself absolutely and necessarily determined to live, and talk, and act like other people in the common affairs of life. But notwithstanding that my natural propensity, and the course of my animal spirits and passions reduce me to this indolent belief in the general maxims of the world, I still feel such remains of my former disposition, that I am ready to throw all my books and papers into the fire, and resolve never more to renounce the pleasures of life for the sake of reasoning and philosophy.' Hume, *A Treatise of Human Nature*, 1.4.7.

2. For further discussion of these aspects see Peter Hicks, *Truth: Could it be True?* (Carlisle: Solway, 1996), chapters 8–10.

3. I have suggested in *Truth: Could it be True?* that the notion of love as something that enriches and is enriched in relationship could provide a

basis for an understanding of truth in terms of enriching and promoting wholeness.

4. Existentialism tended to assert that for a choice to be truly free (and so authentic) it had to be subject to no influence whatever; choosing some course of action *for a reason* was a sign of unauthenticity. So choice had to be irrational. This in turn meant that it was amoral, and, in effect, meaningless. Such has ceased to be choice at all, and has degenerated into mere randomness.

19. Conversion and certainty

1. J. Wesley, sermon on 'The New Birth', *Sermons on Several Occasions* (3 vols.; London: Wesleyan Conference Office, 1874–76), vol. 2, pp. 65–66.

2. *Ibid.*, p. 66.

3. J. Wesley, *A Farther Appeal to Men of Reason and Religion*, part II, III.22.16–17, in G. R. Cragg (ed.), *The Works of John Wesley* (Oxford: Clarendon, 1975), vol. 11, p. 269.

4. In the past, many evangelicals, especially those in the Calvinistic tradition, emphasized the more sombre side of such encounters, and the resulting conviction of sin. Today, the stress tends to be more on the power and grace of God in revealing himself to the individual, modelled, perhaps, on those who encountered God in Christ during his earthly ministry.

5. At this point evangelicals are very close to Kierkegaard's dictum: 'An objective knowledge of the truth of Christianity, or of its truths, is precisely untruth.' S. Kierkegaard, *Concluding Unscientific Postscript*, trans. D. F. Swenson and W. Lowrie (Princeton: Princeton University Press, 1941), p. 201. The issue for evangelicals is that truth must affect and change us, not merely be known by the mind.

6. C. S. Lewis, *Surprised by Joy* (London: Collins, 1959), p. 179. Lewis's conversion appears to have been a protracted affair (perhaps as befits a thinker), though he picked out three significant final stages: on the top of a bus (*ibid.*); alone in his room at Magdalen, when he 'gave in, and admitted that God was God, and knelt and prayed: perhaps, that night, the most dejected and reluctant convert in all England' (*ibid.*, p. 182); and on the way to Whipsnade one sunny morning: 'When we set out I did not believe that Jesus Christ is the Son of God, and when we reached the zoo I did. Yet I had not exactly spent the journey in thought. Nor in great emotion . . . They have spoilt Whipsnade since then. Wallaby Wood, with the birds singing overhead and the bluebells underfoot and the Wallabies hopping all round one, was almost Eden come again' (*ibid.*, pp. 189–190).

7. *Metanoia*, the New Testament word traditionally translated 'repentance', means 'change of mind'; but its implication is much more than cerebral: it entails change in the whole of the person and each part of life.

8. 'There is within the human mind, and indeed by natural instinct, an awareness of divinity. This we take to be beyond controversy.' Calvin, *Institutes of the Christian Religion* 1.3.1, ed. J. T. McNeil, trans. F. L. Battles (Philadelphia: Westminster, 1960), p. 43. Calvin's interest was the sphere of theological truth and, on balance, he seems to have held that in practice the amount the unregenerate person believes or lives the truth of God is negligible. 'This bare and external proof of the Word of God should have been amply sufficient to engender faith, did not our blindness and perversity prevent it. But our mind has such an inclination to vanity that it can never cleave fast to the truth of God; and it has such a dullness, that it is always blind to the light of God's truth. Accordingly, without the illumination of the Holy Spirit, the Word can do nothing. From this, also, it is clear that faith is much higher than human understanding. And it will not be enough for the mind to be illumined by the Spirit of God unless the heart is also strengthened and supported by his power. In this matter the Schoolmen go completely astray, who in considering faith identify it with a bare and simple assent arising out of knowledge, and leave out confidence and assurance of heart. In both ways, therefore, faith is a singular gift of God, both in that the mind of man is purged so as to be able to taste the truth of God and in that his heart is established therein.' *Ibid.*, 3.2.33, pp. 580–581.

9. 'There is a natural relation between truth, whether speculative, aesthetic, moral, or religious, and the mind of man. All such truth tends to produce an effect suited to its nature, unless counteracted by inadequate apprehension or by the inward state of those to whom it is presented. This is of course true of the Word of God. It is replete with truths of the highest order; the most elevated; the most important; the most pertinent to the nature and the necessities of man; and the best adapted to convince the reason, to control the conscience, to affect the heart, and to govern the life.' C. Hodge, *Systematic Theology* (3 vols.; London: Nelson; New York: Charles Scribner, 1871–73), vol. 2, p. 655. For this knowledge to become saving knowledge, however, the supernatural work of the Spirit is required: 'The Scriptures clearly teach that the mere outward presentation of the truth in the Word, does not suffice to the conversion or sanctification of men; that the natural, or unrenewed man, does not receive the things of the Spirit of God, for they are foolishness unto him; neither can he know them; that in order to any saving knowledge of the truth, i.e. of such knowledge as produces holy affections and secures a holy life, there is need of an inward supernatural teaching of the Spirit,

producing what the Scriptures call 'spiritual discernment.' *Ibid.*, vol. 1, p. 67.

10. J. I. Packer, *'Fundamentalism' and the Word of God* (London: Inter-Varsity Fellowship, 1958), pp. 113–114.

11. Hodge, *Systematic Theology*, vol. 3, p. 107.

12. For instance: 'I rest in Thine almighty power;/The name of Jesus is a tower,/That hides my life above . . ./Assured that Thou through life shalt save,/And show Thyself beyond the grave/My everlasting Friend.' C. Wesley in *The Methodist Hymn Book* (London: Methodist Conference Office, 1933), hymn 531. 'Blessed assurance, Jesus is mine;/O what a foretaste of glory divine!' F. J. van Alstyne, *ibid.*, hymn 422.

13. Packer, *'Fundamentalism'*, p. 96.

14. Hodge, *Systematic Theology*, vol. 3, p. 107.

20. God's truth

1. 'The divine inspiration of the Holy Scripture and its consequent entire trustworthiness and supreme authority in all matters of faith and conduct'; the Evangelical Alliance Basis of Faith. 'We believe in the *Holy Scriptures* as originally given by God, divinely inspired, infallible, entirely trustworthy'; World Evangelical Fellowship Statement of Faith. '[Scripture's] text is word for word God-given; its message is an organic unity, the infallible Word of an infallible God, a web of revealed truths centred upon Christ'; J. I. Packer, *'Fundamentalism' and the Word of God* (London: Inter-Varsity Fellowship, 1958), pp. 113–114. 'We affirm the divine inspiration, truthfulness and authority of both Old and New Testament Scriptures in their entirety as the only written Word of God, without error in all that it affirms, and the only infallible rule of faith and practice'; Article 2, The Lausanne Covenant, in J. D. Douglas (ed.), *Let the Earth Hear His Voice* (Minneapolis: World Wide Publications, 1975), p. 3. 'We affirm that Scripture, having been given by divine inspiration, is infallible, so that, far from misleading us, it is true and reliable in all matters it addresses. We deny that it is possible for the Bible to be at the same time infallible and errant in its assertions. Infallibility and inerrancy may be distinguished, but not separated. We affirm that Scripture in its entirety is inerrant, being free from all falsehood, fraud and deceit . . . We affirm the propriety of using inerrancy as a theological term with reference to the complete truthfulness of Scripture. We deny that it is proper to evaluate Scripture according to standards of truth and error that are alien to its usage or purpose. We further deny that inerrancy is negated by Biblical phenomena such as a lack of modern technical precision, irregularities of

grammar or spelling, observational descriptions of nature, the reporting of falsehoods, the use of hyperbole and round numbers, the topical arrangement of material, variant selections of material in parallel accounts, or the use of free citations'; Articles XI to XIII, the Chicago Statement on Biblical Inerrancy, in N. L. Geisler (ed.), *Inerrancy* (Grand Rapids: Zondervan, 1979), p. 496.

2. C. Hodge, *Systematic Theology* (3 vols.; London: Nelson; New York: Charles Scribner, 1871–73), vol. 1, p. 56.

3. All the points Thielicke raises in criticism of verbal inspiration seem to rest on his strong 'either/or' approach, for instance his belief that empirical and transcendent statements cannot stand side by side in the Scriptures, and that it is not acceptable to call both Jesus and the Bible 'the Word of God'.

4. Mt. 16:24–25; Phil. 1:1.

5. New Testament examples of integration are Jn. 7:16–17 (understanding and will) and Rom. 12:1–2 (body, spirit and mind).

Index